教育部人文社会科学研究项目"构式语法视角下的汉语元语言否定研究"

（编号：19YJC740046）

本成果受到浙江海洋大学外国语学院学科建设经费资助，在此致谢

认知语言学视角下的现代汉语元语否定研究

Metalinguistic Negation in Modern Chinese:
A Cognitive Linguistic Approach

龙　磊　著

浙江工商大学 出版社

ZHEJIANG GONGSHANG UNIVERSITY PRESS

·杭州·

图书在版编目(CIP)数据

认知语言学视角下的现代汉语元语否定研究 / 龙磊
著. -- 杭州:浙江工商大学出版社,2024.4
ISBN 978-7-5178-6006-8

Ⅰ.①认… Ⅱ.①龙… Ⅲ.①现代汉语—研究 Ⅳ.
①H109.4

中国国家版本馆 CIP 数据核字(2024)第084425号

认知语言学视角下的现代汉语元语否定研究

RENZHI YUYANXUE SHIJIAO XIA DE XIANDAI HANYU YUANYU FOUDING YANJIU

龙 磊 著

责任编辑	张莉娅
责任校对	韩新严
封面设计	望宸文化
责任印制	包建辉
出版发行	浙江工商大学出版社
	(杭州市教工路198号 邮政编码310012)
	(E-mail:zjgsupress@163.com)
	(网址:http://www.zjgsupress.com)
	电话:0571-88904980,88831806(传真)
排 版	杭州朝曦图文设计有限公司
印 刷	杭州宏雅印刷有限公司
开 本	710mm×1000mm 1/16
印 张	18.5
字 数	307千
版 印 次	2024年4月第1版 2024年4月第1次印刷
书 号	ISBN 978-7-5178-6006-8
定 价	68.00元

List of Main Abbreviations

ASP   Aspect

BCC   Beijing Language and Culture University (BLCU) Chinese Corpus

CL   Classifier

GEN   Genetic

ICA   Intersubjective Construal Adjustment

INT   Interjection

PRT   Particle

QM   Question Marker

Preface

 This book is concerned with metalinguistic negation (MN) in modern Chinese. Contrary to ordinary descriptive negation (DN), MN is characterized as a marked, non-truth-functional use of negation. In recent years, several accounts have been proposed by researchers working within both pragmatics and cognitive semantics to characterize the nature of MN, i.e. whether it is a matter of semantic ambiguity or pragmatic ambiguity, and where the alleged ambiguity resides. Undoubtedly, these studies shed valuable insights into many respects of the phenomenon. However, restricted by theoretical frameworks and the intuitive approach, they fail to provide a sufficient explanation of the cognitive motivations and conceptual mechanisms underlying the meaning representations of MN.

 This study is intended to develop a new theoretical model [i. e. the intersubjective construal adjustment (ICA) model] based on Verhagen's model of intersubjectivity and Langacker's model of construal, with an aim to present an alternative account of MN in modern Chinese. It is argued that the "ambiguity" of negation in natural language does not purely reside at the semantic level, nor does it purely reside at the pragmatic level. Rather, it resides at the conceptual level. This can be termed as the "conceptual ambiguity" position. A distinction is made between "intrasubjective construal adjustment" and "intersubjective construal adjustment". We propose that MN expressions are the linguistic manifestations of the adjustment of alternate construals of the same state of affairs between different conceptualizers. Specifically, the speaker invites the addressee to consider and abandon a particular way of construal, and to update the common ground by suggesting another way of construing the same situation.

As for the methodology, this study adopts a usage-based approach, focusing on the real use of MN in modern Chinese. BCC and the Internet are two major data resources. In terms of the representational effects it normally produces, a comprehensive classification of MN in modern Chinese is proposed. Four major types of MN are identified, namely strengthening denials, identifying denials, positioning denials, and formal denials. An in-depth description is also provided for the variety of semantic patterns. Based on the ICA model, we give a systematic analysis of the cognitive mechanisms underlying the meaning representation of each type of MN. It is argued that: (1) strengthening denials are generated through intersubjective adjustment of alternate construals based on parameters of construal such as scale, specificity, scopes of attention, modal ground, and action chain schema; (2) identifying denials are derived from intersubjective construal adjustment concerning parameters of construal such as prototypicality, domains, "trajector/landmark" alignment, identity ground, and mental scanning; (3) positioning denials are manifestations of similar adjustment processes concerning parameters of construal such as viewing arrangement, profiling, deixis, individuation, relationality, and frames; (4) formal denials involve intersubjective adjustment of different sanctioning relations arising from alternate ways of categorization.

This study adds further evidence that cognitive linguistic theories can provide useful perspectives for the studies of some traditional research topics in pragmatics. Verhagen's model of intersubjectivity and Langacker's model of construal focus on different aspects of "cognition" (i.e. intrasubjective and intersubjective) and different types of meaning representations (i. e. constructional and non-constructional). Therefore, they can be fruitfully integrated, yielding new explanatory power that founders of both models may have not anticipated. The ICA model proposed here not only incorporates the explanatory power of previous cognitive semantic accounts but also allows us to account for a wide variety of MN phenomena in modern Chinese. At the methodological level, this study shows that the usage-based approach helps to reveal the diversity of semantic patterns of MN in modern Chinese systematically, and overcome the limitation of the intuition-based approach, endowing the linguistic account with a higher level of descriptive and explanatory adequacy than previous attempts. Therefore, this approach deserves more attention in its own right in the further research of MN.

Contents

List of Tables

List of Figures

Chapter 1

Introduction

1.1 Background of the Study

Negation in natural languages is an intriguing phenomenon. From Aristotle to the present day, it has been the focus of attention of a very large number of philosophers and linguists. The present study is concerned with an irregular or a marked use of negation, labeled as metalinguitic negation by Laurence Horn. According to Horn (1985, 1989), negation does not always fulfill the same function in different contexts. He makes a descriptive/metalinguistic dichotomy of negation: DN is a truth-functional use of negation, objecting to the truth condition of a proposition, whereas MN is a non-truth-functional use of negation, objecting to a previous utterance on any ground whatever, including implicature, presupposition, connotation, and linguistic forms such as pronunciation, morphology, and register. Some typical cases of DN and MN are given in (1) and (2):

    (1) Typical Cases of DN

        a. The capital of China is not Shanghai.

        b. I haven't finished my homework.

        c. Tom does not work very hard.

    (2) Typical Cases of MN

        a. The king of France is not bald—there is no king of France.

b. Some men are not chauvinists—all men are chauvinists.

c. He didn't call the [pólis], he called the [polís].

d. I didn't manage to trap two mongeese—I managed to trap two mongooses.

e. Now, Cindy, dear, grandama would like you to remember that you're a young lady: Phydeaux didn't shit the rug, he soiled the carpet.

f. I'm not his daughter—he's my father.

(Horn, 2009)

The sentences in (1) are examples of DN, which are ordinary and unmarked uses of negation in natural language. Each of them is a description of the state of affairs in the world. By contrast, the sentences in (2) are examples of MN, used not to describe states of affairs but to express one's objection to the non-truth-conditional content of the previous utterance. Their targets of objection are (a) presupposition, (b) scalar implicature, (c) phonological realization, (d) morphology, (e) register or style, and (f) focus and connotation.

According to Horn, the difference between the two types of negation is not to be found at the semantic level but at the pragmatic level: at the semantic level, negation operator is a unitary truth-functional operator, while at the pragmatic level, truth-functionality is replaced by the function of rejection, making possible the use of negation in a non-truth-conditional way. The difference is analyzed as a case of "pragmatic ambiguity" rather than semantic ambiguity.

Over the past few decades, a large number of studies of MN have been conducted since Horn's pioneering work. While the dichotomy of DN and MN has been widely accepted, the "pragmatic ambiguity" account has triggered heated discussion. Some researchers basically accept Horn's account, often in a modified form (e.g. Burton-Roberts, 1989a, 1989b; Shen, 1993; Pitts, 2005). Others reject this view and propose alternative accounts for the phenomenon. One approach is advocated by researchers working in the framework of relevance theory. They argue that the negation operator in natural language is always truth-functional;

MN should be characterized as involving "echoic use" or "metarepresentation" in the negative scope (Carston, 1996; Carston & Noh, 1996; Noh, 2000). Davis (2010, 2011, 2016) offers an alternative perspective that diverges from both the conventional and relevance-theoretical viewpoints. Davies concurs that the negation operator is unequivocal but advocates for the semantic ambiguity thesis. He suggests that MN is most effectively interpreted as an idiom that has evolved from generalized conversational implicatures.

MN in English has also garnered some attention from researchers within cognitive semantics. For example, in developing his theory of frame semantics, Fillmore (1985) characterizes DN and MN as "within-frame negation" and "cross-frame negation" respectively. Following Fillmore, Mamaridou (2000) suggests that MN emerges from the inappropriateness of applying a particular idealized cognitive model (ICM) to a situation. In a similar vein, Gao (2003) treats MN as a rejection of a particular way of categorizing an entity within a context.

While existing accounts of MN have uncovered many interesting aspects of this phenomenon, there are some limitations in both descriptive and explanatory dimensions. Descriptively, they are intuition-based rather than usage-based. Authentic data, especially those found in corpora, has so far played a rather minor role in developing these accounts. On the other hand, they are mainly based on observations of English. MN in non-Indo-European languages, such as Chinese, has not received much scrutiny in the literature. In terms of explanatory aspects, as mentioned above, most of the studies are based on theoretical models in pragmatics. To date, with few exceptions in cognitive semantics, research into the cognitive structures and mechanisms underpinning MN's meaning representation remains sparse.

The present study aims to offer a novel explanation for MN, focusing on observation of MN in modern Chinese. Specifically, our primary objective is to enhance previous insights from cognitive semantic studies by delivering a comprehensive explanation of MN in modern Chinese. Theoretically, we develop a new model (i.e. the intersubjective construal adjustment model) based on a combination of the model of intersubjectivity proposed by Verhagen (2005, 2009) and the model of construal proposed by Langacker (1987, 2008, 2013, 2015). To ensure our account is grounded in an adequate description of the phenomenon, this study adopts a usage-based approach by looking into the authentic data retracted from a corpus and the Internet. Subsequently, it systematically characterizes the various types of MN. The main goal of this book is to offer an in-depth analysis of the conceptual principles and processes underlying the meaning representations of MN.

1.2 Rationale for the Study

This study is primarily motivated by the desire to have a thorough understanding of the cognitive motivation behind MN drawing on cognitive-linguistic insights on the related issues. Issues with MN are tied to the semantics/pragmatics distinction itself (Mamaridou, 2000). Specifically, the controversy over the "ambiguity" of negation stems from different conceptions of the boundary between semantics and pragmatics. A growing number of researchers, particularly those working in cognitive linguistics (e. g. Fauconnier, 1985; Lakoff, 1987; Langacker, 1987; Sweetser, 1990), realize that the boundary between semantics and pragmatics is not so clear-cut as previously thought. Cognitive linguistics equates meaning construction with conceptualization, a dynamic process where linguistic expressions act merely as "prompts" for conceptual operations grounded in our encyclopedic knowledge (Evans & Green, 2006). According to this view, linguistic meaning is not purely constructed at the semantic level, or at the pragmatic level. Rather, it should be characterized at the conceptual level. Thus, cognitive linguistic theories prompt us to re-evaluate the nature of MN and offer a potential alternative solution for the related problems.

In recent years, many researchers begin to explore the potential synergies between cognitive linguistics and pragmatics (e.g. Zhang & Cai, 2005; Tendahl & Gibbs, 2008; Tendahl, 2009; Jiang, 2011), and how cognitive linguistics might shed light on the traditional topics in pragmatics (e. g. Fauconnier, 2006; Mamaridou, 2000; Kleinke, 2010). To our knowledge, with few exceptions in cognitive semantics as mentioned above, there has been scant research into how our conceptual structure and operations contribute to constructing the meaning of MN. Cognitive linguistics encompasses far more than just the cognitive semantic approach. The potential efficacy of other theoretical models that provide complementary perspectives and analytical tools for this phenomenon remains unexplored.

Another crucial consideration is the methodological requirement. Previous research on MN in Chinese was confined to a few intuitive data, with insufficient focus on systematically describing the semantic patterns of MN in Chinese. So far, none of the discussed analyses have utilized actual contextualized data for making linguistic generalizations. Over the last few decades, corpora have become prominent in linguistic research. Corpus data can not only give a more accurate and complete picture of the usages of MN but also provide typical examples attested in authentic contexts. We aim to base our explanatory account on a descriptively adequate account of MN in Chinese. Thus, by using authentic data collected from corpora of modern Chinese and the Internet, we propose a new classification of MN in terms of the types of representational effects it generally produces. In addition to the frequently discussed examples, the new classification can incorporate various other types of MN previously unaddressed in earlier accounts.

An additional consideration is a typological one. Until now, the majority of existing literature has focused on the structure and function of MN in Indo-European languages, with a particular emphasis on English. However, MN in non-Indo-European languages, like Chinese, has been largely overlooked. Claims made in the previous studies are often biased by the data from the language under investigation. A detailed examination of MN in Chinese not only aids in validating numerous theoretical and empirical claims in the existing accounts but also serves as a test for the explanatory capacity of cognitive linguistic theories when applied to languages beyond English.

1.3 Research Objectives

Given the above rationale, the present study aims to present a novel interpretation of the cognitive mechanisms underlying the meaning representation of MN in modern Chinese by adopting a usage-based approach (rather than the intuition-based approach). For its descriptive objective, this study intends to propose a more comprehensive classification of this phenomenon based on authentic data collected mainly from a corpus and the Internet. As to the explanatory objectives, based on a combination of Verhagen's model of intersubjectivity and Langacker's model of construal, it will develop previous insights within cognitive semantics on the meaning construction processes of various types of MN, namely strengthening denials, identifying denials, positioning denials and formal denials.

1.4 Significance of the Study

This study is intended to make a theoretical contribution by providing a deeper insight into "ambiguity" of negation and presenting a systematic and in-depth analysis of the meaning construction of various types of MN in modern Chinese. It adds further evidence of the explanatory potentiality of cognitive linguistic theories for the analysis of traditional pragmatic issues, bringing new insights into an ongoing dialogue between pragmatics and cognitive linguistics. The newly developed theoretical model demonstrates how the model of intersubjectivity might be fruitfully combined with the model of construal. It not only incorporates the key aspects of the previous cognitive semantic accounts, but also offers greater explanatory power in understanding the cognitive motivations behind MN.

Methodologically, it illustrates the significant contributions of authentic data towards enhancing both the descriptive and explanatory adequacy of pragmatic phenomena. Recently, there is an increasing awareness that linguistic study needs to be grounded in authentic data, especially those extracted from a corpus, within both pragmatics (e.g. Romero-Trillo, 2014, 2015, 2016; Aijmer, 2013; Aijmer & Rühlemann, 2015) and cognitive linguistics (e.g. Stefanowitsch & Gries, 2007). Until now, the majority of illustrative examples in MN studies have been invented rather than contextualized. Adopting a usage-based approach, this study shifts from the traditional intuitive approach, showcasing the advantages of corpus methodology in describing and explaining of MN. Although not experimental or quantitative, it evinces a higher degree of reliability on linguistic grounds. The usage-based approach could be extended cross-linguistically, paving the way for comparative studies of MN in Chinese and other languages in the world.

1.5 Organization of the Book

This book consists of ten chapters. Chapter 1 offers an overall introduction to the research. The first section introduces the research background of MN, while the second section delves into the study's rationale, covering its theoretical, methodological, and typological considerations. The third section concerns the research objectives, and the fourth one discusses the significance of the study.

Chapter 2 presents a review of the state-of-the-art research of MN, including four different theoretical accounts of MN, namely the standard accounts, the relevance-theoretical accounts, the "idiom" account, and the cognitive semantic accounts. Subsequently, a critical evaluation of these perspectives is conducted to validate the theoretical and methodological approaches employed for analytic purposes.

Chapter 3 discusses the theoretical considerations and analytical framework for the present study. This chapter introduces relevant insights in Verhagen's model of intersubjectivity and Langackers' model of construal. It is demonstrated that the two models provide complementary insights into the "ambiguity" of negation and meaning construction of MN. By merging the strengths of the two theoretical constructs, a new cognitive-linguistic model for analyzing MN is proposed.

Chapter 4 describes the methodology used in the present study. It begins with an explication of the central tenets of a usage-based approach to MN and how it can inform the present research. Following the introduction of data sources and the method of data collection and identification, a quantitative analysis of the corpus data is presented. This includes the frequencies of various forms of MN and their overall distributions across the genres of literature, newspaper, conversation, and technology.

In Chapter 5, a comprehensive classification of MN in modern Chinese is proposed based on the data collected. Four major types of MN are identified in terms of the representational effects MN generally produces. They are strengthening denials, identifying denials, positioning denials, and formal denials. Subspecies of each category of MN are described in detail.

Chapter 6 offers a cognitive linguistic exploration of the cognitive processes involved in the meaning construction of strengthening denials, encompassing scalar strengthening denials, granular strengthening denials, partonomic strengthening denials, epistemic strengthening denials, and directional strengthening denials. This chapter illustrates how the five types of identifying denials emerge from intersubjective adjustment of alternate construals, grounded in cognitive principles such as scale, specificity, scopes of attention, epistemic ground, and action chain schemas.

Chapter 7 delves into the meaning construction of identifying denials, encompassing categorical identifying denials, facet identifying denials, relational identifying denials, identity identifying denials, and sequential identifying denials. It demonstrates how the five types of identifying denials are produced through the adjustments of alternate construals between two subjects of conceptualization, based on parameters like prototypicality, domains, "trajector/landmark" alignment, common ground, and mental scanning.

Chapter 8 explores the cognitive processes behind the derivation of the five types of positioning denials: relativistic positioning denials, causative positioning denials, deictic positioning denials, structural positioning denials, and evaluative positioning denials. This chapter aims to show that positioning denials result from intersubjective adjustments of alternate construals related to a number of parameters such as viewing arrangement, action chain profiling, deixis, individuation and relationality, and frames.

Chapter 9 deals with the cognitive activity leading to three types of formal denials: phonological denials, collocation denials, and stylistic denials. It demonstrates that formal denials emerge from intersubjective adjustment of different ways to categorize the same entity. Introducing the notion of "sanction" proposed in Langacker's cognitive grammar, we suggest that the meaning construction of formal denials involves varying sanctioning relations between the sanctioning structure and target structure.

Finally, Chapter 10 summarizes the key findings of the book and outlines how this research enriches current studies. The book concludes with a discussion on the study's limitations and offers suggestions for future research.

Chapter 2

Literature Review

This chapter presents a systematic review of existing studies of MN. As previously mentioned, MN has been characterized through various accounts based on different theoretical frameworks. This review will elucidate four theoretical accounts of MN: standard accounts, relevance-theoretical accounts, "idiom" account, and cognitive semantic accounts. The purpose of this chapter is to critically evaluate existing accounts of MN to justify the theoretical and methodological approach adopted in this study.

2.1 The Standard Accounts of MN

As highlighted in Chapter 1, the "pragmatic ambiguity" account proposed in the pioneering work of Horn (1985, 1989) has received considerable attention over the past few decades. Many researchers share some fundamental agreement with Horn, though they sometimes diverge from the "pragmatic ambiguity" account on various issues. Notably, Burton-Roberts' (1999) contributions merit discussion. Following Noh (2000), Burton-Roberts's account, alongside the "pragmatic ambiguity" account, is considered a standard account of MN in this context.

2.1.1 The "Pragmatic Ambiguity" Account

Horn is not the first scholar to note the "duality of use" of linguistic negation. He (1985) recognizes that much the same observation has already been made in Ducrot (1972, 1973), Grice (1967), Wilson (1975), among others (cf. Horn 1985). Ducrot (1972) notes that negation in natural language fulfills two functions: "descriptive" and "métalinguistique". The negation that cancels a presupposition, exemplified by Russell's (1905) famous sentence "The King of France is not bald—there is no king of France." illustrates the metalinguistic function of negation. Building on Ducrot's work, Horn contends that often linguistic negation doesn't simply describe a situation but signals the speaker's reluctance to affirm a proposition for reasons beyond its truthfulness.

As outlined in Chapter 1, the grounds of MN extends beyond presupposition to encompass non-propositional elements like implicature, pronunciation, morphology and register. MN is depicted as a device for objecting to a previous utterance on the ground that it is unassertable. According to Horn, "assertable" means "felicitously assertable" or "appropriately assertable", encompassing all forms of marked negation. Yoshimura (2013) summarizes the features of DN and MN in Table 2.1.

Table 2.1 Horn's Dichotomy of Negation

Category	DN	MN
Status of the operator	Truth-functional operator	Non-truth-functional operator
Focus of negation	The truth or falsity of a proposition	The assertability of an utterance
—	Propositional content	Any aspects of an utterance
Function	Taking a proposition P into a proposition not-P	Objecting to an utterance ("I object to U")

Horn (1985, 1989) interprets the noticeable "duality of use" in linguistic negation as "pragmatic ambiguity". Before this explanation, Horn identifies two distinct views on negation's variability: the "ambiguity" position and the "monoguity" position. Advocates of the "ambiguity" position claim that natural language negation is semantically ambiguous, and the marked negation can be semantically analyzed in terms of truth. This viewpoint is embraced, in one way or another by researchers like Russel (1905), Karttunen and Peters (1979) and proponents of three-valued logic. The assumed ambiguity is contested by proponents of the "monoguist" position, including philosophers and linguists like Atlas (1977, 1979, 1989, 2005, 2012), Kempson (1975) and Gazdar (1979a, 1979b), who maintain that all instances of negation in natural language share a single truth-functional operator.

As a pragmatist, Horn attempts to reconcile the discrepancies between the two camps. He argues that neither of the two approaches captures how the two principal varieties of negation differ from each other. This oversight occurs because most analyses of negation's variability concentrate on its semantics, neglecting pragmatic aspects. The distinction between DN and MN is asserted to exist not semantically, but pragmatically. Agreeing with monoguists, Horn posits that negation is a singular phenomenon that can be semantically analyzed based on truth. However, the truth-functional role of the negation operator is maintained only in its descriptive usage; in metalinguistic contexts, it shifts to contesting the "appropriateness" of an utterance. Therefore, this distinction is interpreted as "pragmatic ambiguity", distinct from the "semantic ambiguity" proposed by ambiguists. The concept of "pragmatic ambiguity" can also apply to other linguistic operators like "and", "or", and "if", according to Horn (1985).

Horn introduces various diagnostic criteria for identifying this unique category of negation in English. In English, MN is typically characterized by a range of non-semantic features, such as resistance to morphological incorporation, inability to activate negative polarity items, distinctive intonation, specific distributional traits of but-conjunctions, and the potential to induce a "garden-path" effect.

Resistance to morphological incorporation: in English, *not* typically can be incorporated onto a lexical item as the *im-*, *un-* or *in-* prefixes, as seen in *impossible*, *unhappy* and *inaccurate*. These morphologically incorporated forms are truth-functionally identical to their non-incorporated counterparts. However, in metalinguistic negation, these incorporated forms are typically deemed unacceptable. Consider the following examples, drawn from Horn (1985):

(1) a. It's⎰not possible/*impossible⎰for you to leave now—it's necessary.

　　b.⎰not probable/*improbable⎰but certain.

　　c.⎰not likely/*unlikely⎰but certain.

　　d.⎰not interesting/*uninteresting⎰but certain.

Inability to activate negative polarity items: negative polarity items (NPIs) refer to words like "any", "ever", and "at all". Typically found in negative and other downward-entailing contexts, NPIs convey low quantitative and high informative significance. It is argued that NPIs demonstrate asymmetrical grammatical behavior between DN and MN. Specifically, they can only occur in DN but are not permitted in MN. For example, NPIs such as *any* and *at all* can be licensed by ordinary descriptive negation, as shown in (2) a and (3) a. However, they should be excluded by the metalinguistic use of negation, as seen in (2) b and (3) b:

(2) a. Tom did not buy ANY book in the bookstore; he likes borrowing books from the library.

　　b. *Tom did not buy ANY book in the bookstore; he brought all of them.

(3) a. Mary does not like Jack AT ALL; instead, she hates him very much.

　　b. *Mary does not like Jack AT ALL; she loves him.

Distinctive intonation: The descriptive use of negation is characterized by normal stress on the negation operator and a final fall. For example, in (3) *not* receives stress and is given the same or a higher pitch compared to *like*. However, in the metalinguistic use of negation, stress is typically put on the lexical item in the scope of negation. The negative clause is ended with what Ladd (1980) terms the "fall-rise" contour, as an intonation cue for the following rectification clause.

Concessive/contrastive *but*-conjunctions: Another diagnostic for the distinction between DN and MN in English lies in the distributional characteristic of *but*-

conjunctions, which can be either concessive or contrastive. Horn (1985) observes that MN predominantly appears in contrastive contexts and can be clarified through various means; yet, specific morphosyntactic limitations apply to contrastive *but*-conjunctions. For example, the rectification can be achieved using "but" or a complete finite clause, but not both simultaneously. Consider (4):

(4) a. It isn't hot, but scalding.

b. It isn't hot—it's scalding.

c. *It isn't hot, but it' s scalding.

(Horn, 1985)

It is argued that these *but*-conjunctions are acceptable within the context of descriptive negation, where they are often interpreted as concessions and accompanied by a distinct intonation contour. Consider (5):

(5) a. I do not love Peter, but I like him.

b. The king of France is not bald, but he has very scarce hair.

c. Tom did not steal all the money, but he stole some of it.

Garden-path effect: Metalinguistic uses of negation are also different from descriptive ones in that the former generally produce a garden-path effect. Horn (2009) claims, "The metalinguistic understanding typically requires a second pass and the effect is typically that of an ironic 'unsaying' or retroactive accommodation." For example, in (4), the first part of the utterance may garden-path the hearer because the default interpretation is typically the descriptive one, i.e. *it is cold* or *it is at least warm*.

Horn's work has also received considerable attention from many Chinese linguistic researchers over the past decade. Among them, Shen (1993) represents a pioneering effort to examine MN in modern Chinese. DN and MN are respectively termed as "semantic negation" and "pragmatic negation" to highlight the different aspects of meaning they negate. The former is characterized as denying the semantic content (i.e. truth condition) of a proposition, whereas the latter involves pragmatic content (i.e. felicity condition) of the proposition. Shen categorizes MN in Chinese into five types: (a) MN derived from the maxim of quantity; (b) MN derived from the maxim of order; (c) MN used to deny implicatures concerning styles and connotations; (d) MN used to deny presupposition; (e) MN concerning the felicity conditions on phonology and grammar. MN is characterized by specific formal and functional features: It always includes a quotation of a previous utterance, a correction or explanation of an affirmative utterance, and the propositions in the negative and corrective clauses embody the same speech act. These views fundamentally align with Horn's. However, Shen demonstrates the validity of the DN/MN dichotomy in a language unrelated to English and provides insightful discussions on some syntactic, morphological, and semantic features characteristic of MN in Chinese. Operating within the neo-Gricean theory of conversational implicature, Xu (1994) renames MN as "implicature negation" and divides it into two categories: negation of scalar implicature and negation of stereotypical implicature. They are generated by the Q-principle and the R-principle in Neo-Gricean pragmatics, respectively. Agreeing with Shen and Xu's accounts, Zhang (1999) further explores how pragmatic negation is restricted by structural form, lexical meaning, and context. It is argued that these restriction factors are interrelated and collectively influence the expression of MN.

While Horn's insightful description of MN's properties merits commendation, his theoretical account has sparked significant debate over the years. A particularly contentious issue is the true nature of the so-called "pragmatic ambiguity". Its validity is supported mainly by references to similar analyses, like Donnellan's attributive/referential distinction, Wertheime's exploration of modal "ambiguity", and Grice's examination of scalar predication from a one-sided/two-sided perspective. However, this concept is not clearly defined in Horn's works and lacks a recognized status in pragmatics (Foolen, 1991). This notion has sparked numerous debates regarding its interpretation (e.g. Burton-Roberts, 1989a, 1989b; Foolen, 1991; Carston & Noh, 1996). Among these, Burton-Roberts critically assesses

Horn's work, providing valuable insights into the interpretation of MN and its differentiation from DN.

2.1.2 The "Semantic Contradiction" Account

Burton-Roberts (1989a, 1989b) concurs with Horn that DN diverges from truth-functional negation. However, he highlights a contradiction in Horn's stance: MN is described both as "an extended metalinguistic use of a fundamentally truth-functional operator" and as "irreducible to the standard truth-functional operator". (Horn, 1985) Agreeing with Horn, Burton-Roberts maintains that negation is semantically clear-cut and that MN is a pragmatic phenomenon. Yet, he delves deeper into investigating the dynamics between DN and MN, questioning their directionality and which is primary versus derivative.

Burton-Roberts asserts that a pragmatic analysis of MN necessitates an understanding of the logical semantics of negation. Specifically, he posits that the descriptive, truth-functional interpretation is foundational, and the metalinguistic, non-truth-functional interpretation is derived from it pragmatically. When interpreting a MN utterance, the addressee typically perceives the negative clause as descriptive and truth-functional negation. This leads to a semantic contradiction between the negative clause and the corrective clause (i.e. the rectification). The interpretation of MN becomes possible only after this semantic contradiction is induced. Consider (6):

(6) I'm not meeting a woman this evening; I'm meeting my wife!

(Burton-Roberts, 1989b)

The corrective statement contradicts the initial clause under the assumption that meeting one's wife inherently means meeting a woman. Upon noticing the semantic contradiction, the listener is compelled to re-evaluate the default interpretation and undertake a pragmatic reanalysis of the initial clause. This perspective on MN interpretation closely aligns with Horn's concepts of "double processing" and "garden-path" effects associated with MN. However, Burton-

Roberts (1989a) goes further to explain the distinctive behavior of MN compared to DN, drawing on the "use-mention" distinction. This distinction is rooted in Sperber and Wilson's (1981) analysis of irony. Simplified, when a linguistic expression is used to highlight or discuss states of affairs, it is "used"; when it draws attention to or discusses the expression itself, it is "mentioned". Sperber and Wilson (1986) argue that the fundamental semantic trait of ironic statements is their status as "mentions" (as opposed to "uses") of a proposition. Following this theory, the differentiation between DN and MN is framed as a distinction between "use" and "mention". MN is considered a specific form of mention, or (semi-) quotation, entailing the mention of a proposition previously used in discourse.

Burton-Roberts (1989b) posits that interpreting MN as mention is particularly useful for explaining the arch, often ironic tone frequently associated with this form of negation. This interpretation helps elucidate the diagnostic properties of MN outlined in the preceding section. According to him, mention produces a sealing-off effect, isolating the mentioned expression from its immediate linguistic context within the sentence. Consequently, negation outside this seal cannot activate a negative polarity item or be prefixally attached to a word inside the seal. The sealing-off effect of mention is also thought to explain why the double negation inference rule is inapplicable in MN. Consider (7):

(7) Marry isn't not happy; she is ecstatic.

Through double negation, the negative clause implies that Mary is happy, a notion that conflicts with the corrective statement that she is ecstatic. Clearly, applying the double negation rule distorts the speaker's intended message in this sentence. The failure of the double negation rule in this instance is due to *not happy* being "mentioned" rather than "used", thereby isolating it from the external negation operator *not*.

To sum up, Burton-Roberts questions the validity of "pragmatic ambiguity" as a means of distincting between DN and MN. He examines the challenges Horn encounters in his explanation and puts forward several key points. MN is considered to stem from a "semantic contradiction" between the negative clause and the rectification. The dichotomy of DN and MN ultimately hinges on whether the related linguistic expression is "used" or "mentioned". Despite Burton-Roberts' critical stance towards Horn's perspective, they share some fundamental agreements. Most importantly, they both recognize the role of truth conditions in the analysis of natural language, thus considering DN primary and MN derivative. Standard interpretations of MN have been contested by researchers in the relevance theory framework, both theoretically and empirically.

2.2 The Relevance-theoretical Accounts of MN

Scholars utilizing relevance theory propose a novel perspective on MN, emphasizing its relationship with our overarching cognitive abilities. In the next section, two relevance-theoretical accounts, namely the "echoic use" account and the "metarepresentation" account will be discussed.

2.2.1 The "Echoic Use" Account

Relevance theory offers a cognitive perspective on thought and communication. Unlike neo-Gricean pragmatic theories, which posit that pragmatic inference is required solely for deriving implicatures, relevance theorists view human inference as absolutely essential for understanding language. Pragmatic inference encompasses more than just deriving implicatures and fairly obvious processes such as disambiguation and reference assignment; it extends to subtler processes that make contribution to the truth condition of the utterances. This point is termed the "strong underdeterminacy thesis", which asserts that an utterance's encoded meaning requires significant pragmatic enrichment before the truth-conditional content can be determined (Carston & Noh, 1996). According to them, the distinction between the two negation uses lies not in the negation operator itself but in the negated content: the former is used descriptively, whereas the latter is used echoically.

Within relevance theory, "echoic use" is intimately linked to humans' inherent ability to represent another representation due to some resemblance in content or form, i. e. the metapresentational ability (Sperber & Wilson, 1986; Wilson & Sperber, 1988, 1992). Echoic use is described as a form of metarepresentation where the speaker conveys their attitude towards the metarepresented content. Specifically, a representation is considered echoically used when the speaker attributes it to someone else (not themselves at the moment of utterance) and demonstrates a specific attitude towards the negated content, spanning from full agreement to outright rejection. Consider (8):

(8) A: Your father's car is not old; it is pretty new.

B: Your father's car is not old; it is antique.

The negative clause in (8) A is a standard truth-functional negation, which is a description of a state of affairs in the world where the hearer's father has a new car rather than an old one. The negative clause in (8) B is marked, metalinguistic use of negation, negating the inadequate application of the word *old* because of its weaker semantic strength. The content negated in (8) B is typified by echoic use, where *old* is reiterated from an earlier statement.

Carston (1994, 1995) contends that the characteristics Horn and Burton-Roberts ascribe to MN are not fundamental: MN statements don't invariably entail a preceding utterance; they aren't all semantic contradictions; certain MN instances don't necessitate explicit clarification clauses; they might not induce a garden-path effect; at times, the metalinguistic application isn't overtly signaled by prosodic features. Rather, the accurate generalization is that all MN instances involve "echoic use", where the speaker's attitude conveyed can be either explicit or implicit. The explicit objection manifested in MN contrasts with irony, wherein the speaker's dissociative stance is implied rather than overtly stated. Compare (8) with (9):

(9) A: I heard that Tom's girlfriend is a gorgeous woman.

(When they found that Tom's girlfriend was very ugly.)

B: (Sarcastically) Tom's girlfriend is a gorgeous woman.

In (9), speaker B's remark is ironic, not serving as a truth-conditional description of reality but rather as an echoic statement to voice objection to A's viewpoint. Here, the speaker's dissociative stance is implied, as discerning their disagreement with A relies on interpreting contextual cues. In contrast, in (8), the speaker's dissociative attitude is explicitly indicated through the use of the negation operator. Unlike linguistic expressions that employ verbs like *say,* the echoic use in MN isn't explicitly denoted by linguistic indicators. Put differently, the negated content in MN features implicit echoic use.

The perspective that MN entails echoic use is echoed by Sandt, even though his work is conducted beyond the confines of relevance theory. To grasp the explanatory scope of Carston's theory more fully, a concise exploration of Sandt's contributions is warranted. Sandt (2003) distinguishes between negation and denial: negation applies to sentences and is truth-functional, whereas denials target utterances, amending information content stemming from an earlier utterance. MN is characterized as a denial of any "information content" that is echoed from a preceding utterance. The negated material of MN includes not only the non-truth-conditional content (such as presupposition, implicature, style, and register) but also propositional content, for example, the proposition *Shanghai is the capital of China*. Consequently, both propositional and non-propositional denials constitute a coherent category.

Sandt's account encounters numerous challenges. One of them is that MN can be formed by echoing the linguistic material from a previous utterance that is not declarative in nature (Noh, 2000). Consider (10):

(10) A: It is cold outside?

B: It is not cold outside; it is downright freezing.

B's remark clearly exemplifies metalinguistic negation. Yet, it doesn't serve as a denial of A's utterance's information content, given that A's statement is not declarative. B's utterance is obviously a metalinguistic use of negation. However, it is not a denial of the information content of A's utterance since what A said is not declarative. Another problem is that MN needs not to be used in response to a previous utterance. Consider (11):

>(11) A: Meinong thought that Vulcan is hot.
>
>   B: Vulcan is not hot: it does not exist.

(Davis, 2011)

In (11), B denies Meinong's thought that Vulcan is hot, rather than what A said. Nor does B deny what A presupposes or implicates since A presupposes or implies nothing about Vulcan's existence or nature.

The limitations inherent of Sandt's account of MN can be addressed through the relevance-theoretical notion of "echoic use". Wilson (2000) delineates three principal forms of metarepresentation: public representations, such as utterances; mental representations, like thoughts; and abstract representations, including sentences and propositions. Thus, "echoic use" emerges as a comprehensive category that not only covers scenarios addressed by Sandt but also extends to instances eluding his framework (Noh, 2000).

Assuming the strong underdeterminacy thesis discussed above, Carston and Noh (1996) view the negation operator *not* (and other operators like *as*, *or* and *if*) as uniformly truth-functional in all cases of negation, and hold that there is substantial pragmatic enrichment of the echoed linguistic material at the level of the proposition expressed (or what is said). Consider (12):

>(12) They didn't have a baby and get married; they got married and
>   have a baby.

(Horn, 1989)

According to Horn, this sentence is not a descriptive and truth-functional negation, but a metalinguistic and non-truth-functional one. This is because the negation targets the manner implicature that arises from the sequence of the conjuncts, namely the idea that they didn't have a baby *and then* get married.

However, relevance theory posits that this aspect of meaning should be categorized as an "explicature", a technical term for *what is said* or *directly meant*, rather than "implicature". (Sperber & Wilson, 1986; Carston, 1988) As such, it constitutes a segment of the truth-functional content and, accordingly, falls within the scope of the negation operator.

Characterizing MN as a type of echoic use and being truth-conditional implies that this category is not necessarily confined to cases that are usually recognized. In other words, propositional content may also be the target of MN.[①] The rationale is that, within relevance theory, the concept of "echoic use" pertains not just to non-truth-conditional content but also to the truth-conditional content of a previous utterance (Carston, 1996). Consider (13):

> (13) A: Do you like to play table tennis after class?
>
> B: I don't want to play table tennis; I'd like to play basketball.

In B's response, the truth-conditional content of playing table tennis is negated, but this also incorporates echoic use, similar to the typical cases of MN discussed earlier. The reason why this form of negation isn't commonly classified as MN is the difficulty in differentiating it from the standard descriptive use of negation.

To sum up, in the "echoic use" account the negation operator of MN is analyzed as being truth-functional as that of DN, but without the ambiguity as Horn claims. The ambiguity lies in the nature of the linguistic items within the scope of negation: DN involves a descriptive use of these items, whereas MN is distinguished by its implicit echoic use.

2.2.2 The "Metarepresentation" Account

The "echoic use" account is further revised and refined in Noh (2000). Noh

---

① As mentioned above, Sandt (2003) holds the similar view that propositional denials can be considered instances of MN.

concurs with Carston that MN and DN both utilize a standard truth-functional negation operator, yet the content within their scopes differs in nature. However, he disputes Carston's assertion that the negated content pertains to "echoic use" as previously defined. Instead, he characterizes MN purely as a form of metarepresentation, not necessarily reflecting the speaker's attitude. He reasons that when a speaker echoes merely a portion of the proposition or a single aspect of the linguistic form, it's challenging to assert that the utterance conveys a dissociative attitude. Compare (14), from Noh (2000):

> (14) A: The teacher used the rod of love to make us learn better.
>
> B1: He didn't use the rod of love; he simply used violence.
>
> B2: But some teachers didn't use the rod of love; they simply used violence.

Both responses in (14) B1 and (14) B2 serve as instances of MN, as the basis for negation lies not in the propositional content but in the connotation of the phrase *the rod of love*. The negation in (14) B1 can be interpreted as reflecting the speaker's dissociative attitude towards the phrase. However, the negation in (14) B2 does not appear to convey the speaker's dissociative attitude towards it. It merely provides an accurate depiction of the teacher's actions as described in A's statement; the rejection pertains solely to the phrase's applicability to other teachers.

Drawing on relevance-theoretical research on metarepresentation (Sperber & Wilson, 1986; Wilson & Sperber, 1988, 1992; Blakemore, 1992), Noh (2000) identifies two forms of metarepresentation: one related to conceptual content resemblance and the other to linguistic form resemblance. When the former is negated, it is regarded as an interpretive or metaconceptual negation. Conversely, denying the latter results in what is considered genuine metalinguistic negation. These two negation types are collectively referred to as metarepresentational negation.

Interpretive negation is also termed attributive interpretive negation, implying that the negated material encompasses the semantic content of either an attributed utterance (public representation) or an attributed thought (private representation). Consider (15) and (16):

> (15) A: She is happy.
>
> B: She is not happy. She has a problem with her husband these days.
>
> (16) A: No more whisky. You said you would have an important meeting tomorrow morning.
>
> B: I'm not drunk. Give me another glass.
>
> Noh (2000)

In (15), the focus of metarepresentation is the semantic content of A's statement. And in (16), the metarepresented material is A's thought that the speaker is drunk. Both the two examples illustrate the metarepresentational use of negation, with the negated contents being, respectively, a public representation (an utterance) and a private representation (a thought) that can be attributed to certain sources.

Characterizing MN as the metapresentation of formal linguistic properties enables a broader understanding of MN utterances beyond previous accounts and aids in elucidating its purported characteristics. Consider (17) - (19), from Noh (2000):

> (17) A: Mary is sometimes late.
>
> B: Mary is not {sometimes/*ever} late; she is always late.
>
> (18) She is {not happy/*unhappy}; she is ecstatic.
>
> (19) Max isn't not very tall; he is a dwarf.
>
> ≠ * Max is very tall; he is a dwarf.

As discussed previously, the negative polarity item *ever* in (17) cannot be replaced by the positive polarity item *sometimes*. In (18), the negated material *happy* is resistant to lexical incorporation. And in (19), the double negation rule is not applicable. The inability to replace these with semantically equivalent utterances is ascribed to the characteristic of metalinguistic metarepresentation. That is, it's not their semantic content that's being represented, but rather their linguistic form.

This division is also claimed to explain why attributive interpretive negation does not meet the alleged diagnostics for MN. That is, morphological incorporation, the double negation rule, and negative polarity items are all applicable to this form of negation. As illustrated above, instances such as (15) and (16) involve the metapresentation of an utterance. However, they might also be categorized under DN, as the speakers refute the truth conditions of the utterances according to Horn's interpretation.

Noh endorses Carston's original account that MN is as always truth-functional as DN once the metarepresentational element is properly analyzed. However, he gives a more detailed analysis of how the metarepresented material in MN is unpacked based on relevance theory. According to Noh, metarepresentation in the negative clause contributes to the proposition it expresses and should be pragmatically enriched in order to have a determinate truth-conditional content. The understanding process of MN is guided by the principles of relevance and relevance-theoretical interpretation strategies (Sperber & Wilson, 1986, 2002; Wilson & Sperber, 2002; Sperber, Cara & Girotto, 1995). Consider (20):

> (20) A: Did you see two mongeese yesterday?
>
> B: I didn't see two mongeese; I saw two mongooses.

When interpreting B's utterance, guided by the principle of relevance, the hearer will adopt the most accessible reading. Obviously, the proposition expressed by A's utterance is not relevant in its own right. Then the first accessible reading satisfying the hearer's expectation of relevance will be the metarepresentional one because of the morphological resemblance between the utterance of A and B. This interpretation will achieve the expected degree of relevance thereby. Accordingly, the hearer selects this interpretation in accordance with the relevance-theoretical comprehension strategy. The metarepresented material is then incorporated into a descriptive expression and assigned a truth condition, as shown in (21):

(21) a. Not [You saw two mongeese]; you saw two mongooses.

b. Not [you bought what is properly expressed as mongeese];

[you bought what is properly expressed as mongooses]

The logical form of (20) B can be represented as (21) a. The metarepresented morphological plural *mongeese* is embedded within the phrase "what is properly expressed" to indicate its attributed use. This yields a fairly determinate proposition with its own truth condition.

To sum up, Noh gives an updated relevance-theoretical account of MN by analyzing it as a case of metarepresentaional use, without necessarily expressing the speaker's attitude. Metarepresentational negation is categorized into metalinguistic negation which pertains to the metarepresentation of form, and interpretive negation which concerns the metaprcsentation of content. The metarepresented content needs to be pragmatically enriched to achieve determinate truth-conditional content. Furthermore, the process of pragmatic enrichment is steered by the quest for optimal relevance, following the relevance-theoretical comprehension strategy.

2.3 The "Idiom" Account of MN

Davis (2010, 2011, 2013, 2016) proposes the "idiom" account of MN as an alternative pragmatic approach. Davis highlights the inappropriateness of the term "metalinguistic negation", emphasizing that it accurately pertains only to phonological or morphological examples of MN. To rectify this, he introduces "irregular negation" as a replacement for the term "metalinguistic negation". The sentence obtained by omitting the negation operator is termed the root. Davis contends that the ambiguity does not reside in the negation operator itself but in the facets of meaning it seeks to negate. Specifically, the negation is a logically regular one when the speaker denies what the root asserts, and the negation is irregular when the speaker objects to the implicatures of the root. Consider (22), from Davis (2016):

    (22) a. The sun is not larger than some planets.

        b. The sun is larger than some planets. (Root)

        c. The sun is larger than just some planets. (Implicature of Root)

        d. The sun is not larger than just some planets. (Denial of Root Implicature)

Contrary to the views of researchers like Horn, Burton-Robert, Sandt, and Carston, Davis (2013, 2016) posits that objecting to a prior statement is not essential or unique to irregular negations. What is denied in a MN is a specific implicature of the root itself, which may not have been previously stated. Following Grice's (1967) distinction of speaker meaning and word meaning, Davis (2013) differentiates between speaker implicature and sentence implicature: speaker implicature refers to what the speaker means by saying something else; sentence implicature is what the sentence of that form may be conventionally used to implicate. It is argued that the implicature of the root of negation is not speaker implicature but sentence implicature, i.e. "generalized conversational implicature" in Gricean pragmatics. Contrary to the belief that negation can counter any implicature (Horn, 1985, 1989; Burton-Roberts, 1989; Sandt, 1991), Davis argues that irregular negation cannot deny the "particularized conversational implicature" of a previous utterance.

In Davis (2016), irregular negations are classified into six types: limiting implicature denial, strengthening implicature denial, ignorance implicature denial, metalinguistic implicature denial, evaluative implicature denial and presupposition-canceling denial. Different types of irregular negations deny different root implicatures. It can be illustrated by (23):

(23) a. The sun is not larger than some planets: it is larger than all planets.

b. Mary did not meet a man at the bar; she met her husband.

c. The water is not at most warm: it is known to be freezing cold.

d. That's not a tomäto: it's a tomāto.

e. Vulcan is not hot: it does not exist

f. Midori's performance was not somewhat flawed; it was nearly flawless.

Limiting implicature denial and strengthening implicature denial are respectively generated by Horn's Q-principle and R-principle (Horn, 1989). Limiting implicature denials, also known as "scalar implicature denials", refer to cases of irregular negations in which the speaker objects to a stronger proposition implicated by the root. For example, the target of the negation in (23) a is the limiting (or scalar) implicature of its root, i. e. the sun is not larger than all planets. Strengthening implicature refers to cases in which a stronger proposition is implicated. For example, *Mary did meet a man at the bar* has a strengthening implicature that *Mary met an unrelated man at the bar.* This implicature is denied by the speaker in (23) b. Ignorance implicature refers to implicature that the speaker does not know whether the proposition expresses in the root is true. For example, *The water is at most warm* induces the ignorance implicature "I do not know whether the water is warm". (23) c is used to deny this ignorance implicature. Metalinguistic implicature denials refer to the type of negation used to deny the appropriateness of (phonological or morphological) form, style or register, such as in (23) d. The negation in (23) e is used to deny the presupposition of the root, rather than its truth condition. Evaluative implicature denials involve denying the positive or negative evaluation conveyed by the root, as is shown in (23) f.

According to Davis, evaluative implicature denials are considered "live" implicatures, setting them apart from other forms of irregular negations that are more akin to fixed expressions or idioms. This difference stems from the nature of their interpretation: the intended meaning of evaluative implicature denials only becomes apparent with specific contextual focus, unlike the more straightforward interpretation of other irregular negations. In the case of evaluative implicature denials, the connection between their conventional (regular) and derived (irregular) meanings is less direct. This nuanced relationship does not apply to other negation types, such as limiting (or scalar) implicature denial, strengthening implicature denial, ignorance implicature denial, metalinguistic implicature denial, and presupposition-canceling denial, which have a more direct transition from their general to specific meanings. These fives idioms are hypothesized to be evolved from GCI, which gradually become conventional through frequent use, like literal meanings of dead metaphor. Or, put it differently, the irregular meaning of these negations has begun as implicature, but gradually becomes an additional sense of the negation. Let us illustrate this idea with the limiting implicature denials with "some". Given that "some" can be used in the form of the sentence "S Vs some O" to mean "S Vs just some O", there is no reason for "S does not V some O" not to mean "S does not V just some O". Similar to the former, the latter usage can also be conventionalized with frequent uses, giving rise to the irregular sense of sentences of the form "S does not V some O". This irregular sense gradually becomes the direct, rather than indirect meaning of the sentence. The same is true of strengthening implicature denials, ignorance denials, metalinguistic implicature denial, and presupposition-canceling denials.

Irregular negations significantly differ from conventional idioms regarding both compositionality and productivity. Unlike typical idioms, which are phrase-based and lack compositionality, irregular negations are sentence-based and exhibit partial compositionality. Compare the typical idiom *throw in the towel* with the irregular negation *the sun is not larger than some planets*. Davis (2013) elucidates that irregular negations, lacking fixed forms, can be non-compositional yet exhibit high productivity, and makes a distinction between two types of idioms: "fixed-form" idioms and "free-form" idioms. "Fixed-form" idioms are syntactically rigid, offering minimal compositionality and productivity, whereas "free-form" idioms, despite having a set structure, are somewhat compositional. As a result, irregular negations demonstrate greater productivity than typical idioms. Finding new examples of limiting-implicature denials in daily conversation is straightforward, like *Marry did not eat some of the chocolates; she ate all* and *Some students were not absent yesterday; all students were absent.* Irregular negations are non-compositional mainly because their meanings do not solely stem from their lexical components and syntactic structures. Instead, irregular negations derive their idiomatic meanings through the conventional use of general sentence forms to convey broad conceptual frameworks.

To sum up, Davis argues against pragmatic ambiguity theories that MN is derived from regular interpretations using conversational or cognitive principles. They are unusual because the roots of negation are conventionally used to express the corresponding implicature (or explicature in terms of the relevance framework). The irregular uses of negation result from the idiomaticity of generalized conversational implicatures. Similar to conventional idioms, the connection between the irregular meaning and the semantically encoded meaning is "semantic" rather than "pragmatic". Consequently, the distinction between DN and MN is characterized by "semantical ambiguity" rather than "pragmatical ambiguity".

2.4 The Cognitive Semantic Accounts of MN

Cognitive semantics emerged in the 1970s, responding to the limitations of the truth-conditional approach to semantics, which fails to take into consideration of the cognitive processes of human beings. Within cognitive semantics, the exploration of meaning constituents not addressed by truth-conditional semantics has become a significant area of interest. MN serves as a compelling example to demonstrate the explanatory strength of cognitive semantic theories regarding non-truth-conditional meaning aspects. Meaning constituents that can not be captured by truth-conditional semantics become an interesting and important topic within cognitive semantics. MN constitutes a good case to show the explanatory power of cognitive semantic theories on non-truth-conditional aspects of meaning. This section will explore three cognitive semantic accounts, namely the frame-denying account, the ICM-denying account, and the dynamic categorization account.

2.4.1 The Frame-denying Account

This account is proposed by Charles Fillmore based on his model of frame semantics (Fillmore, 1977, 1982, 1985). At the heart of frame semantics is the concept of a "frame", a comprehensive knowledge structure shaped by our interactions with the world. Unlike formal semantics, which relies on a truth-conditional model of meaning, cognitive semanticists believe that linguistic meaning is organized around the frames that provide context for understanding linguistic expressions.

A language often provides various frames for a single situation to be conceptualized. As Fillmore (1982) puts it, "From a frame semantics point of view, it is frequently possible to show that the same 'facts' can be presented within different framings, framings which make them out as different 'facts'." For instance, a person reluctant to spend money might be labeled either *stingy* or *thrifty*. These two terms refer to the same situation but are interpreted through different frames, offering unique evaluations. While *stingy* is contrasted with *generous*, representing a negative assessment of the behavior's treatment of other people, *thrifty* is contrasted with *wasteful*, representing a positive assessment of the behavior's management of money or other resources.

According to Fillmore (1985), frame semantics readily accommodates the interplay between truth and negation. The ability to frame a single situation in various ways enables the representation of negation in two distinct manners. Consider (24):

> (24) a. Mary is not stingy; he is generous.
>
>   b. Mary is not stingy; he is downright thrifty.

In (24) a, the speaker acknowledges the "stingy-generous" scale but declines to assess Mary's behavior as being on the "stingy" end. By contrast, in (24) b, the speaker rejects the scale of measurement in question as being in error. This means Mary's behavior should not be evaluated in terms of the "stingy-generous", but rather of the "thrifty-wasteful" one.

Following the observation, Fillmore distinguishes between "within-frame negation" (also known as frame-accepting negation) and "cross-frame negation" (also referred to as frame-rejecting negation). For within-frame negation, the situation's frame is accepted, and one aspect is contrasted with others, exemplified by stating *Mary is not stingy but generous*. In cross-frame negation, the situation's frame is rejected in favor of contrasting with alternative frames, for instance, *Mary is not stingy but thrifty*. Clearly, instances identified as "cross-frame negation" fall under the category of MN. Fillmore's contributions are pioneering efforts to demonstrate how MN is driven by our conceptual frameworks.

2.4.2 The ICM-denying Account

Mamaridou (2000) proposes this account based on the concept of ICMs, as proposed by Lakoff (1987). ICMs are termed "idealized" because they generalize a spectrum of experiences rather than depict particular instances of an experience (Evans & Green, 2006). In other words, ICMs are abstract frameworks that may not cover every conceivable real-world scenario. According to this approach, the meaning of a word is determined by its corresponding ICM. One frequently cited example is the concept of a bachelor, which is interpreted through a schematic marriage ICM, incorporating knowledge about the typical marital status of a bachelor. Echoing Fillmore (1985), Mamaridou contends that a speaker may either endorse an ICM by dismissing situations that don't align with it or refuse the ICM's relevance to the situation. For instance, in (24) b, the rejection targets the ICM evoked by the word *stingy* due to its implied negative assessment; in *Tom does not regret quitting the job because he did not quit*, the focus is on dismissing the ICM evoked by the word *regret*.

2.4.3 The Dynamic Categorization Account

This account is proposed by Gao (2003) who argues that the pragmatic studies of MN are problematic because researchers generally adopt an objectivist view of truth, without taking context and human cognition into consideration. This is in line with Lakoff and Johnson (1980) and Lakoff (1987) who propose that truth is based on understanding and not inseparable from our cognitive abilities of categorization. Adopting a dynamic perspective on truth, Gao considers MN to be truth-functional as DN, highlighting the adaptability of human categorization. Essentially, multiple categories may be apt for a given context; if a speaker deems the category selected by another as inappropriate for the context, they can employ MN to refute the truthfulness of that other party's statement.

2.5 Problems with the Existing Accounts

Without question, the accounts explored above offer a range of perspectives and valuable insights into the study of MN. Yet, they exhibit notable shortcomings in terms of descriptive accuracy and explanatory depth. This section delves into the limitations inherent in both pragmatic and cognitive semantic approaches.

2.5.1 Problems with the "Pragmatic Ambiguity" Accounts

It's clear from the preceding discussion that there's yet to be a universal agreement on the nature and origins of MN. Scholars immersed in varied theoretical paradigms exhibit divergent stances on the concept of negation's "ambiguity". On the standard account, it is a matter of "pragmatic ambiguity" and the negation operator has both truth-functional function and non-truth-functional function. By contrast, the division of DN and MN in both the relevance-theoretical account and the idiomatic account is a matter of "semantic ambiguity". In the former account, the negation operator is uniformly truth-functional in both DN and MN, and the "ambiguity" lies in their different representational natures, i.e. "representational ambiguity". And in the latter account, the negation operator is not ambiguous, either; the ambiguity resides in whether the root of negation is used literally or idiomatically.

As discussed previously, Horn himself is far from clear on the definition of "pragmatic ambiguity" and the inherent relation between DN and MN. It seems that the "ambiguity" account of the negation operator not only violates our intuition but receives little support from empirical research. Noh et al. (2013) report a set of eye-tracking experiments on the processing of MN. It shows that there are no significant differences in the subjects' processing times at the rectification clauses between MN and DN. Thus, it provides no empirical support for Burton-Roberts' claim that negation is interpreted as descriptive by default and the metalinguistic interpretation is derived from a pragmatic reanalysis. Rather, the result is consistent with the relevance-theoretical view that the interpretation process is governed by the principle of relevance, under which the type of interpretation is chosen because it yields greater cognitive effects with less processing effort.[①]

The "non-ambiguity" view of the negation operators also seems to be supported from studies of data from Korean, Chinese, Arabic, and Greek (Carston & Noh, 1996; Zhao, 2011). Findings show that there are no negation operators in at least these languages that are exclusively used for the expression of MN. However, the echoic and metarepresentational accounts of MN based on relevance theory are not without problems. The reason is that echoicity or metarepresentation is neither a necessary condition nor a sufficient condition of MN. On the one hand, obviously, not all the MN examples are used to criticize a prior utterance in response to an assertion of their root. On the other hand, DN may also be used echoically to reject a previous utterance. Consider (25), from Carston (1996):

(25) A: Isn't it tiring for you to drive to work?
B: I don't drive to work; I jog.

---

① But see an ERP experiment reported in Lee (2016) in support of the "pragmatic ambiguity" account.

Contrary to the standard account, Noh (2000) interprets speaker B's reply as an instance of MN rather than DN. Noh argues that MN is applicable for negating any represented content, encompassing both the non-truth-conditional and truth-conditional dimensions of a preceding statement.

Evidently, the relevance theory's interpretation of MN diverges from Horn's original dichotomy between DN and MN, particularly concerning their truth-functional roles. In the perspective of relevance theory, Horn's MN is conceptualized as a variant of "metarepresentational negation". Wilson (2000) further obscures the distinction between DN and MN, asserting that any sentence negation employing an explicit negation operator should be viewed as metarepresentational. According to this framework, "descriptive negation" involves rejecting a non-attributive proposition, while "metarepresentational negation" concerns attributive propositions. This is categorized as "metalinguistic" when denying formal aspects and "interpretive" when refuting semantic aspects of a proposition. As the negation operator consistently acts upon metarepresentations, the echoic or metarepresentational application no longer serves as the hallmark of the traditional MN category.

The claim that all forms of negation entail metarepresentation aligns, to some extent, with the intersubjective perspective on linguistic negation discussed in this study. Metarepresentation, by definition, involves the representation of another representation. Consequently, negation introduces an additional layer of representation, potentially attributed to either a different conceptualizer (whether known or unknown) or the same conceptualizer at varied times. In the forthcoming chapter, as delineated in Verhagen's (2015) model of intersubjectivity, the conventional meaning of the negation operators resides in their function of coordinating conceptualization of different individuals, not just describing the state of affairs. Thus, these two theoretical frameworks might be more accurately regarded as complementary rather than opposing. However, this discussion will not be expanded further at this juncture. It is pertinent to note that relevance theory, which adopts a formalistic stance towards language and a truth-conditional approach to semantic meaning, confines its exploration of the negation operator to its truth-functional properties, overlooking its conceptual functions. Additionally, relevance theory embraces a modular conception of the mind, attributing our ability to metarepresent cognitive states to a theory-of-mind module within our cognitive system. This perspective is supported by the works of scholars such as Sperber (1994, 2001, 2005), Sperber and Wilson (2002), Wilson (2005), and Wilson and Sperber (2004), and resonates with the theoretical contributions of Chomsky (1975) and Fodor (1983, 2001). Despite its focus on the cognitive aspects of pragmatic communication, this approach has been criticized for its limited engagement with our conceptual system and the conceptual processes that underpin utterance production.[①]

The idiomatic explanation also falls short of being satisfactory. One of the central claims of this account is that MN solely arises from and targets GCI. This perspective fails to account for the nuanced ways in which MN interacts with different types of conversational implicatures. Take the case of "limiting (or scalar) implicature denials" as an example. According to the idiomatic view, only semantically weaker lexical items in Horn scales are allowed to enter the negative scope of MN. It is because, according to neo-Gricean pragmatists such as Horn (1984, 2009), Levinson (2000), and Huang (2014), only Horn scales can generate GCI, ad hoc scales can only give rise to context-dependent implicatures, i. e. particularized conversational implicatures (PCI). However, previous studies such as Carston (1999) and Lee (2005) indicate that MN can be derived from both kinds of scales. In other words, both GCI and PCI can be the targets of MN.

---

① Tendahl (2009) posits that it's entirely plausible to move away from the modular view of the mind in favor of the insights provided by relevance theory, particularly those concerning communication, metarepresentation, and cognitive principles. Cognitive linguists define metarepresentation—or "echoing"—as a cognitive process that constructs a conceptual structure reflective of one previously engaged. This opens up potential synergies between the relevance theory's approach to metarepresentation and the cognitive theories, including the models we will explore in the next chapter. Although this subject offers a fascinating exploration path, it exceeds the scope of our current discussion in this book.

Another significant limitation of current pragmatic research is its lack of descriptive adequacy. Predominantly, these studies depend on the researchers' intuition and a constrained selection of invented data, rather than on systematically gathered empirical evidence. In this context, real language corpora have been notably underutilized. Up to now, a comprehensive framework for classifying MN, grounded in a systematic analysis of authentic data, remains absent. Research that does not incorporate real language corpora risks overlooking the multifaceted nature of MN. Consider, for instance, the scalar instances of MN. Echoing Horn (1989), prior investigations into this variant of MN have predominantly concentrated on instances emanating from standard Horn scales, that is, lexical arrays characterized by entailment relations. However, analysis of our corpus data reveals a significant prevalence of MN arising from non-entailing lexical frameworks, encompassing ranked entities, actions and attributes, stages and prerequisites of processes, whole/part relationships, instance-of dynamics, generalized/specialized relations, among other relational types outlined in Hirschberg (1991).

Furthermore, the majority of MN examples analyzed in prior research predominantly feature literal expressions. However, an exploration into both English and Chinese reveals that MN can be intricately expressed through figurative language, with a notable emphasis on metaphorical constructions. Regrettably, such metaphorical expressions of MN have seldom been considered within existing classification frameworks. Consider (26) and (27):

(26) Man is not man, but a wolf to those he does not know.
(Plautus' quote)

(27) 病后的虚弱要是也由医院负责的话,医院就不是医院,而是养老院了。(BCC)

Bing hou de xuruo yaoshi ye you yiyuan fuze de hua, yiyuan jiu bu shi yiyuan, er shi yanglaoyuan le.

disease after GEN weakness if also PSV hospital responsible PRT that simply not hospital PRT but nursing. home PRT

If a hospital were responsible for a patient's weakness after illness, it would no longer be a hospital, but a nursing home.

Moreover, current pragmatic analyses and classifications predominantly derive from observations of negative utterances in English, overlooking the linguistic diversity and nuances present in other languages. A wealth of research indicates that the mechanisms of negation in Chinese significantly diverge from those in English across multiple dimensions (Biq, 1989; Yeh, 1995; Zhao, 2011; Tan, 2016). A crucial distinction is the greater flexibility of negation operators in Chinese, which enjoy more liberty in syntactic positioning and collocation within negative scopes compared to their English counterparts. For instance, Wei (2019) demonstrates that the ensuing examples of MN are prevalent and productive in Chinese, yet markedly scarce in English. Consider (28) and (29):

> (28) 今晚我看的不是电影，而是情怀。(BCC)
>
> *Jinwan wo kan de bu shi dianying, er shi qinghuai.*
>
> tonight I watch GEN not movie but sentiment
>
> Tonight, what I experienced wasn't just a movie; it was an emotional journey.
>
> (29) 你们喝掉的不是酒，而是法官的形象。(BCC)
>
> *Nimen hediao de bu shi jiu, er shi faguan de xingxiang.*
>
> you drink away GEN not wine but judge GEN image
>
> What you've consumed isn't merely wine; it's the dignity of your role as a judge.

The hallmark of this form of negation is the seamless connection between negative and corrective clauses via the rhetorical technique known as zeugma. This variant of MN construction is distinguished by its profound empathetic and expressive impacts, making it a prevalent choice in contemporary Chinese discourse. Nonetheless, this particular aspect of MN might have been overlooked in scholarly discussions. Furthermore, it is an open question as to how these expressions can be effectively integrated into established classification frameworks.

2.5.2 Problems with the Cognitive Semantic Accounts

Researchers in the field of cognitive semantics have provided insightful analyses of MN. In several critical aspects, our perspective aligns closely with the theories proposed by Fillmore (1985), Mamaridou (2000), and Gao (2003). However, cognitive semantic interpretations share similar descriptive limitations with pragmatic analyses. These interpretations largely focus on English, with scant attention to the systematic exploration of cognitive processes involved in producing and interpreting MN in non-Indo-European languages, like Chinese. As demonstrated in Chapter 4, MN manifests in a more varied and diverse manner in Chinese compared to English.

Similar to proponents of relevance theory, supporters of cognitive semantic interpretations often subscribe to the notion of a singular "truth-functional" negation operator. However, they fail to explicitly explore the role these negation operators play at the conceptual level in constructing the meaning of MN. Cognitive linguistics typically rejects the "truth-conditional" approach to linguistic meaning, favoring a conceptual view of semantic representation. Language expressions are seen as "prompts" that facilitate the construction of richer conceptualizations. Given these foundational assumptions, it becomes crucial to delineate the types of cognitive activities conventionally prompted by the negation operator.

Another issue with cognitive semantic interpretations is their explanatory inadequacy. The cognitive semantic notions such as "frame", "ICM" and "categorization", despite their usefulness in characterizing the intuitive examples of MN, only constitute a small part of the much wider range of construal operations revealed in the realm of cognitive linguistics. Evans and Green (2006) suggest that cognitive linguistics comprises two complementary approaches: cognitive semantics and cognitive (approaches to) grammar. The former explores the interplay between experience, embodied language, and cognition, while the latter focuses on the symbolic linguistic units constituting language. Verhagen's model of intersubjectivity and Langacker's model of construal belong to the cognitive approaches to grammar. In the next chapter, we will explore the synergistic potential of these two models in enhancing our understanding of cognitive semantic interpretations. Significantly, current cognitive semantic approaches tend to overlook the rich diversity of cognitive activities that may operate in a manner similar to those already identified. This oversight is partly due to inherent methodological limitations within cognitive semantic interpretations themselves, which, at their best, provide only a partial or somewhat coarse-grained insight into the cognitive mechanisms that underpin the derivation of MN. By integrating insights from the mentioned models, we aim to address these gaps, offering a more comprehensive and nuanced perspective on cognitive processes involved in MN.

2.6　Research Gaps and Research Questions

The literature review clearly shows that despite numerous attempts to explain the nature and mechanisms of meaning in MN, all proposed generalizations have fallen short of satisfaction. This section summarizes the identified research gaps and introduces the research questions that this study aims to address. Concerning the descriptive inadequacies, studies on MN have largely relied on intuitive approaches. This reliance on intuition, while valuable, highlights a significant gap in empirical evidence and methodological rigor. Corpus linguistics is well-justified within both pragmatic (Romero-Trillo, 2008) and cognitive linguistic research (Stefanowitsch & Gries, 2007; Stefanowitsch, 2011), demonstrating its critical role in revealing authentic language patterns. Despite its proven utility, the adoption of corpus linguistics for a deeper understanding of MN in everyday communication has been surprisingly sparse in existing studies.

This limitation is further compounded when considering linguistic diversity. Research on MN in non-Indo-European languages, including Chinese, is scarce compared to the predominant focus on English. This disparity underscores the need for more extensive exploration and validation of MN theories across diverse linguistic landscapes. Given the substantial morphosyntactic and semantic differences in MN between modern Chinese and English, a systematic and detailed exploration of MN's diverse patterns in modern Chinese is not just beneficial but essential. Such an investigation promises to enrich our understanding of MN by incorporating perspectives from a linguistically and culturally distinct context, thereby broadening the scope of current research.

Regarding the issue of explanatory gaps, the majority of existing research primarily focuses on unveiling the pragmatic motivations behind the phenomenon, with cognitive motivations receiving considerably less attention. While the echoic and metarepresentational perspectives grounded in relevance theory offer significant insights from a cognitive-oriented standpoint for understanding MN, they tend to overlook the influence of our conceptual system and cognitive operations in the generation and interpretation of MN due to their modular view of the mind. Additionally, cognitive semantic approaches, constrained by their theoretical frameworks and reliance on intuition-based methodologies, fail to fully elucidate the cognitive mechanisms underlying MN. This situation highlights the need for a more integrated approach that bridges the gap between pragmatic and cognitive dimensions to provide a comprehensive understanding of MN.

Addressing prior research's descriptive limitations, this study employs a usage-based approach to investigate MN in Chinese, with a particular emphasis on *bu* (不) as the negation operator. This study will analyze authentic data, capturing negation's usage across spoken and written communication, to ensure a comprehensive understanding of its application. A comprehensive classification scheme will be proposed, focusing on the representational effects characteristic of MN. To overcome the explanatory gaps identified in existing literature, this study will introduce a novel theoretical framework by synthesizing Verhagen's model of intersubjectivity with Langacker's model of construal. Leveraging this integrated framework, the research will reinterpret the "ambiguity" of negation and conduct a detailed examination of MN's semantic patterns. This study aims to elucidate:

(1) Are the two types of negation (i.e. DN and MN) primarily pragmatically ambiguous, semantically ambiguous, or ambiguous in other ways?

(2) What semantic patterns of MN in modern Chinese emerge from a

systematic analysis of data primarily drawn from authentic texts?

(3) How are the processes of MN influenced by the general cognitive processes that shape our world conceptualization? And what specific cognitive activities support the meaning representations of the various semantic patterns of MN?

2.7 Summary

This chapter has systematically reviewed the extensive body of literature on MN, encompassing diverse theoretical perspectives such as the standard accounts, the relevance-theoretical accounts, the "idiom" account, and the cognitive semantic accounts. Despite the valuable insights and interpretations offered by these studies, they exhibit significant limitations in terms of descriptive accuracy and explanatory depth. In response to a critical evaluation of these limitations, this study has formulated three sets of research questions aimed at addressing the identified gaps, drawing on principles from cognitive linguistics and pragmatics.

Chapter 3

Theoretical Considerations and Analytical Framework

Building upon the critique of existing MN accounts outlined in Chapter 2, this chapter aims to construct an alternative theoretical framework that more accurately explicates MN's meaning mechanisms. Initially, we explore Verhagen's model of intersubjectivity, examining its relevance for dissecting negation's "ambiguity". Subsequently, Langacker's model of construal is discussed, highlighting its utility in analyzing meanings beyond truth conditions. The ensuing sections will demonstrate the synergistic potential of integrating these two theories, culminating in the proposal of a pioneering cognitive-linguistic model for MN.

3.1 Verhagen's Model of Intersubjectivity

Building on the observations from Chapter 2, it becomes clear that existing MN analyses have largely overlooked the intricate relationship between negation operators and their role in conceptualization. Addressing this gap, Verhagen's model of intersubjectivity emerges as a pivotal framework. It offers a cognitive perspective on the conventional meaning of linguistic negation, as detailed in Verhagen's (2005, 2007, 2015) works. This section will delineate the core tenets of Verhagen's model, with a particular emphasis on its intersubjective approach to understanding linguistic negation.

3.1.1 Theoretical Background and Central Claims

In recent years, the cognitive-functional approach to grammar has increasingly highlighted the subjectivity of language users in underlying meaning representation. However, despite this growing interest, the phenomenon of intersubjectivity—how individuals understand and relate to the mental states of others—has received comparatively less attention. Verhagen's exploration of intersubjectivity leverages insights from Anscombre and Ducrot's theory of argumentation and Langacker's cognitive grammar to offer a fresh perspective on language use. According to Anscombre and Ducrot, the conventional function of a linguistic expression is not merely to convey information but to influence the thoughts, attitudes, or behaviors of another individual. They argue that normal language use is inherently "argumentative", challenging the view that sees linguistic meaning primarily in terms of the information provided by expressions. From this "argumentative" standpoint, the primary role of an ordinary expression is to serve as an argument for some conclusion, with its informational content playing a secondary role.

Another important theoretical foundation for Verhagen's model is Langacker's concept of cognitive construal. Langacker's cognitive grammar posits that each linguistic expression embodies a specific construal or "way of seeing" a scene or situation. This conceptualization process between a speaker (or hearer) and reality is defined as a "construal relationship" (Langacker, 1987). Verhagen (2005, 2007) highlights that this relationship's essence is effectively illustrated by the "viewing arrangement" concept, as delineated by Langacker (1987, 1991). This arrangement is instrumental in understanding how individuals mentally structure and communicate their perceptions, as depicted in Figure 3.1:

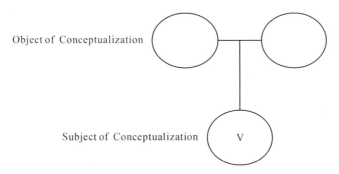

Figure 3.1 A Viewing Arrangement

Figure 3.1 serves as a visual representation of the construal relationship within the framework of cognitive grammar as proposed by Langacker. In this diagram, two distinct levels are illustrated to differentiate between the objects and subjects of conceptualization. The upper level focuses on the object of conceptualization, which is the situation or scene being linguistically described. This is depicted through two circles that symbolize the entities involved in the situation, connected by a horizontal line that represents the relationship between these entities. The lower level, referred to as the "ground", encompasses the subject of conceptualization, primarily the speaker. This level encapsulates the speech event and its participants—the speaker and the hearer—their shared knowledge, and the surrounding circumstances, emphasizing the contextual foundation of linguistic expressions. A vertical line extending from the speaker to the object of conceptualization symbolizes the construal relationship, highlighting the cognitive and perceptual pathway through which the speaker conceptualizes and articulates the situation.

However, as critiqued by Verhagen (2005), this model does not adequately distinguish between different speech act participants, namely the speaker and the hearer. It also overlooks the human capacity to understand and internalize other states of mind during the conceptualization process. Addressing these shortcomings, Verhagen proposes a revision in Figure 3.2, which introduces an explicit distinction between the speaker and the hearer at the lower level and adds an additional node to represent the subjective perspective. This modification aims to refine the theoretical model of language to better account for linguistic meanings that arise from cognitive coordination between interlocutors.

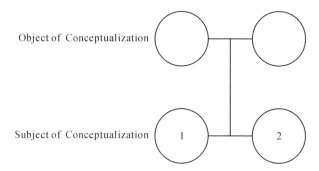

Object of Conceptualization

Subject of Conceptualization

1

2

Figure 3.2 The Construal Configuration and Its Basic Elements

Obviously, in Figure 3.2 another subject of conceptualization (conceptualizer 2) has been explicitly incorporated into the construal configuration. The "ground" thus consists of two subjects of conceptualization: the "communicator", represented by the right circle, and the real or conceived "addressee", represented by the right circle. The lower horizontal line indicates the coordination relationship between the two conceptualizers, while the vertical line captures the relationship of joint attention between the conceptualizers and the object of conceptualization. Thus, the ground is actually the "common ground" shared by the two interlocutors (Clark, 1996; Sinha, 1999; Langacker, 1987). Broadly, the point of this model is that the first conceptualizer takes responsibility for the utterance, and is engaged in the intersubjective coordination relation with another conceptualizer based on the shared knowledge, beliefs and attitudes, and the communicative event. It follows that the meaning of a linguistic utterance arises from the process in which the speaker invites the addressee to jointly attend to an object of conceptualization in some specific way, and to update the common ground.

Verhagen (2005) asserts that this construal configuration, characterized by shared attention and intersubjective coordination, underlies all linguistic usage events. This model accommodates scenarios where an actual speaker or addressee may not be present, suggesting that linguistic utterances inherently involve attributing cognitive capabilities and intentions to conceptualizers, whether real or imagined. In essence, even in the absence of a direct interlocutor, the act of communication presupposes the presence of another mind capable of interpreting and responding to the utterance.

It is worth noting that in Langacker's subsequent work, there is increasing attention on the intersubjective dimension of construal relation. The scheme offered in Langacker (2008) also incorporates the role of the hearer in the meaning expressions. And the intersubjective engagement has received explicit and detailed consideration in Langacker (2015):

> Being social creatures, we recognize the existence of other conceptualizers who engage us as objects just as we engage them. And through our further capacity for simulating another subject's experience, we achieve the intersubjective awareness crucial for cognitive development, language acquisition, and linguistic interaction. Canonical language use involves conceptual engagement in each of two dimensions. Along one axis the interlocutors engage one another, intersubjective awareness being one component of their interaction. Contributing to this awareness is their joint apprehension, along the other axis, of the expression's form and meaning.

This perspective resonates with the ideas presented by Verhagen, particularly regarding the significance of the intersubjective dimension in linguistic communication, its evolutionary underpinnings, and its role in cognitive development and language acquisition. Both scholars acknowledge the fundamental importance of understanding how individuals use language not only to convey information but also to engage with each other on a conceptual level. However, despite the common ground shared by Langacker and Verhagen, Verhagen's model presents certain advantages for the specific aims of this study. These advantages include the following:

(1) Unified framework for perspectivization: Verhagen offers a comprehensive

framework that integrates various phenomena of perspectivization. This unified approach facilitates a deeper understanding of how speakers position themselves and others within the narrative or discourse, enabling a nuanced analysis of perspective-taking in language use.

(2) Refined characterization of intersubjective-coordination activities: Verhagen's model provides a detailed characterization of the activities involved in intersubjective coordination. This refined depiction enhances our comprehension of how interlocutors align their cognitive and conceptual resources during communication, contributing to a more precise understanding of the dynamics of linguistic interaction.

(3) Insights into the conventional function of negation: Verhagen's analysis extends to the conventional function of negation and its conceptual implications. By examining negation-related phenomena at the conceptual level, Verhagen opens new avenues for addressing the so-called "ambiguity" of the negation operator in pragmatic studies. This perspective offers valuable insights into how negation is employed in language to modulate meaning, challenge assumptions, and navigate complex conceptual landscapes.

In summary, while Langacker's contributions significantly deepen our understanding of the intersubjective dimension of construal relations and highlight its crucial role in linguistic communication, it is Verhagen's model that offers particular advantages for this study. Specifically, Verhagen provides unique analytical tools and perspectives, especially through his novel insights into the conventional function of negation and related conceptual phenomena. This approach not only sheds light on the often-discussed "ambiguity" of the negation operator in pragmatic studies but also introduces a compelling perspective that is particularly relevant for dissecting the cognitive intricacies associated with MN in our investigation.

3.1.2 The Conventional Function of Negative Operator

A central claim of Verhagen's research is that there is a range of linguistic expressions whose meaning is best characterized in terms of cognitive coordination between subjects of conceptualization, rather than a description of the world. In other words, their linguistic meanings are conventionally associated with the level S of intersubjective coordination, but not the vertical connection between the subject of conceptualization and the object of conceptualization. These linguistic phenomena include negation and negation-related constructions, concessive constructions, complementation and discourse connectives.

With regard to negation, it is suggested that the intersubjective approach makes it possible to formulate how the function of sentential negation differs from that of morphological negation and the corresponding affirmative expression. Consider (1), from Verhagen (2005, 2007):

> (1) a. Mary is not happy. On the contrary, she is feeling really depressed.
>
> b. #Mary is unhappy. On the contrary, she is feeling really depressed.
>
> c. #Mary is a bit sad. On the contrary, she is feeling really depressed.

While all three statements suggest Mary's unhappiness, only the first aligns coherently with the phrase "on the contrary". This discrepancy highlights the unique function of sentential negation: it doesn't just negate a proposition but also establishes a cognitive framework that contrasts with the following statement. This is achieved by creating two mental spaces with opposing views on the same issue, with the "not" operator signaling this bifurcation. By contrast, morphological negation and the corresponding affirmative expression lack such functions of setting up another mental space contrasting with the base space, thus making (1) b and (1) c incoherent. The function of "not" in (1) a is illustrated in Figure 3.3.

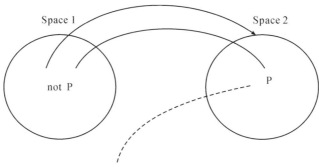

On the contrary, she is feeling really depressed.

Figure 3.3 "On the contrary" Relates to Evoked Mental Space

Therefore, negation operator "not" and other negative expressions cannot be considered as merely relating language to the object of conceptualization, with a function of reversing the truth value of a proposition. Rather, they should be characterized as linguistic means of cognitive coordination, functioning to invite the addressee to reject a particular epistemic stance towards some idea, particularly one that the addressee might entertain himself/herself. In other words, truth-functionality reversal is neither the primary function nor the conventional meaning of negation, but the by-product of the intersubjective coordination function of negation.

The intersubjective model makes it possible to secure rigidity for negation without positing an independent dimension of negative meaning. As discussed in the previous chapter, this has not received sufficient support from cross-linguistic studies. In line with this model, the alleged "ambiguity" of negation should reside at the conceptual level and is intimately tied to the coordination relationship between the two conceptualizers. Given its conceptual nature, our view of the "ambiguity" of negation can be termed the "conceptual ambiguity" view. It is intended as an alternative account to the "semantic ambiguity" view and the "pragmatic ambiguity" view. Then, the question that immediately arises is: how the alleged "ambiguity" might be related to the intersubjective coordination? In Verhagen's works, there is no consideration of the distinction of DN and MN, much less how the latter is derived. To pursue this topic, we need to outline

Langacker's model of construal, which could inform the investigation of the cognitive grounding of the non-truth-conditional meaning of a proposition.

3.2 Langacker's Model of Construal

This section delves into Langacker's model of construal, highlighting its pivotal role in unraveling the conceptual "ambiguity" inherent in linguistic negation. Initially, we outline the core principles of Langacker's framework that directly inform our analysis of negation. Subsequently, we explore three distinct classifications of construal operations, offering insights into their relevance for understanding the multifaceted nature of negation.

3.2.1 Construal Operations and Alternate Construal

The concept of construal stands at the heart of Langacker's cognitive grammar, marking a pivotal departure from traditional truth-conditional semantics. Unlike the latter, which equates linguistic meaning with its correspondence to factual states in the world, cognitive grammar posits that meaning encompasses not only the conceptual content but also a particular construal of content. Conceptual content is roughly comparable to truth conditions, a state of affairs, or the objective situation described, while construal introduces a dynamic element, layering the content with subjective interpretation and perspective (Langacker, 2015).

A fundamental assertion of Langacker's framework is that each linguistic expression embodies a specific construal relationship between the speaker and the described situation. This relationship signifies merely one among myriad possible interpretations of the same state of affairs, highlighting the rich complexity and variability in human cognition and communication. For illustration, refer to Figure 3.4 in Langacker (2008):

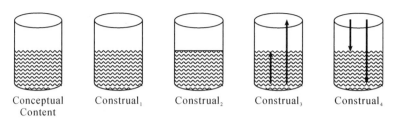

Conceptual Content   Construal₁   Construal₂   Construal₃   Construal₄

Figure 3.4 Examples of Construal

As illustrated in Figure 3.4, a single conceptual content—specifically, a glass containing a certain volume of liquid—can be interpreted through various lenses, each leading to a distinct construal. Although this content might initially appear neutral at the conceptual level, its linguistic representation inherently demands a specific mode of construal. Figure 3.4 highlights four such construals, each delineated by bold lines, leading to unique linguistic expressions: (1) *the glass with water*; (2) *the water in the glass*; (3) *the glass is half-full*; (4) *the glass is half-empty*. Each of them is derived from a particular way of viewing the same conceptual content.

Although the distinction between content and construal is not clear-cut[1], it is useful for expository purposes, because it captures aspects of linguistic meaning that cannot be sufficiently analyzed in terms of truth conditions or the object of conceptualization (Langacker, 2008; Verhagen, 2007). For Langacker, the semantic difference of many linguistic expressions does not lie in the conceptual content in question, but in the particular way of construal they impose.

Langacker's model of construal posits a significant capability in humans: the ability to alter their perspective on the same situation, effectively "transforming one conceptualization into another that is roughly equivalent in content but distinct in the manner of its construal" (Langacker, 1987). This concept, known as construal transformation, is likened to the psychological phenomenon of "mental rotation". Humans are not limited to perceiving a physical object from a single

---

[1] The distinction is not easy to draw because, on the one hand, a linguistic expression always represents certain conceptual content, and on the other hand, any content is represented linguistically in a particular way of construal.

viewpoint; they can also shift or rotate this viewpoint, either mentally or physically. This capability suggests that the process of transforming one's construal of content is not just possible but is an inherent part of human cognition, treated as a cohesive event. An example provided to elucidate this concept involves the mental rotation of a triangle, as depicted in Figure 3.5:

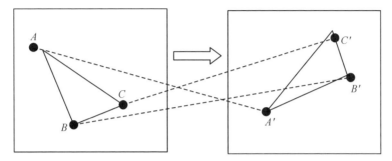

Figure 3.5　Mental Rotation of a Triangle

In Figure 3.5, the triangle presented in the left box represents a visual image captured from a standard, or canonical, viewpoint. Conversely, the triangle in the right box illustrates the result of a viewpoint transformation. The dotted lines serve to highlight the correspondences between the sides and angles of the triangles in each box, demonstrating that the transformation process yields not merely two disparate images but rather a unified, coherent entity. Langacker extends this concept of mental transformation beyond the visual domain, positing its relevance in the realm of semantic structure as well. To illustrate this, consider (2), from Langacker (1987):

(2) a. I will go to Chicago tomorrow.

　　b. I will come to Chicago tomorrow.

In this scenario, where (2) a and (2) b are spoken during a call to someone in Chicago, the usage of go and come serves as a prime example of viewpoint manipulation. The term go in (2) a positions the speaker's current location as the journey's origin, whereas come in (2) b adopts the perspective of the listener in

Chicago, effectively shifting the speaker's location into a conceptual one. This linguistic choice demonstrates how the same event can be construed differently based on viewpoint. Langacker (1987) further elaborates that this ability to modify construal is not limited to perspectives but extends across all conceivable parameters of construal. Understanding this broad spectrum of construal adjustments is fundamental for a thorough comprehension of the cognitive processes that underpin the creation of MN.

3.2.2 The Diversity of Construal Operations

The study of construal operations occupies a significant place in cognitive linguistics.[①] This research has led to the identification and classification of various construal operations, with the frameworks proposed by Langacker, Talmy, and Croft and Cruse being among the most influential. The original classification is proposed in Langacker (1987). Langacker terms the construal operations as "focal adjustment", which includes three parameters in this classification: (1) selection, (2) perspective, and (3) abstraction. Selection is rooted in human beings' capacity to focus on certain aspects of a scene and ignoring others. Perspective pertains to the real or psychological position from which a scene is observed. It is subdivided into four categories, namely, figure/ground alignment, viewpoint, deixis, and subjectivity/objectivity. Finally abstraction is related to the level of specificity the speaker uses to describe a scene. This classification has undergone several revisions in his later works (Langacker, 1991, 1999, 2008, 2015). The most recent version can be seen in Langacker (2015), represented in Figure 3.6.

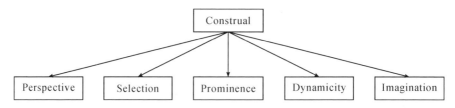

Figure 3.6 Classification of Construal Operations in Langacker

---

① In the present study, the concepts "construal operations", "cognitive principles" of conceptualization, and "parameters of construal" are used interchangeably.

The new classification brings the originally proposed construal operations into a new umbrella, along with some refinement and extension. One of the most notable developments is that a new category of "imagination" is added to this classification. The concepts of "mental spaces" (Fauconnier, 1985), "metaphor" (Lakoff & Johnson, 1980), and "blending" (Fauconnier & Turner, 2002) have been analyzed as reflecting the mental capability of extensionality, i. e. the capacity for entertaining multiple entities as part of a single experience in the same representational space (Langacker, 2015).

Another prominent classification system is proposed by Leonard Talmy who proposes a four-way classification of these cognitive operations under the name of imaging systems: (1) structural schematization, (2) deployment of perspective, (3) distribution of attention, and (4) force dynamics (Talmy, 1988). Later, this classification is sightly altered in Talmy (2000) under the name of "schematic systems". The revised classification can be represented in Figure 3.7.

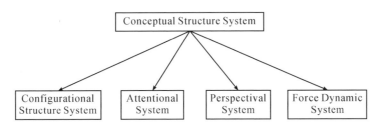

Figure 3.7 Classification of Construal Operations in Talmy

The classifications of construal operations by Langacker and Talmy, while foundational, have been critiqued by Croft and Cruse (2004) for their lack of comprehensiveness. Specifically, they argue that these frameworks fail to account for important dimensions such as image schemas and framing, which are pivotal for a holistic understanding of how cognitive operations shape language and thought. In response, they introduce a classification system that aligns more closely with the general cognitive capacities identified in psychology and phenomenology, offering a broader perspective on the cognitive mechanisms underpinning language processing. This enriched classification is presented in Table 3.1.

Table 3.1 Classifications of Construal Operations in Croft and Cruse

General Cognitive Processes	Construal Operations	
	Main Category	Subcategory
Attention/Salience	Selection	Profiling; metonymy
	Scope (dominion)	Scope of predication; search domains; accessibility
	Scalar adjustment	Abstraction; schematization
	Dynamics	Fictive motion; summary/sequential scanning
Judgement/Comparison	Categorization (framing)	—
	Metaphor	—
	Figure/ground	—
Perspective/Situatedness	Viewpoint	Vantage point; orientation
	Deixis	Spatiotemporal deixis (including spatial image schemas); epistemic deixis (common ground); empathy
	Subjectivity/Objectivity	—
Constitution/Gestalt	Structural schematization	Individuation; topological/geometric schematization; scale
	Force dynamics	—
	Relationality (entity/ interconnection)	—

Obviously, frame and ICM have been incorporated into the classification system, along with a wider variety of construal operations. This broadened perspective underscores that excluding any construal operations beyond frames and ICMs from the analysis of non-truth-conditional meanings is unwarranted. Given this, it is reasonable to propose that a theoretical framework, inspired by Langacker's model of construal, could offer a more nuanced and comprehensive exploration of non-truth-conditional meaning. This approach not only acknowledges the established importance of frames and ICMs but also opens up the analysis to a wider spectrum of cognitive operations, potentially providing a richer understanding of meaning beyond truth conditions.

3.3 Developing an Integrated Approach to MN

This section is dedicated to the potential synergies between Langacker's model of construal and Verhagen's model of intersubjectivity in accounting for MN. Based on the discussion of their complementarity, a new cognitive-linguistic model of MN will be developed ultimately.

3.3.1 Complementarity of the Two Models for MN Analysis

Given the discussion, it's evident that while Langacker's and Verhagen's models focus on different aspects of language, they share essential views on the non-objective components of linguistic meaning, such as those that are construed or not directly tied to truth conditions. These shared perspectives offer a nuanced understanding of the cognitive mechanisms behind MN, challenging traditional interpretations of negation in language.

Related observations in these two models present a serious challenge to the "ambiguity" view of the negation operator. In the standard account, Horn describes the descriptive, truth-functional use of the negation operator as primary and basic, and the metalinguistic, non-truth-functional use as "special", "marked" and "extended", not reducible to the truth-functional operator (Horn, 1985). Obviously, for Horn, the primary function of negation in natural language should be understood in terms of the relation between language and the world. To use Verhagen's construal configuration, negation operators are characterized by Horn as primarily operating on the upper level of the construal relation. However, as discussed in the previous section, this "ambiguity" view of negative operators is fairly restricted because denoting the state of affairs is just part of the conventional meaning of a negation operator.

Given the conventional function (or meaning) of negation consists in its intersubjectivity coordination rather than truth-functionality, it follows that the negation operator itself is not ambiguous, whether semantic or pragmatic, nor does the negation operator later acquire some other meaning in use, via some pragmatic process. Rather, the "ambiguity" should be accounted for at the conceptual level, in terms of the conceptual process it prompts for the intersubjective coordination activity. More specifically, the "duality of use" of negation should be viewed as being intimately tied to the intersubjective coordination between different conceptualizers. However, it remains unclear how the "duality of use" is conceptually motivated and how MN might be related to the intersubjectivity coordination between two subjects of conceptualization.

Langacker's model of construal illuminates how the non-truth-conditional meanings of propositions can be conceptually motivated, playing a pivotal role in elucidating the emergence of non-truth-conditional aspects of meaning. This model facilitates the understanding about how propositions that are functionally equivalent in truth value can describe the same situation differently. Nevertheless, while cognitive grammar adeptly addresses the diversity of meaning construction and the human ability to transform construals, it does not fully explore the cognitive foundations of linguistic negation nor how different conceptualizers can synchronize their alternate construals of the same situation—a process vital for dynamic intersubjective coordination.

Different construals of the same situation are not only fundamental for an individual's interaction with the world but also for how individuals communicate and understand each other. Tomasello's study has significantly contributed to our understanding by highlighting that entities or events can be categorized not solely on an individual basis (intrasubjectively) but also through shared perspectives (intersubjectively). This categorization is deeply influenced by the speaker's communicative intentions and the listener's current attentional state, suggesting a dynamic interplay between the speaker and listener during communication.

To deeply understand the dynamics of construal adjustments, it is crucial to differentiate between intrasubjective and intersubjective construal adjustments. An intrasubjective construal adjustment involves an individual's internal process of managing and shifting between different interpretations of the same situation. This process is pivotal for personal cognition, as it allows individuals to navigate through multiple perspectives or interpretations internally before expressing or acting upon one. Such adjustments are not merely about choosing one interpretation over another but involve dynamically shifting how one conceptualizes and engages with various aspects of a situation. Consider (3) - (5):

(3) 两万余所中小学齐动员，在美丽山东、平安山东、幸福山东建设
中打出了少先队旗帜。[①]

Liang wan yu suo zhong-xiaoxue qi dongyuan, zai meili Shandong, ping'an Shandong, xingfu Shandong jianshe zhong dachule Shaoxiandui qizhi.

two ten. thousand CL middle primary school all mobilize in beautiful Shandong safe Shandong happy Shandong construction in show PRT Young. Pioneers banner

More than 20,000 primary and secondary schools have been mobilized, playing the banner of the Young Pioneers in construction of a "Beautiful Shandong, Safe Shandong, and Happy Shandong".

(4) 当你看风景的时候，风景也在看着你！这一路走来，沿途中的
风景也一并随着走过。[②]

Dang ni kan fengjing de shihou, fengjing ye zai kanzhe ni! Zhe yi lu zoulai, yantu zhong de fengjing ye yibing suizhe zouguo.

When you kook. at scenery GEN time scenery also ASP look. at-ASP you this on. the. way walk come along. the. way in GEN scenery also together follow-ASP come. up

When you look at the scenery, the scenery is also looking at you! When you come here, the scenery along the way will follow you all the time.

---

① https://baijiahao.baidu.com/s?id=1685483095943864519&wfr=spider&for=pc.

② http://www.xbtw.com/meiwen/180.html.

(5) 酸甜苦辣皆为宝,苦—辣—酸—甜才是福。 [①]

Suan-tian-ku-la jie wei bao, ku—la—suan—tian cai shi fu.

sourness sweetness bitterness spiciness all as treasure bitterness
spiciness sourness sweetness only is blessing

While sourness, sweet, bitterness and spiciness are all treasures
of lives, only the experience of the four flavors bitterness-
spiciness-sour-sweet in sequence is a blessing.

The sentence in (3) involves alternate profiling of domains. The adjectives
meili, ping'an, xingfu select the cognitive domains location, society, and people
respectively from the same domain matrix. This selection involves an
intrasubjective adjustment where the focus shifts between these domains to
emphasize different aspects of the campaign. (4) illustrates an intrasubjective
adjustment between real and fictive motion. The observer's role shifts from a
passive viewer to an active participant in the scene, changing the figure/ground
relation and enhancing the emotional and philosophical depth of the interaction
with nature. Similarly, the proverb about life's flavors in (5) demonstrates intrasubjective
adjustments between summary and sequential scanning. The speaker intends to
emphasize the importance of experiencing these flavors in a specific sequence,
suggesting a deeper appreciation and understanding of life's complexities through
sequential experiences.

On the other hand, an intersubjective construal adjustment occurs when
individuals engage in communication, aiming to achieve a mutual understanding
or consensus regarding a situation. The different ways to construe the same
situation often reflect the speaker's unique perspective on the related state of
affairs and fulfill various discursive objectives. For instance, in a hypothetical
scenario such as Figure 3.4, one could interpret a glass as half-full (construal$_3$) or
half-empty (construal$_4$), metaphorically signaling the speaker's optimistic or
pessimistic outlook on life, respectively. A speaker might also modify a specific

---

[①] http://www.xici.net/403.

construal—whether existing or potential—to influence the listener's perception of the situation.

The process of construal adjustment can occur both implicitly and unconsciously, or explicitly and deliberately. While most studies in cognitive grammar treat alternate construal as an implicit and unconscious process, in actual communication, speakers may consciously reject a particular construal and replace it with an alternative perspective of the same situation. For example, if a speaker wishes to counteract the pessimistic tone conveyed by the statement *the glass is half-empty*, they might explicitly correct it by asserting *the glass is not half-empty; it is half-full*. This example illustrates intersubjective cognitive coordination, where different interpretations of the same glass of water are reconciled.

This coordination relies on the "common ground" shared between the speaker and the listener, encompassing their mutual knowledge, including experiences related to life and drinking. Moreover, this common ground is continually updated through the intersubjective adjustment of interpretations, ensuring that communication remains dynamic and contextually relevant. This ongoing adjustment not only facilitates clearer communication but also enhances the shared understanding between individuals, reflecting the complex interplay of perspectives in human interactions.

Intersubjective coordination can be achieved through various mechanisms. Meaning representations can be constructed through either constructional or inferential methods, or a combination of both. The construction "not X but Y" serves as a constructional variant of the lexical item "not". Conventionally, "not" establishes a relationship at the intersubjective level by creating two mental spaces with opposing viewpoints, suggesting that the perspective of conceptualizer 2 (typically the addressee) should be replaced by that of conceptualizer 1 (usually the speaker).

In this constructional variant, "not X but Y", the segment "but Y" functions to clarify the actual viewpoint of the latter, effectively rectifying or specifying the intended perspective. Therefore, "not X but Y" conventionally facilitates intersubjectivity coordination between two mental spaces that encapsulate the differing viewpoints expressed by X and Y. According to Langacker's theory of construal, the two related lexical items or propositions represent alternate construals of the same situation. The meaning representation in the form of "not X but Y" is achieved through the integration of these two contextualized lexical items or propositions within the overarching abstract construction.

Construction grammar posits that the conceptual structure of a non-constructional expression becomes subordinate to a constructional one when it is incorporated into the latter. Thus, when X and Y are integrated into the intersubjective construction "not X but Y", the overall meaning representation profiles an intersubjective adjustment of alternate construals of the same situation. Essentially, the speaker invites the addressee to jointly focus on a specific construal, and to update the common ground by introducing another construal of the same situation. This process not only clarifies the speaker's intention but also enhances mutual understanding by aligning the perspectives of both the speaker and the addressee through a shared linguistic framework.

Drawing on the insights from the two models, we propose that the "ambiguity" of negation does not purely reside at the semantic level, or pragmatic level, as some might assume. Rather, it is a manifestation of the intersubjective coordination of different aspects of conceptualization. The so-called "descriptive", "propositional", or "truth-conditional" negations entail two opposite epistemic stances towards conceptual content of a proposition, whereas "metalinguistic", "non-propositional", and "non-truth-conditional" negations arise from two opposing stances towards a particular way of construing its conceptual content. In terms of construal configuration, the former case focuses on the upper level, while the latter emphasizes the connection between the upper and lower levels. By way of illustration, let us consider (6):

    (6) a. The glass is not half-empty—it is downright full. (DN)

       b. The glass is not half-full—it is half-empty. (MN)

The two negative sentences share the same negation operator which brings into prominence different aspects of construal relation. While the primary focus of argument in (6) a is the conceptual content expressed in the root, the main focus of argument is the way of construal represented in the root and a set of associated assumptions.①

Of course, while the two propositions in (6) b (i.e. *the glass is half-full* and *the glass is half-empty*) are truth-conditionally equivalent, not all cases of MN contain strictly truth-conditionally equivalent expressions like the ones in this example. Consider the so-called implicature negation in (7) and (8):

(7) Jack does not have THREE cars—He has FOUR.

(8) I did not meet a woman yesterday—I met with my wife.

In each sentence, the propositions in the negative clause and the corrective clause do not seem to have the same truth conditions. According to the standard account, the negated meaning constituent in (7) is the implicature "Jock does not have *just* three cars", and in (8) is the implicature "I did not meet a woman other than my wife". Remember in the relevance-theoretic accounts, MN also involves denying the truth condition of a proposition. According to this view, the meaning constituents being negated in the sentences constitute part of the truth-conditional content of the related utterances. Correspondingly, the negation operator in the two examples also operates at the upper level of the construal configuration. This view is also consonant with the dynamic categorization account, which is based on the dynamic view of truth condition in cognitive linguistics. Here, it is worth stressing again that the distinction between content and construal is not at all clear-cut. As Langacker (2008) points out, the conceptual content can only be evoked neutrally at the conceptual level; as soon as it is represented by language, a particular way of construal will be imposed. To say that the negation operator mainly operates on the mode of construal is not meant to deny the meaning

---

① Following Davis (2013, 2016), the notion "root" here and elsewhere in the study denotes the proposition that results from removing the negation operator.

impact it has at the upper level. Instead, it is just a matter of focus. Despite the blurred boundary, the distinction of conceptual content and mode of construal is essential for explaining non-truth-conditional or non-propositional aspects of meaning in a traditional sense.

The idea that MN is linked to denying a specific way of interpreting a situation is not new. It fundamentally underpins the cognitive semantic frameworks previously discussed. Similar concepts, such as frame-shifting, have already been identified in these studies. However, beyond framing, there exists a broader range of construal operations that have been overlooked in the literature. Alternation processes tied to these operations can also lead to MN utterances, much like frame-shifting. By integrating these operations into our analytical toolkit, the present study has the potential to enhance the explanatory power of cognitive linguistic theories on this phenomenon.

3.3.2 The Intersubjective Construal Adjustment Model of MN

Based on the preceding discussion, an integrated model for the meaning mechanism of MN can be established. This model integrates key aspects of Langacker's model of construal and Verhagen's model of intersubjectivity in a single formulation, with the aim to provide a cognitively plausible account of MN. The central assumption is that MN is a linguistic manifestation of the intersubjective coordination activity concerning alternate construals of the same situation. In broad terms, the point of an MN utterance is that the speaker invites the addressee to "consider and abandon" (Verhagen, 2005) a particular construal, as represented in the root, and instructs him/her to accept an alternative construal of the situation, as represented in the rectification. Given its key assumption, i.e. an MN utterance involves adjustment of alternate construals between two subjects of conceptualization, this model is termed as intersubjective construal adjustment

(ICA) model of MN.[①] Figure 3.8 diagrams the main structure of this model.

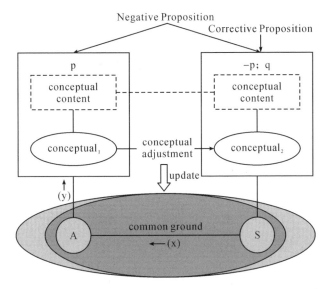

Figure 3.8 The Intersubjective Construal Adjustment Model of MN

In Figure 3.8, the two largest blocks represent the mental spaces evoked by the negative proposition that consists of a negation operator and a root proposition. This is in line with the claim of Verhagen's model that negation conventionally prompts two distinct mental spaces with opposite viewpoints: the thought that p is valid, and the thought that p is not valid. As discussed previously, the corrective proposition functions to specify the exact thought of the speaker. In this sense, it fills in the second mental space with a detailed conceptual representation q. The block in connection with the oval embodies Langacker's view that conceptualization consists of both the conceptual content and the way of construing the content. As indicated by the dotted line, the

---

① It is evident that MN involves not only rejecting others' statements but also one's own prior utterances or thoughts. This act of self-correction can be seen as a form of self-reflection, where individuals reassess and revise their previous beliefs in response to new information or upon reconsideration. This process represents a type of internal intersubjective coordination, wherein speakers engage in a dialogue with their past selves. Such internal dialogue is analogous to the external intersubjective coordination, where individuals adjust their views through interactions with others.

conceptual content (roughly correspondent to "truth condition") designated by p is not profiled. Instead, what is brought into prominence is the way of construing the conceptual content (as indicated by the solid line). The correspondence line linking to its counterpart in the right block indicates that the conceptual content in the other mental space is also valid. However, the two mental spaces contain different ways of construing the shared conceptual content: $construal_1$ and $construal_2$.

The horizontal level of the model basically shares the same structure with the level S in Verhagen's model. That is, S and A represent the speaker and the addressee, respectively. They engage in cognitive coordination by means of the utterance, with respect to some object of conceptualization. Specifically, the speaker invites (indicated by $(x) \rightarrow$) the addressee to consider and abandon the ways of construal ($construal_1$) as expressed in p (indicated by $(y) \rightarrow$), and encourages acceptance of the alternate construal expressed in q. The intersubjective construal adjustment process is based on the common ground between the two subjects of conceptualization, and updates the common ground by suggesting an alternative way of construing the same conceptual content. Based on Langacker's model, we hypothesize that diversity of construal operations make it possible for the speaker to adjust one's mode of construal in a number of parameters (not restricting to framing and categorization), thus giving rise to various kinds of MN.

3.4 Summary

In this chapter, the related claims of Langacker's model of construal and Verhagen's model of intersubjectivity have been compared from a theoretical point of view, highlighting the fact that both have different foci and can shed light on different aspects of MN analysis. Whereas the former model offers a cognitive plausible explanation for the conventional meaning of the negation operators, the latter model elucidates how the non-truth-conditional aspects of meaning can be generated at the conceptual level. Drawing on insights and tools from both models, the present chapter has developed a new cognitive-linguistic model for MN that offers an analytic framework for subsequent chapters.

Methodology

This chapter addresses the methodology and data used in the study. Unlike previous studies which typically rely on elicited data, this study employs a usage-based approach to MN. It begins with an explication of the central tenets of this approach and its potential to illuminate new aspects of MN research. Subsequently, the chapter will provide a detailed description of the data sources, along with the methods used for data collection, identification, and analysis. Finally, an analysis of corpus data will be presented, aiming to enhance understanding of the formal and functional properties of MN in modern Chinese.

4.1 A Usage-based Approach to MN

As discussed in Chapter 2, previous research on MN has several deficiencies. One significant deficiency is the lack of attested language data in previous MN studies. Instead, they often rely on a handful of invented examples, and their hypotheses have not been tested with authentic data. Although systematic observation of MN in real communication is beneficial, there have been few attempts to describe and theorize MN using authentic data.

The usage-based approach is a functionalist approach, used to investigate linguistic phenomena by focusing on language use within specific contexts. It originated from the rejection of the distinction between competence and performance proposed by Chomsky. The central premise is that language knowledge stems from its actual use in communication. In other words, knowledge of the language is actually knowledge of how language is used (Langacker, 1990; Barlow & Kemmer, 2000; Bybee, 2006, 2010, 2013; Bybee & Hopper, 2001; Tomasello, 2003). Language structure emerges from language use. (Michael Tomasello, 2003)

Given its assumption that the use of utterances in real communication shapes the organization of our linguistic system, investigation of language system should be based on the analyses of authentic data. As Evans and Green (2006) put it, "Language structure cannot be studied without taking into account the nature of language use." In cognitive linguistics, the usage-based approach is extensively applied to study language knowledge, change, and acquisition (Evans & Green, 2006). This approach aligns well with cognitive linguistics' fundamental assumptions about language's nature and cognitive basis. Consequently, it is strongly advocated in cognitive grammar (Langacker, 2008) and various schools of construction grammar (Croft, 2007; Fried, 2010).

The usage-based approach manifests in various forms. Recent works illustrate usage-based studies employing experimental, quantitative, and qualitative methodologies, either individually or in combination (Barlow & Kemmer, 2000; Bybee & Hopper, 2001). The advantage of corpus linguistics is clear: a study isn't truly usage-based unless it utilizes actual usage data, readily observable in corpora or online. Corpus linguistics can help ground linguistic analysis on a firmer basis of objective observation. As Sanders and Spooren (2007) put it:

> Cognitive linguistics is the study of language in use; it seeks to develop so-called usage-based models (Barlow & Kemmer, 2000) and in doing so increasingly relies on corpora of naturally occurring discourse that make it possible to adduce cognitively plausible theories to empirical testing.

In this study, the description and theoretical explanation of MN are primarily based on a careful analysis of naturally occurring data rather than invented ones. This approach ensures that our analysis authentically reflects the actual use of language, aligning with the usage-based research paradigm in cognitive linguistics. Specifically, the methodology of this study combines quantitative and qualitative methods. On the one hand, the data description in the subsequent section is quantitative, employing statistical methods to measure and analyze language patterns found in the corpus. This approach allows for objective and replicable findings that can be generalized across similar linguistic contexts. On the other hand, the classification and explanation in the following chapters are primarily qualitative, focusing on the interpretation and contextualization of the phenomena observed. This involves a detailed examination of how specific constructions are used in real-life interactions and the cognitive and social functions they serve. By integrating both quantitative and qualitative methods, the study provides a comprehensive view of MN, capturing both the broad patterns and the nuanced details of its use.

4.2 Sources of Data

With the exception of very few examples that are taken from the literature, the data for this study has been drawn from two sources: BCC and Internet searches. BCC is the primary source of data, which is established by Beijing Language and Culture University. This corpus is chosen from among a number of electronic corpora available for two reasons. First, it is a large corpus, composed of digital texts with over 32 billion Chinese characters, which offers a significantly larger sample of MN than other corpora. Second, it contains both spoken and written texts from a variety of sources, which facilitates precise and detailed descriptions of the structural and semantic behavior of MN in modern Chinese. BCC is reputed to provide a comprehensive view of the language used in verbal communication of modern Chinese people (Xun et al., 2016).

There are five sub-corpora in this corpus, namely literature corpus, conversation corpus, newspaper corpus, technological discourse corpus, and a multi-field corpus. Among them, the multi-field corpus is established based on the aforementioned three sub-corpora. That is, it contains texts from the genres of literature, conversation, newspaper, and technological discourse. This corpus is intended by the founders to serve as a balanced corpus, offering a wide-ranging view of actual usage of the relevant linguistic patterns. In order to make our generalization more reliable, the multi-field corpus serves as the source of extraction for each construction of MN.

While BCC is big enough, our experience with this corpus is that it somewhat lacks in capturing the diversity of semantic patterns of MN, particularly novel expressions. This necessitates a versatile search tool that can have access to ample online instances of MN in multiple contexts and situations. In recent years, the Internet as an important data source has received considerable attention from researchers in the field of linguistics (Kilgarriff & Grefenstette, 2003; Renouf, 2003; Bergh & Zanchetta, 2008; Fletcher, 2007). One of its advantages is that it facilitates the search for complex language structures which is not commonly found in standard corpora, which is an advantage of a large corpus (Sinclair, 1991, 2001, 2004). The second advantage is that Internet data is consistently updated by language users in multiple contexts, which allows us to study highly novel expressions that are gaining acceptance in a given language community. Therefore, linguistic data from the Internet is used as one additional resource to complement the evidence extracted from BCC.[①]

4.3 Data Collection and Identification

Negation in modern Chinese manifests in various forms. The primary negators are "不" (*bu*) and "没" (*mei*). Additionally, expressions such as "哪里" (*nali*), "什么" (*shenme*), and "还" (*hai*) also convey negation. However, MN typically appears in specific discourse structures such as "不是 X, (而)是 Y" [*bu shi X, (er) shi Y*], which negates a previous statement and introduces a corrective or contrasting statement. This structure is crucial for understanding the dynamics

---

① For the sake of brevity and clarity, unnecessary linguistic contexts of MN in many examples have been eliminated or modified.

of agreement and disagreement in modern Chinese discourse.

As noted by Shen (1993), another significant form of MN is "Y, (而) 不是 X" [Y, (*er*) *bu shi X*], where the corrective clause precedes the negative clause. This inversion highlights the corrective focus before negating the initial assertion. The analysis in this section will concentrate on these major forms of negation using "不", specifically excluding non-canonical negative expressions such as "哪里", "什么", and "还". Additionally, variations that deviate from structures involving "是" (*shi*) or "而是" (*er shi*) like (1) and (2) are not considered, as they do not fit the typical patterns of MN discussed here:

(1) 他不是"喜欢"打麻将——都走火入魔了。

   Ta bu shi "xihuan" da majiang—dou zouhuorumo le.

   he not like play mahjong even obsessed PRE

   He doesn't like playing mahjong—he is obsessed with it.

(2) 我不喝牛奶，我要喝巧克力牛奶。

   Wo bu he niunai, wo yao he qiaokeli niunai.

   I not drink milk I want drink chocolate milk

   I don't drink milk; I want to drink chocolate milk.

In cases of MN which are represented by *bu shi X, (er) shi Y* construction, *Y* is used as the rectification of the inappropriate expression *X*. Both *X* and the corrective counterpart *Y* can be realized by a clause or non-clausal string of words. This construction of MN has two constructional variants: *bu shi X, er shi Y* and *bu shi X, shi Y*, as illustrated in (3) and (4):

(3) 全队十几个人的眼睛里面，冒出来的不是目光，而是火焰，是战
   斗的意志！(BCC)

   *Quandui shiji ge ren de yanjing limian, mao chulai de bu shi
   muguang, er shi huoyan, shi zhandou de yizhi!*

   whole team a-dozen-CL people GEN eyes inside burst come-out

   GEN not gaze but flame but fight GEN will

Inside the eyes of a dozen people in the team, there was not a gaze, but a flame, burning with the will to fight!

(4) 我点点头，不是没信心，是很没信心，我就是把我的朋友都叫来，也打不过人家十万人呀。(BCC)

Wo diandian tou, bu shi mei xinxin, shi hen mei xinxin, wo jiu shi ba wo de pengyou dou jiaolai, ye da bu guo renjia shiwan ren ya.

I nod head not not confidence am very not confidence I even BA I GEN friends all call come still beat not over them 100,000 people PRT

I nodded. And I was not diffident, but very diffident. Even if I called all my friends, I could not defeat 100,000 people.

The second form of MN is characterized by the use of "不" or "不是" as discourse markers. This form of negation occurs when a proposition containing element X is first asserted by another speaker or by the speaker themselves. Following this assertion, the negators "不" or "不是" are employed not merely to negate the truth value of the proposition, but to challenge its appropriateness or relevance in the given context. Subsequently, a corrective clause or fragment containing element Y is introduced, providing an alternative perspective or rectifying the initial statement. The structural dynamics of this form of MN can be seen in two constructional variants, which will be demonstrated in (5) and (6):

(5) 女孩在讲台上的甜甜笑意多像当年她到自己家去时脸上挂着的笑容啊！不，简直是一模一样！(BCC)

Nühai zai jiangtai shang de tiantian xiaoyi duo xiang dangnian ta dao ziji jia qu shi lian shang guazhe de xiaorong a! Bu, jianzhi shi yimoyiyang!

girl on podium-on GEN sweet smile so like once she come self home go when face-on hung-ASP GEN smile PRT not simply is exactly-the-same

The sweet smile on the girl's face as she stood on the podium resembled so much the smile she had when she first came to his house! No, it was exactly the same!

(6) 他在机房玩了一会儿后,心情就变好了。我也无语了,不是! 是彻底无语了! (BCC)

Ta zai jifang wanle yihuir hou, xinqing jiu bianhao le. Wo ye wuyu le, bu shi! Shi chedi wuyu le!

he in computer-room play-ASP for-a-while after mood simply turn good-PRT I got speechless PRT not am totally speechless PRT

He was in a better mood after playing in the computer room for a while. I was speechless, no, totally speechless!

MN in the construction *Y, (er) bu shi X* forms a contrast with the above two forms with respect to the information structure: the root and the rectification are arranged in a different order. There are also two variants of this construction, exemplified by (7) and (8):

(7) 我可能有时会有霸气,但绝不会霸道……我觉得这是演员的权利,而不是名演员的权利。①

Wo keneng youshi hui you baqi, dan jue bu hui badao ⋯ wo jue de zhe shi yanyuan de quanli, er bu shi ming yanyuan de quanli.

I may sometimes will have mighty but never will bossy I think this is actor GEN right but not famous actor GEN right

I might sometimes be assertive, but I am never overbearing ... I believe this is the right of an actor, not just the right of a famous actor.

(8) 我爱你,是爱,不是喜欢,我只爱你一个,如果你不相信,我可以

---

① https://card.weibo.com/article/m/show/id/2309404375116376104898.

发誓。(BCC)

Wo ai ni, shi ai, bu shi xihuan, wo zhi ai ni yi ge, ruguo ni bu xiangxin, wo keyi fashi.

I love you be love not like I just love you one-CL if you not believe I can swear

I love you. It is love, not like. You are the only one I love. And if you don't believe me, I can swear about it.

Taken together, three major forms of MN of negative utterances will be focused in this study, namely *bu shi X, (er) shi Y, bu* or *bu shi* as discourse marker, and *Y, (er) bu shi X*. Data extraction in BCC is facilitated by a set of user-friendly and powerful corpus search formulas. All sentences in these constructions can be easily accessed mechanically. For each data extraction, the balanced corpus is capable of randomly displaying up to 10,000 search lines from the total yielded tokens, which users can then download. This feature ensures that researchers have access to a diverse and representative sample of language usage, facilitating robust analysis of metalinguistic negation in modern Chinese. Below is part of the web page in which MN in the construction of *bu shi X, er shi Y* is retrieved by means of the search formula of [不是 *, 而是]. The symbol * represents continuous language fragments.

The identification of MN examples was theory-driven. That is, it is based on previous research on the forms and semantic-pragmatic features of MN. The definition of MN provided by Davis (2016) serves as the working definition which serves as the basis for the data identification. Davis (2016) uses "irregular" instead of "metalinguistic" for the general category and defines MN as follows:

An irregular negation [...] is used to express the negation of a proposition other than the proposition expressed by the "root" of the negation, the root being the sentence that results from removing the not.

Following Carston (1996, 1998) and Noh (2000), presuppositional negation is left aside in the present study because it is highly controversial whether they can be treated as cases MN or not. We will return to this point in the next section.

The downloaded tokens were converted to Microsoft Excel and examples that are judged to be MN were identified. In modern Chinese, most MN lack fixed linguistic forms, making direct extraction from BCC and the Internet challenging. In other words, the same construction might express both DN and MN. Consequently, retrieving MN examples from actual discourse cannot be purely mechanical. Instead, researchers have to manually sort them from BCC and the Internet. In other words, the analytical technique was interactive, combining automatic searches with human judgment (Biber, Conrad & Reppen, 1998). After eliminating unwanted data, a total of 1,759 tokens of MN were identified. Table 4.1 shows the number of MN instances in different data resources.

Table 4.1 Number of MN in Different Data Resources

Item	BCC				Internet	Total
Genre	Literature	Conversation	Newspaper	Technology		
Number	608	861	124	31	135	1,759

4.4 Analysis of Corpus Data

Corpus data serves as an invaluable methodological resource, refining our understanding of the semantic patterns and cognitive motivations behind MN utterances. It also provides insights into their frequencies and genre distribution. These aspects will be further explored in subsequent chapters. This section presents a corpus-based analysis using data from BCC. We focus on examining the frequency of various MN constructions and their distribution across genres, aiming to deepen our understanding of their formal and functional properties.

4.4.1 Frequencies of Various Forms of MN

Given the unique representational characteristics of different forms of MN, their varying prevalence is expected. A statistical analysis of the frequency of these forms within the corpus provides valuable descriptive insights. Table 4.2 illustrates the prevalence of MN, detailing the percentages of the three main constructions and their variants.

Table 4.2 MN in the Four Sub-corpora of BCC

ID Tag		Total Matching Lines	Frequency	Percentage	Average Percentage
pattern	variants				
A	A1	10000	490	49.0‰	64.0‰
	A2	9750	769	78.9‰	
B	B1	9543	172	18.0‰	12.2‰
	B2	9760	62	6.4‰	
C	C1	9924	50	5.0‰	11.2‰
	C2	4646	81	17.4‰	

Note: A = *not X, (er) shi Y*   A1 = *bu shi X, er shi Y*   A2 = *bu shi X, shi Y*
    B = discourse marker *bu (shi)*   B1 = discourse marker *bu*   B2 = discourse marker *bu shi*
    C = *Y, (er) bu shi X*   C1 = *Y, erbu shi X*   C2 = *Y, bu shi X*

Based on the data in Table 4.2, the *bu shi X, (er) shi Y* construction is significantly more prevalent in MN constructions than other types. This high frequency suggests its universality and importance in the language. The predominant use of *bu shi X, (er) shi Y* highlights its advantages in expressing negation, likely due to its semantic clarity which allows for a clear contrast between elements within a sentence. In contrast, the lower frequencies of the discourse markers *bu (shi)* and *Y, (er) bu shi X* constructions indicate their more specialized or contextual usage. Figure 4.1 shows the frequencies of the three major constructions of MN:

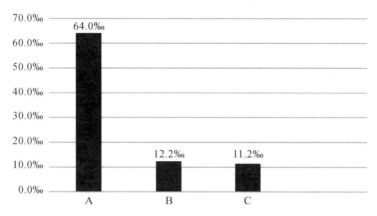

Figure 4.1 Frequencies of Three Major Constructions of MN

Further observations arise from a detailed analysis of the distribution of the constructional variants. As Figure 4.2 shows, MN in the form of *bu shi X, shi Y* demonstrates the highest frequency among the six variants, whereas its sister variant *bu shi X, er shi Y* is significantly lower. This indicates that the former is preferred over the latter, contradicting the common view that MN is typically represented by the form of *bu shi X, er shi Y* (e.g. Shao & Wang, 2010; Wang, 2012). The frequency difference of the sister variants for each construction reflects the intensity of disagreement each variant conveys. Specifically, the more favored variant induces a sharper contrast between the root proposition and the corrective proposition, expressing a stronger emotional response from the speaker than its counterpart. As for *bu shi X, (er) shi Y*, *shi* is a focus marker, which is more concise than the conjunction *er shi*. Thus, *bu shi X, shi Y* can produce higher degree of contrastive meaning effect than *bu shi X, er shi Y*. Similarly the higher frequencies of MN represented by *bu* as a discourse marker and in the construction *Y, bu shi X* are also more concise than their sister variants. This lends additional support to our hypothesis that the more concise and emphatic variants are favored over their counterparts in each construction.

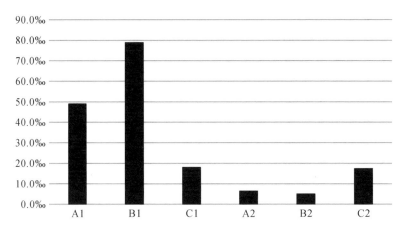

Figure 4.2 Frequencies of the Six Constructional Variants of MN

4.4.2 Genre Distribution of MN

BCC provides further insight into the distribution of MN across different genres. Table 4.3 below shows the frequency of MN in literature, conversation, newspaper, and technological discourse.

Table 4.3 Genre Distribution of MN in BCC

Category	Literature		Conversation		Newspaper		Technological Discourse		Total	
	n	Percentage	n	Percentage	n	Percentage	n	Percentage	n	Percentage
Frequency	608	37.4%	861	53.0%	124	7.6%	31	1.9%	1624	100%

As Table 4.3 shows, while MN is used in both spoken and written forms, it occurs more frequently in conversation (53.0%) and literature (37.4%), than in newspaper (7.6%), and technological discourse (1.9%).

The highest frequency of MN in conversation supports the traditional view that MN tends to occur in interactive contexts. Typically, it is used to counter previous utterances or unspoken thought, rather than merely describing situations. The distribution of MN across the four genres also sheds light on the ongoing debate regarding the rhetoric function of MN. In previous studies, whether MN is a rhetorical device is still a controversial issue. Ni (1982), Wu (1983, 1986) and

Kong (1998) characterize MN as a special rhetorical device in Chinese, whereas Shen (1993) maintains that creating rhetorical effect is not the main function of MN. The high distribution of MN in literature indicates that MN is more likely to be recruited for rhetorical purposes. This observation is further reinforced by considering the fact that the conversational data in BCC are not from spontaneous, face-to-face interactions, but from Internet texts of Weibo.[1] As a popular social media in China, Weibo serves as a key venue for the creation of innovative expressions, primarily among young users. MN meets their demand for innovative and rhetorical expressions to articulate opinions and sentiments on social and personal matters.

4.5 Summary

This chapter has detailed the methodology utilized in this study, beginning with an overview of the usage-based approach, a cornerstone within cognitive linguistics that emphasizes the importance of empirical data in understanding language patterns. We have discussed the primary data sources: BCC and various Internet platforms, highlighting how these resources complement each other in providing a robust dataset for analysis. The methods of data collection and identification have been elaborated to illustrate the efficacy of a corpus-based approach in exploring linguistic phenomena, specifically the usage of MN. The subsequent analysis of the data from BCC underscores the dynamic nature and behavior of MN in actual language use. This approach not only facilitates a deeper comprehension of MN but also enhances our understanding of its rhetorical and interactive roles across different genres and contexts.

---

[1] There are many reasons for failure to use spontaneous, face-to-face conversation, such as ethical issues and transcribing problems; the situation is frustrating because even in "spoken" corpora, spontaneous, face-to-face conversations are not fully represented (Newman, 2010).

Chapter 5

Towards a New Classification of Metalinguistic Negation

In light of the limitations identified in the current classification of metalinguistic negation (MN) as discussed in Chapter 2, this chapter introduces a refined classification scheme, grounded in authentic data, to better capture the nuanced semantic patterns of MN in modern Chinese. The new classification divides MN into four primary categories: strengthening denials, identifying denials, positioning denials, and formal denials. Each category, along with its respective subcategories, will be thoroughly explored to demonstrate their distinct functions and contexts of use. This systematic and comprehensive framework aims to provide a clearer, more detailed understanding of the versatile roles MN plays in linguistic interactions.

5.1 Criterion for the Classification and Major Categories of MN

The primary criterion for the classification is the diverse semantic and pragmatic effects that MN (specifically, the corrective clauses) typically produces. According to Moeschler (2019), it is the corrective clauses, rather than the negative clauses, that are responsible for the semantic and pragmatic differences between different uses of negation. He contends that the three main uses of MN, i. e. descriptive negation, scalar predicates negation, and presupposition negation yield distinctive representational effects (or propositional, cognitive effects): DN erases previously known information from the context, while scalar cases of MN strengthen the root of negation, and presupposition negation eliminates both the explicature and the presupposition of the root. It follows that the three uses of negation can be described not just at the semantic level (scope and entailment), but at the level of their representational/propositional/cognitive effects. Although his study primarily focuses on two types of irregular uses of negation—scalar cases, and presuppositional cases—similar analyses could be extended to other cases of MN.

Critic might argue that a corrective clause is not strictly necessary for an utterance of MN, as shown by Carston (1996) and Noh (2000). However, as Kay (2004) points out, even though MN may not always manifest in an overt phrase or clause, rectification remains an essential aspect of interpreting MN. The addressee can still derive the intended cognitive effect through contextual clues, even in the absence of overt rectification.

Four major types of MN can be identified in terms of the different representational effects of their corrective clauses or fragments: strengthening denials, identifying denials, positioning denials and formal denials. According to Sperber and Wilson (1995), there are various kinds of cognitive effects, such as implication, strengthening, revision, contradiction, or elimination. Strengthening denials are associated with the "strengthening" effect in the sense that the corrective part confirms and reinforces the assumption held by another individual. In a strengthening denial, the root and the rectification contain lexical items varying in the strength of information, i.e. the former being informational weaker than the latter. The corrective utterance aims to strengthen the positive counterpart (i.e. root) of the negative utterance. Identifying denials involve the "revision" effect in the sense that the speaker intends to revise the interlocutor's default assumption of a state of affairs. In an identifying denial, the root is pragmatically enriched into a new proposition in a default way. The rectification does not function to strengthen the root, but to identify what is not consistent with the stereotypical state of affairs denoted by the root. Positioning denials reflect most clearly the "contradiction" effect because the root and the rectification represent two opposing perspectives. The rectification is neither intended to strengthen the root, nor to identify a non-stereotypical state of affairs, but to manipulate the physical or psychological positions represented in the root. Lastly, formal denials have an "eliminating" effect because they are used to correct wrong habitual or contextual usages of certain linguistic items. In a formal denial, a lexical item in the root is misused on the ground of its formal (phonological, morphological, syntactic, or stylistic) realizations. The rectification is intended to show that the formal realization in the context is incompatible with its conventional usages. Each of the four types of denials can be further divided into several sub-types of MN, as we will describe in the next sections. Taken together, our classification of MN can be illustrated in Figure 5.1.

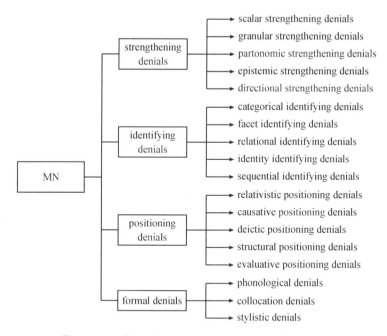

Figure 5.1 Classification of MN in Modern Chinese

5.2 A Detailed Description of Different Types of MN

Having provided a sketch of the classification of MN in modern Chinese in terms of the representational effects of the rectification, in this section each type of MN and its subspecies will be elaborated mainly based on authentic data.

5.2.1 Strengthening Denials

Strengthening denials generally can be paraphrased by adding *just* or *only* to scalar items, such as *The tea is not (just) hot but scolding* (Horn, 1985, 1989). As previously discussed, strengthening denials extend beyond the so-called "scalar implicature" negation in pragmatics. Considering various ordering relations between lexical items or propositions in the root and the rectification, strengthening denials are further divided into scalar strengthening denials, granular strengthening denials, partonomic strengthening denials, epistemic strengthening denials and directional strengthening denials.

5.2.1.1 Scalar Strengthening Denials

The term "scale" occurs in sightly varying forms in different frameworks. Scalar cases of MN are typically linked to lexical sets based on unilateral entailment relations between linguistic expressions. Besides Horn scales, there are various kinds of non-entailment contrast sets that can give rise to MN. To date, the most comprehensive classification of these ordering relations has been made in Hirschberg (1991). According to Hirschberg, lexical relations that support scalar implicature include quantifier orderings, models, logical connectives, numerical orderings, indefiniteness and definiteness, ranked entities, states, actions and attributes, temporal implicatures, spatial orderings, process stages and prerequisites, whole/part relation, type/subtype, instance-of, and generalized/specialization relations. Although these contrast sets do not give rise to scalar implicature in terms of an entailment scale, they do invoke kinds of quasi-scales on which strengthening denials can be generated.[1]

Obviously, the class of partially ordered sets is not a heterogeneous category. It includes both entailing and non-entailing lexical sets. Moreover, the non-entailing relations include both linear and hierarchical relations. In this study, the

---

[1] Lee (2005) makes similar observations about MN in English.

term "scalar strengthening denials" is used in a fairly restricted sense, referring to negative expressions that are generated on the basis of linear ordering relations. Denials generated by lexical sets with hierarchical orderings, such as whole/part, type/subtype, instance-of and generalized/specialization relations, are treated as other types of strengthening denials.

Scalar strengthening denials can be further divided into standard and non-standard types. Standard scalar strengthening denials are generated on the basis of true scales, also known as Horn scales. According to Horn (1984, 2004, 2009), prototypical or true scales are established on the basis of unilateral entailment relations between linguistic expressions. The speaker's assertion of a weaker value suggests he/she wasn't in a position to assert a stronger value within that scale. The non-literal meaning induced by true scales is called "scalar implicature" in (neo-) Gricean theories (Horn, 1984, 2004, 2009; Levinson, 2000). This meaning constituent is the upper-bounded meaning of a scalar expression. It is treated as a proper pragmatic inference, rather than a semantic entailment. In this type of denials, the corrective clause often contains a semantically stronger lexical item which unilaterally entails the weaker linguistic expression in the negative clauses. Consider (1) - (4):

(1) 不是一些历史书,而是所有历史书都是这么写的。(BCC)
   Bu shi yixie lishi shu, er shi suoyou lishi shu dou shi zheme xie de.
   not some history book but all history book all are so write PRT
   Not some history books, but all history books are written like this.

(2) 他们不是可能,而是一定会哗变。(BCC)
   Tamen bu shi keneng, er shi yiding hui huabian.
   they not possible, but certain will mutiny
   It is not just possible but certain for them to mutiny.

(3) 他看到的不是一个人,而是三个人。(BCC)
   Ta kandao de bu shi yi ge ren, er shi san ge ren.
   he see GEN not one-CL person but three-CL person

What he saw was not one person, but three.

(4) 这道菜不是很成功,而是非常成功! (BCC)

Zhe dao cai bu shi hen chenggong, er shi feichang chenggong!

this-CL dish not very successful but extremely successful.

This dish is not very successful, but extremely successful.

In (1) - (4), the negated lexical item and its counterpart in the rectification constitute an ordered set with semantic entailment relation. Typically, in environments involving standard negation, the focus is on negating the lower-bound, truth-conditional meaning of the lexical items. However, in these examples, the negation targets the upper-bound, non-truth-conditional meaning. For instance, in (1), the speaker negates the upper-bound meaning of *yixie* ("some"), which implies "not all", rather than its lower-bound meaning of "at least some".

Scalar strengthening denials can also be generated by non-entailment contrast sets. Though the lexical items in these sets are not unilaterally entailed, they vary in informational strength. According to neo-Gricean pragmatics, the use of the former gives rise to a similar Q-implicature that the use of the latter does not hold. Consider the contrast set <divorce, separate>. According to Levinson (2000) and Huang (2014), this contrast set is a non-entailment scale because one can get divorced without being separated. Nevertheless, the use of the item *separate* in a sentence can induce a non-entailing quantity implicature that they haven't get "divorced" yet. A scalar strengthening denial is generated by denying the appropriateness of using an informationally weak lexical item to describe a state of affairs. Consider (5) - (7):

(5) 支援还没有到,两个小时内所有的防线都被攻破,不是被攻破,
而是被消灭! (BCC)

Zhiyuan hai meiyou dao, liang ge xiaoshi nei suoyou de fangxian dou bei gongpo, bu shi bei gongpo, er shi bei xiaomie!

support yet not arrive two-CL hour in all defense all PSV

breach but PSV breach but PSV eliminated

The support had not yet arrived. Within two hours, all the defense lines had been breached. Actually, it had not been breached; it had been eliminated.

(6) 这么多士兵要吃掉多少东西啊！李长官这次不是破费了，而是破产了。(BCC)

Zheme duo shibing yao chidiao duoshao dongxi a! Li zhangguan zhe ci bu shi pofei le, er shi pochan le.

so many soldiers will eat-ASP how.much thing PRT Li officer this-CL not spend-a-lot ASP but go.broke ASP

How much food will be eaten by so many soldiers! This would not just render Officer Li strapped; it will make him broke.

(7) 听说他使得一把铁斧，谁跟他打起来，就不是斩手了，而是斩首，砍脑袋！(BCC)

Tingshuo ta shide yi ba tiefu, shui gen ta da qilai, jiu bu shi zhan shou le, er shi zhan shou, kan naodai!

it. is. said he use one-CL iron axe whoever with he fight-ASP just not cut hand ASP but cut hand cut head

I heard that he had an iron axe. And whoever fights him will not just chopped off the hands, but the head!

All these examples contain contrast sets that can form scales wherein the items on the left are informationally stronger than those on the right. In each example, the speaker denies not the truth condition of the root proposition but the non-literal meaning (i. e. "just X") it may induce. For example, in (5) *gongpo* ("breached") is informationally stronger than *xiaomie* ("eliminated"), but it does not semantically entail it. As in the case of Horn scale, the use of the infomationally weaker *gongpo* in (5) gives rise to a similar non-literal meaning that the defence line has not been eliminated.

Scalar strengthening denials also include denials that are based on metaphorically constructed scales. Unlike canonical strengthening denials, metaphorical scalar-strengthening denials feature metaphorically rectified expressions. These denials can be categorized into single-metaphorical ones and double-metaphorical types. In the former, the negative clause literally describes the state of affairs, while the corrective clause employs a metaphorical expression. The metaphorical rectification serves to scale up the concept expressed by its counterpart in the root proposition to an unrealistic level. Consider (8) - (10):

(8) 在他们眼中,这胖子挥舞着的不是拳头,而是两把大铁锤! 是的,一拳就够了。(BCC)

Zai tamen yan zhong, zhe pangzi huiwuzhe de bu shi quantou, er shi liang ba da tiechui! Shide, yi quan jiu gou le.

in they eyes-in this fat-man wave-ASP GEN not fist but two-CL big iron hammer yes one punch simply enough ASP

In their eyes, the fat man was not waving fists, but two big iron hammers! Yes, one could not stand even one punch.

(9) 中国的高铁速度好快啊,高铁司机不是在开火车,而是在开火箭。(BCC)

Zhongguo de gaotie sudu hao kuai a, gaotie siji bu shi zai kai huoche, er shi zai kai huojian.

China GEN high-speed railway speed so quick INT high-speed railway driver not ASP drive train but ASP drive rocket

China's high-speed railway is so fast. The drivers are not driving trains, but rockets.

(10) 非洲的太阳简直不是太阳,而是火炉! 它能直接把你烤成北京烤鸭。(BCC)

Feizhou de taiyang jianzhi bu shi taiyang, er shi huolu! Ta neng zhijie ba ni kaocheng Beijing kaoya.

Africa GEN sun simply not sun but stove it can soon BA you roast-become Peking. Roast. duck

The sun in Africa is not a sun, but a stove! It can roast you into a Peking Roast Duck.

In the above sentences the constrast sets <*quantou* "*fist*", *tiechui* "*iron hammer*">, <*huoche* "*train*", *huojian* "*rocket*">, and <*taiyang* "*sun*", *huolu* "*stove*"> form three non-entailing scales. In (8), the contrast set is formed in terms of weight. The speaker does not deny that the man is waving his fist. Rather, he/she intends to mean that *quantou* is not an informationally adequate expression to describe the weight of the fist. And this is the reason why it is being rejected and replaced by the word *tiechui*. The latter is located in a higher position than the former on the scale of weight. This sentence is intended to mean that the man's fist is so heavy like an iron hammer. In the same vein, the root in (9) and (10) can also induce the non-literal meaning (i.e. "just X") through their metaphorical rectifications.

In cases of double-metaphorical negations, both the negative clause and the corrective clause contain metaphorical items that can form a scale. The infelicitous metaphor in the root, often idiomatic, is informationally weak than another metaphorical item in the rectification. Consider (11) - (13):

> (11) 这种比赛结果不是给巴西人泼了一盆冷水,而是一场倾盆大雨。①
>
> *Zhe zhong bisai jieguo bu shi gei Baxi ren po le yi pen leng shui, er shi yi chang qingpendayu.*
>
> this CL match result not give Brazilians pour ASP one-CL cold water but one-CL heavy.downpour
>
> This result is not like pouring a basin of cold water on the enthusiasms of Brazilians, but like a heavy downpour.
>
> (12) 他说余校长不再是老狐狸了,而是狐狸精。老狐狸只会骗人,狐狸精却能迷人。(BCC)
>
> *Ta shuo Yu xiaozhang bu zai shi lao huli le, er shi hulijing. Lao huli zhi hui pian ren, hulijing que neng mi ren.*

① http://sports.sina.com.cn/s/2004-05-19/1107246950s.shtml.

he say Yu principal no. longer be old fox ASP but vixen old

fox only can cheat people vixen but can entice people

He says that Principal Yu is no longer just a cunning fox, but

has become a fox spirit. While a cunning fox merely deceives

people, a fox spirit can truly enchant them.

(13) 小李一听更来气了,实实在在地顶了他一句:"都说你将他当

成干爹,我看不是干爹,是亲爹。"(BCC)

Xiao Li yi ting geng laiqi le, shishizaizai de ding le ta yi ju:

"Dou shuo ni jiang ta dangcheng gandie, wo kan bu shi

gandie, shi qindie."

Du Zhong when hear more irritated ASP sternly PRT retort

ASP he a sentence all say island inside make America treat-

become godfather I think not godfather is biological father

Upon hearing this, Xiao Li became even more infuriated and

retorted firmly, "People say that you treat him as a godfather,

but I don't think it's a godfather; it's a real father."

Both the root and the rectification in each example contain metaphorical expressions. In (11), *po le yi pen lengshui* in Chinese is a metaphorical idiom, and signifies discouragement. This sentence denies not merely the fact that the football competition disappointed Brazilians, but rather the degree of disappointment conveyed by the metaphorical expression. In (12), the sentence does not deny that the man had fox-like traits. Instead, it serves to magnify the negative personalities by describing him as a *hulijing* ("vixen"). This expression allows the speaker to convey more intense negative emotions towards the principal. This pattern is similarly observed in (13).

5.2.1.2 Granular Strengthening Denials

Granular strengthening denials operate within scales defined by type/subtype, instance-of, and generalized/specialization relations, in Hirschberg's (1991) terms. In these scales, the semantic or informational strength of the lexical items is vertically ordered. For example, in the contrast set <dog, spaniel>, *spaniel* is semantically stronger than *dog* because as it entails the latter specifically (Huang, 2020). A granular strengthening denial refines the description of a state of affairs by increasing specificity. It involves two propositions, one with greater specificity than the other. The root proposition is semantically weaker than the rectification proposition because it excludes certain details of the state of affairs being described. In this type of denials, the focus is not on the truth condition of the root but the appropriateness of its less specific lexical choice. Granular strengthening denials are categorized further into qualitative and quantitative granular strengthening types.

A qualitative granular strengthening denial contains two propositions that describe the same entity at different levels of categorization. Thus, there are qualitative differences in the amount of information conveyed between the two propositions. Consider (14) - (16):

(14) "你们汉人有那么多女人，还要女人干什么?"莲柔一听就糊涂了。"注意，不是女人，而是美女……它们之间是有差别的。"(BCC)

Nimen hanren you name duo nüren, hai yao nüren gan shenme?" Lianrou yi ting jiu hutu le. "Zhuyi, bu shi nüren, er shi meinü … tamen zhijian shi you chabie de."

you Han. Chinese have so many woman still want women do what Lian Rou when hear soon confused PRT attention not women but beautiful women they between are have difference PRT

"Why do you Han People still need women since you already have so many?" Lian Rou was confused. "Notice, not women, but beautiful women ... there is a big difference between the two concepts."

(15) 当同事说他工作起来"像一只狼"的时候，他说:"不是一只狼，

是一只饿狼。”[①] (BCC)

Dang tongshi shuo ta gongzuo qilai "xiang yi zhi lang" de shihou, ta shuo: "Bu shi yi zhi lang, shi yi zhi e lang."

when colleague say he work ASP as-if one-CL wolf GEN time

he say not one-CL wolf is one-CL hungry wolf

When his colleagues said he worked "like a wolf", he said, "Not a wolf, but a hungry wolf."

(16) 我们所进行的革命，不是国家革命，而是国家社会主义革命。
我们甚至要在"社会主义"一词之下加着重点。(BCC)

Women suo jinxing de geming, bu shi guojia geming, er shi guojia shehuizhuyi geming. Women shenzhi yao zai "shehuizhuyi" yi ci zhixia jia zhuozhongdian.

we PRT conduct GEN revolution not national revolution but national socialist revolution we even must under socialist a term ZHI under add emphasis

The revolution we are conducting is not a national revolution, but a national socialist revolution. We must add an emphasis under the term "socialist".

The negative clause and the corrective clause in each example respectively represent a relatively general and specific description of the same state of affairs. The speaker does not deny the truth condition of the root proposition, but the appropriateness of categorizing the state of affairs at a rather schematic level. The root proposition is denied by the speaker because it fails to meet the speaker's expectation of information strength. For example, the proposition in (14) is denied because it provides no details about the appearance of the woman. Similarly, the proposition in (15) is denied because it is rather vague about what kind of wolf this person was like. The same analysis can also be applicable to (16).

A quantitative granular strengthening denial also pertains to the fineness of

---

① https://www.sohu.com/a/441455859_120799904.

details in description. However, unlike qualitative cases, the informational asymmetry between the root and rectification propositions is based on quantitative differences rather than qualitative. Specifically, quantitative granular strengthening denials focus on the precision of specifications along specific quantitative parameters, rather than on categorical levels. Consider (17) - (19):

(17) 天没有黑，他却已经看不清，不是看不清，是完全看不见，他已经陷入了无边的黑暗中。(BCC)

Tian meiyou hei, ta que yijing kan bu qing, bu shi kanbuqing, shi wanquan kanbujian, ta yijing xianrule wubian de heian zhong.

sky not dark he but already see not clear not see not clear is totally see not clear he already fall-into ASP boundless GEN darkness-in

It was not dark, but he could not see clearly—no, it is totally invisible, he had fallen into the boundless darkness.

(18) 东方不败笑了一下，问道："没有信心了？"我点点头，"不是没信心，是很没信心。" (BCC)

Dongfang Bubai xiao le yi xia, wendao: "Meiyou xinxin le?" wo diandian tou, "Bu shi mei xinxin, shi hen mei xinxin."

Dongfang Bubai smile-ASP one-CLF ask not confidence PRT I-nod head not not confidence is very not confidence

Dongfang Bubai smiled and asked, "You are lack of confidence?" I nodded my head, "To be frank, I am not lack of confidence; I have no confidence at all."

(19) "这件事难道你就没有一丝好奇？""不是好奇，而是好奇得要命。只是大家还不是很熟，没好意思问罢了。" (BCC)

"Zhe jian shi nandao ni jiu meiyou yisi haoqi?" "Bu shi haoqi, er shi haoqi de yaoming. Zhishi dajia hai bu shi hen shu, mei haoyisi wen bale."

this-CL matter how-can-it-be you simply not a.little curious not curious but curious PRT to.death just we still not very familiar not dare ask PRT

"Aren't you curious about this matter?" "I am not curious, but curious to death. Since we're not very familiar with each other yet, I was reluctant to ask them."

Each example demonstrates the enhancement of a basic proposition by specifying a gradable concept along a quantitative parameter. In (17) the adverb *wanquan* ("totally") specifies the extent of the man's inability to see, intensifying the description of his blindness. In (18), the adverb *hen* ("very") specifies the speaker's level of lack of confidence. Similarly, the expression *yaoming* ("to death") specifies the speaker's extreme degree of curiosity. These linguistic expressions serve to intensify the value of a gradable term, thereby producing a strengthening representational (or cognitive) effect. The same analysis can also be applicable to (19).

Quantitative granular strengthening denials can also occur by specifying an approximate assertion in the root. This happens because that the use of an approximate proposition on certain occasions can induce the implicated meaning that more precise information is not necessary. Consider (20) - (22):

(20) "十年了。"他叹息着。她知道他说的日子是从那个春夜后开始计算的,她远比他记得更清楚,不是十年,是十年一个月零三天。(BCC)

"*Shi nian le." Ta tanxizhe. Ta zhidao ta shuo de rizi shi cong na ge chun ye hou kaishi jisuan de, ta yuan bi ta ji de geng qingchu, bu shi shi nian, shi shi nian yi ge yue ling san tian.*

ten-year ASP he sign-ASP he know he say GEN days is from that-CL spring night after start count PRT she far than he remember PRT more clear not ten-year is ten-year one-CL month plus three-day

"Ten years," He sighed. She realized that the days had been calculated since that spring night. And she remembered it far better than he did—not ten years, but ten years plus one month and three days.

(21) 郭瑜惊道:"你真的三天没吃东西了?"小菊摇头道:"不是三天,是三天半。"(BCC)

Guo Yu jing dao: "Ni zhende san tian mei chi dongxi le?"
Xiao Ju yao tou dao: "Bu shi san tian, shi san tian ban."

Guo Yu surprise say you really three-day not eat thing ASP
Xiao Ju shake head say not three-day is three-day half

Guo Yu was very surprised and said, "You really haven't eaten for three days?" Xiaoju shook his head, "Not just three days, but three and a half days."

(22) "我离开你几年了?"于富贵想了想,然后说:"七八年了吧?" "不是七八年,是整整八年。"(BCC)

"Wo likai ni ji nian le?" Yu Fugui xiang le xiang, ranhou shuo: "Qi-ba nian le ba?" "Bu shi qi-ba nian, shi zhengzheng ba nian."

I leave you how. many year ASP Yu Fugui think ASP think then say seven eight year ASP QM not seven eight year is exactly eight year

Liu Li suddenly squeezed her eyes and said, "Brother-in-law, how many years have we been apart?" Yu Fugui thought for a while, and then said, "Has it been seven or eight years?" "Not seven or eight years. It has been eight years, to be exact."

In each case, the speaker does not intend to refute the truth condition of the root proposition, but rather to question the appropriateness of the approximate quantification. The denial in (20) is used to express the speaker's unwillingness to use the approximate expression *shi nian* ("ten years") to describe the time elapsed since their departure. Similarly, in (21), the denial targets the suitability of using the expression *san tian* ("three days"), which might convey the non-literal meaning of "just three days". The same principle applies in (22).

5.2.1.3 Partonomic Strengthening Denials

Strengthening denials can also be generated by contrast sets formed on the basis of part/whole relationships. As mentioned previously, for some neo-Gricean pragmatists like Hirschberg (1991), part/whole relationship is one type of non-entailment relations that can give rise to Q-implicature. These relationships are also referred to as partonomies, or meronymies. For this reason, strengthening denials induced by contrast sets of part/whole relations can be termed as "partonomic strengthening denials". In such denials, the contrastive concepts between the root and the rectification are of part/whole relations. The intention here is not to refute the truth conditions of the root propositions but to challenge the implicated meaning derived from part/whole hierarchies.

In a canonical partonomic strengthening denial, the root proposition provides the partial description of a particular state of affairs, while the rectification proposition represents the whole picture of the same thing. Consider (23) - (25):

(23) "程文这帮小子把登闻鼓一敲,满宫中都知道了。""不是满宫中,而是整个北京城。" (BCC)

"*Chen Wen zhe bang xiaozi ba dengwen gu yi qiao, man gong zhong dou zhidao le.*" "*Bu shi man gong zhong, er shi zheng ge Beijing Cheng.*"

Chen Wen this-CL guy BA Deng Wen drum once knock whole palace-in all know ASP not whole palace-in but whole-CL Peking city

"As long as Cheng Wen and other guys knocked on Deng Wen drum, all the people in the palace would know about it."

"Not only people in the palace, but people in the whole Beijing city."

(24) 现在,所有的美国大公司,不,应该说几乎所有的美国公司,都在互联网上有自己的地址。 (BCC)

Xianzai, suoyou de Meiguo da gongsi, bu, yinggai shuo jihu suoyou de Meiguo gongsi, dou zai hulianwang shang you ziji de dizhi.

now all GEN American big company not rather almost all GEN

American companies all at internet-at have self GEN address

Nowadays, all big American companies, no, in fact almost all

American companies, have their own addresses on the Internet.

(25) 后来,上海——乃至全国——超市勃然兴起。不是一个柜台
无人售货,而是整个商店无人售货! (BCC)

Houlai, Shanghai——naizhi quanguo——chaoshi boran xingqi.
Bu shi yi ge guitai wuren shouhuo, er shi zheng ge shangdian
wuren shouhuo!

later Shanghai even whole country supermarket suddenly

popular not one-CL counter unmanned sale but whole-CL

supermarket unmanned sale

Later, in Shanghai, even over the whole country, supermarkets

burgeoned. In each supermarket, there's not just one unmanned

counter—all counters are unmanned!

In (23), the imperial palace and Beijing city form a part/whole relationship since the palace is just a small district within the larger city. The initial statement might imply that the sound of the drum is confined to the palace. The second person counters this by clarifying that the sound reaches across the entire city of Beijing, thereby correcting the limited scope of the initial statement. Similarly, in (24) large American companies represent only a subset of all companies in the country, and in (25) an unmanned counter is just a small fraction of the whole supermarket. Each example demonstrates a denial of the adequacy of an incomplete description, aiming to dispel a potentially wrong assumption associated with the utterance.

There exists another type of denials that are generated through metonymic part/whole relations. In these cases, the meaning of the rectification is conveyed through the rhetorical device of metonymy, where the root proposition and the rectification proposition are of a "standing for" relationship. This relationship allows the rectification to represent a broader or different aspect than what is literally expressed in the root. Consequently, this type of denials can be termed as "metonymic partonomic strengthening denials". Consider (26) - (28):

(26) 那场足球赛已经不是两支球队在场上的对决,而是两个城市之间的对决。当时就感觉,没有别的,就是为青岛而战。[①]

Na chang zuqiu sai yijing bu shi liang zhi qiudui zai chang shang de duijue, er shi liang ge chengshi zhijian de duijue. Dangshi jiu ganjue, meiyou bie de, jiu shi wei Qingdao er zhan.

that-CL football match already not two-CL team on field-on GEN showdown but two-CL city between GEN showdown then just feel not other simply is for Qingdao to fight

That football competition was no longer a showdown between two teams on the field, but between two cities. At that time, I have no choice but to fight for the honor of Qingdao.

(27) 腾讯和360之间的斗争其实不是两个公司之间的斗争,而是两个体系、两个阵营之间的竞争。[②]

Tengxun he 360 zhijian de douzheng qishi bu shi liang ge gongsi zhijian de douzheng, er shi liang ge tixi, liang ge zhenying zhijian de jingzheng.

Tencent and 360 between GEN struggle actually not two-CL company between GEN struggle, but two-CL system two-CL camp between GEN competition

The struggle between Tencent and 360 is not actually a struggle between the two companies, but a competition between two systems and two camps.

(28) 谭嗣同不是一个人,而是一个集团……其他五个人都尊敬谭

---

① http://www.chinanews.com/ty/2014/12-23/6903436.shtml.

② https://tech.qq.com/a/20120418/000354.htm.

嗣同,把他视为六君子的核心。①

Tan Sitong bu shi yi ge ren, er shi yi ge jituan … qita wu ge
ren dou zunjing Tan Sitong, ba ta shiwei liu junzi de hexin.

Tan Sitong not one-CL person but one-CL group other five-CL
person all respect Tan Sitong BA him view as Six. Heroes
GEN core

Tan Sitong is not a single person, but a group ... The other
five people all respect Tan Sitong and regard him as the core
of the Six Heroes.

The negation in (26) does not aim to refute the fact that two football teams were competing on the field. Instead, it seeks to challenge the potential implicated meaning that event is not merely a competition between the two football matches. In the corrective clause, the significance of the football match is amplified through the use of metonymy, where the football teams symbolize the cities they represent. Similarly, in (27), the contention is not merely about the companies of Tencent and 360. The sentence aims to highlight the broader implications of the struggle. The proposition in the corrective clause is figurative as no other companies were literally involved in the competition. This interpretation necessarily involves recognizing the metonymic "standing for" relationship between the two companies and the camps they represent. The same is true of the sentence in (28).

5.2.1.4 Epistemic Strengthening Denials

Epistemic strengthening denials are closely aligned with what Davis (2016) terms "ignorance implicature denials". Davis delineates ignorance implicature as distinct from limiting implicature. Ignorance implicature, often triggered by scalar implicatures, serves to indicate a speaker's lack of complete knowledge. For instance, the statement "Some S are P" can imply the speaker's uncertainty about whether all S are P, whereas "X is at least warm" might suggest the speaker does

---

① https://m.xiaoshuodaquan.com/zhonghuadadiguo/579.html.

not know if X is hot. This distinction is crucial: limiting implicature should only be employed when the speaker has sufficient knowledge or near certainty about the subject matter. For example, it would be misleading for a speaker to claim "the children didn't eat all the cakes" without knowing whether all cakes were indeed eaten. Instead, a statement like "The children ate some cakes" would more accurately convey the speaker's uncertainty.

Epistemic strengthening denials can be induced by either lexical items or constructions. The latter are roughly what Huang (2014) calls "Q-clausal implicature". According to Huang (2014), this kind of implicature is induced when there are two constructions X (p) and Y (p) that have different semantic strength but equal brevity, where p is entailed by the former but not by the latter, the use of Y (p) will implicates that the speaker is not sure whether p obtains or not (see also Grice, 1989; Gazdar, 1979a; Levinson, 2000). Semantically, epistemic strengthening denials can be categorized into two types: validity strengthening denials and predictability strengthening denials, following Fowler's (1985) division of epistemic modality. Validity strengthening denials concern the speaker's confidence in the truth of a proposition, reflecting a direct challenge to the assumed truth value. Predictability strengthening denials, on the other hand, relate to the likelihood of future events occurring, addressing the speaker's assessment of future probabilities rather than present or past realities. Consider (29) - (32):

(29) 不几天,野战医院来告状……人家挺客气,用了"据说"和"牵"
这样两个词。"不是'据说'。"工兵不领情:"实实在在全是我们
扛走的。不信我领你去看看。"(BCC)
Bu ji tian, yezhan yiyuan lai gaozhuang … renjia ting keqi,
yong le "jushuo" he "qian" zheyang liang ge ci. "Bu shi'jushuo'."
Gongbing bu lingqing: "Shishizaizai quan shi women kangzou
de. Bu xin wo ling ni qu kankan. "
not few-days field hospital come complain they quite polite
use PRT It-is-said. and pull such two-CL words not it-is-said
sappers not appreciate truly all is we carry-away PRT not

believe I lead you go have-a-look

In just a few days, the field hospital came to complain ... They were quite polite and described the event with the expression "it is said" and "pull". "Not 'it is said'." The engineers didn't appreciate their kindness and said, "It was really us who carried them away. If you don't believe me, I will show you where they are. "

(30) 过去我感到非常伤心的原因,是我好像很荒唐可笑。不是好像,而是确实荒唐。 (BCC)

Guoqu wo gandao feichang shangxin de yuanyin, shi wo haoxiang hen huangtang kexiao. Bu shi haoxiang, er shi queshi huangtang.

in. the. past I feel very sad GEN reason is because I as. if very absurd ridiculous not as.if but really absurd

I felt very sad in the past because it looked as if I was very ridiculous. Actually, it's not "as if"—I am indeed absurd.

(31) 所有的海盗都是人类的敌人,不是一个国家或某一类人民的敌人,而是全人类的敌人。

Suoyou de haidao dou shi renlei de diren, bu shi yi ge guojia huo mou yi lei renmin de diren, er shi quan renlei de diren.

all pirates all are mankind GEN enemy not one-CL nation or enemy but all mankind GEN enemy

All pirates are the enemies of mankind, not the enemies of one country or one kind of people, but the enemies of all mankind.

(32) 他曾经对她说:"不是至少还有你,而是此生只有你。"[1]

Ta cengjing dui ta shuo: "Bu shi zhishao hai you ni, er shi ci sheng zhi you ni."

he once to she say not at. least still have you but this life only you

He once told her, "It's not just that I still have you; it's that in

---

[1] https://www.xxzww.net/read-htm-tid-3188221.html.

this lifetime, I only have you."

All instances of MN in sentences (29) - (32) are examples of validity strengthening denials. They are not used to negate the truth conditions of the roots but rather to deny the so-called "ignorance implicatures" induced by the roots. In (29) the expression *jushuo* ("it is said") will generate the implicated meaning that it is unknown whether it was the sappers who had carried the thing away. This meaning constituent is subsequently refuted by the sapper who acknowledges their actions. In (30), *queshi* ("really") is semantically stronger than *haoxiang* ("as if"). The root proposition implicates that the speaker was not quite sure whether he/she had been really so absurd. Likewise, in (31) the use of semantically weaker expression *huozhe* ("or") implies that the speaker does not know whether both P and Q are true at the same time. By the same token, using *zhishao* ("at least") in (32) implies that the speaker does not know whether the proposition is true or not.

Predictability strengthening denials involve instances of MN where the two propositions predict different likelihoods of a future event occuring. They aim to refute the implied meaning that it is uncertain whether a conceived event will actually occur. Generally, the rectification contains a semantically stronger proposition than the root, indicating the speaker's increased confidence in the occurrence of the same event. Consider (33) - (35):

(33) 黛娜忽然用十分苦涩的声音问："鹰,如果我们……离开这
里——"这时他忍不住道："不是如果,我们一定可以离开这
里!" (BCC)
*Daina huran yong shifen kuse de shengyin wen: "Ying, ruguo
women … likai zheli——" Zheshi ta renbuzhu dao: "Bu shi ruguo,
women yiding keyi likai zheli!"*
Dai Na suddenly use very bitter GEN voice ask Ying if we
leave here then he can-not-help say not if we definitely can
leave here
Dai Na suddenly asked in a very bitter voice, "Eagle, if we ...

get out of here..." Then he couldn't help but said, "Not 'if', we can definitely leave here!"

(34) 两者之间的较量是正常的，不是"倘若"，而是"已经"；至于说"谁能赢"根本就不是现在能够下结论的事情。①

Liangzhe zhijian de jiaoliang shi zhengchang de, bu shi "tangruo", er shi "yijing"; zhiyu shuo "shui neng ying" genben jiu bu shi xianzai nenggou xia jielun de shiqing.

two-CL between GEN conflict is normal PRT not in.case but already as-to tell who will win at-all simply not now draw conclusion GEN matter

As the leaders of two major powers with conflicts of interest, the contest between them is normal. It is not "in case it happens", because it has already happened. As to "who can win", it is simply too early to tell at present.

(35) "真的离开了，就又会怀念了。""唉，也许吧，可是我现在好想好想离开这个学校。""不是也许，而是肯定。" (BCC)

"Zhende likai le, jiu you hui huainian le." "Ai, yexu ba, keshi wo xianzai haoxiang haoxiang likai zhe ge xuexiao." "Bu shi yexu, er shi kending."

really leave ASP simply again will miss PRT PRT perhaps PRT but I now really want really want leave this-CL school not maybe but definitely

"Once you really leave, you'll start missing it again." "Sigh, maybe, but right now I really, really want to leave this school." "It's not maybe; it's for sure."

Similar to validity strengthening denials, predictability strengthening denials do not negate the truth condition of the root proposition but rather refute the "ignorance implicature" generated by the root. In (33), employing the semantically

---

① https://junshi.eastday.com/a/180718002211605.html.

weaker expression *ruguo* ("if") can induce the "ignorance implicature" that the occurrence of the event is uncertain. This implied meaning is dismissed by the speaker, and replaced by a semantically stronger proposition. This pattern is consistent across the other two examples as well.

5.2.1.5 Directional Strengthening Denials

Directional strengthening denials focus on the directional nature of actions within discourse, specifically distinguishing between unidirectional and bidirectional interactions. This category of denials is crucial for understanding how speakers use language to negotiate and redefine the roles and relationships in communicative events. Like other forms of strengthening denials, directional strengthening denials often employ paraphrases such as "not just X" or "not only X". These denials do not contest the state of affairs described in the root propositions but rather challenge the implied meaning that the event is merely unidirectional instead of bidirectional. Consider (36) - (38):

(36) 我说的启蒙就是一个全民的启蒙运动, 不是你启蒙我, 我启蒙你, 而是我们互相启蒙。(BCC)

Wo shuo de qimeng jiu shi yi ge quanmin de qimeng yundong,

bu shi ni qimeng wo, wo qimeng ni, er shi women huxiang qimeng.

I say GEN enlightenment just is one-CL all people GEN enlightenment movement not you enlighten me I enlighten you but we mutual enlighten

The enlightenment I am talking about is a universal enlightenment movement. It is not that you enlighten me or I enlighten you. Rather, we enlighten each other.

(37) 他们留下的只有厌烦和疲倦, 而且他们之间不再是丈夫指责妻子, 而是互相指责, 互相谩骂。(BCC)

Tamen liuxia de zhi you yanfan he pijuan, erqie tamen zhijian

bu zai shi zhangfu zhize qizi, er shi huxiang zhize, huxiang manma.

they leave GEN only boredom and fatigue but they between no. longer be husband blame wife but mutual blame mutual abuse

They were left with nothing but boredom and fatigue. Moreover, the situation was not just that the husband blamed their wives, but they blamed and abused each other.

(38) 虽然我知道你看不见,不过我还是想说,不是你对我依赖,而是我们互相依赖！我们会是一辈子的朋友。(BCC)

Suiran wo zhidao ni kanbujian, buguo wo hai shi xiang shuo, bu shi ni dui wo yilai, er shi women huxiang yilai! women hui shi yi beizi de pengyou.

though I know you blind but I still want say not you on I depend but we mutually depend we will be whole-life GEN friend

Even though I know you can't see it, I'd like to say it's not that you depend on me—we depend on each other! We will be friends for life!

In (36), the event described assigns the role of agent to the speaker and patient to the hearer, indicating a unidirectional flow of action. This characterizes the enlightenment event as proceeding from one participant to another. Conversely, in the rectification, both the speaker and the hearer participate equally, with either capable of being designated as agent or patient. Consequently, this interaction is depicted as bidirectional, reflecting mutual influence. This bidirectional dynamic is consistently observed in the other two examples as well.

5.2.2 Identifying Denials

Unlike strengthening denials, which enhance an assumption by increasing the semantic or informational strength of the root proposition, identifying denials serve to emphasize the discrepancy between a stereotypical state of affairs and the actual context. Identifying denials operate through a "revision" effect, where the speaker intends to revise the interlocutor's default assumption. In these denials, the root is pragmatically enriched into a new proposition by default. The corrective utterance in identifying denials does not aim to strengthen the root but to delineate what is inconsistent with the stereotypical state of affairs denoted by the root.

The meaning constituent being denied by an identifying denial is roughly correspondent to "R-based" implicature discussed in Horn (1989). Although Horn initially argued that MN could reject any prior utterance for various reasons, he later noted in a separate analysis that MN could not negate (Horn, 1989). Contrary to this, Davis (2016) suggests that Horn's perspective might be too broad, asserting that numerous types of R-based implicatures can indeed be negated by MN, a point substantiated by our empirical data. Like strengthening denials, the representational effect of identifying denials arises from the contrast between the rectification proposition and the root proposition. However, while strengthening denials enhance the root by adding stronger or more explicit information, identifying denials often involve a shift or clarification that specifically addresses and corrects the root's implications or assumptions. In terms of the ways in which the representational effect is produced, identifying denials can be sub-divided into categorical identifying denials, facet identifying denials, relational identifying denials, identity identifying denials and sequential identifying denials.

5.2.2.1 Categorical Identifying Denials

Categorical identifying denials enable speakers to assess whether an entity within a specific context fits a predefined category. This is done through stereotypically instantiating a schematic category represented in the root, which gives rise to a more specific proposition. Such denials often reflect the speaker's rejection of classifying an entity or a situation within a traditional category. This type of denials can be further classified into two types: canonical and metaphorical category-identifying cases. Canonical cases involve earnest category-judgement activities, where both the root and the rectification literally represent the same state of affairs. Consider (39) - (41):

(39) 巴黎一向是灯红酒绿,洋溢着欢乐的花都,可波德莱尔偏偏写了一本《巴黎的忧郁》,况且竟不是诗,而是什么"散文诗"。①

Bali yixiang shi denghong-jiulü, yangyizhe huanle de huadu,
ke Bode Laier pianpian xie le yi ben《Bali de Youyu》, kuangqie
jing bu shi shi, er shi shenme "sanwen shi".

Paris always is flamboyant brim-ASP joyful GEN flower. city
but Baudelaire just wrote ASP one-CL Paris GEN sulk
moreover not poem but so-called prose peom

Paris has been well known as a flower city, which is
flamboyant and brimming with joy. However, it was written by
Baudelaire in a collection of poems entitled *Le Spleen de*
Paris. What is more, they are not actually poems, but so-called
"prose poems".

(40) 我经常听她说人家"我觉得你说的像南方英语"或者"你这不
是英文,而是上海英文吧"。 (BCC)

Wo jingchang ting ta shuo renjia "wo jue de ni shuo de xiang
nanfang yingyu" huozhe "ni zhe bu shi yingwen, er shi
Shanghai yingwen ba".

I often hear she criticize others I think you speak GEN like
Southern English or you this not English but Shanghai English
PRE

I often heard her criticizing others, "I think you speak like
Southern English" or "This is not English, but Shanghai
English".

(41) 他掏出一本书看得津津有味,那本不是什么书,而是漫画,是
《龙虎门》。大学中文系的一年级生,日常读物竟是《龙虎门》。
(BCC)

Ta taochu yi ben shu kan de jinjinyouwei, na ben bu shi
shenme shu, er shi manhua, shi《Long-Hu Men》. Daxue zhongwen
xi de yi nianji sheng, richang duwu jing shi《Long-Hu Men》.

---

① http://www.miaoqiyuan.cn/cyjl.m/show-zzjm.html.

he take-out one-CL book read-PRT with. relish that-CL not

what book but cartoon is dragon tiger sect college Chinese

department GEN one-grade student daily readings surprisingly

is dragon tiger sect

He took out a book and read it with great interest. It was not a

serious book but a cartoon, *Dragon and Tiger Sect*. Surprisingly,

as a first-year college student in Chinese department, his daily

reading material is such a cartoon.

Each of the three examples contains a root proposition that can be stereotypically enriched into a more specific proposition. In (39), the lexical item in the negative scope *shi* ("poem") specifically denotes classical poetic works, not merely any form of poetry. This implies that Baudelaire's work, though not a traditional poem, is a prose poem—an unconventional form within the poetic genre. In (40), the term *yingwen* ("English") refers specifically to standard English spoken by native speakers, contrasting with the Shanghai-style English spoken by the non-native speaker. This denial underlines the significant disparity between non-standard and standard English. Similarly, in (41), the term *shu* ("book") is used to denote scholarly or serious literature, not just any printed material. The speaker's point is that the material the boy was engrossed in was not scholarly literature, but rather a comic book.

Certainly, this form of denial extends beyond mere judgments of nominal categories to include verbal categories as well. In the examples provided below, the negated lexical items belong to verbal categories. Here, the speaker is not denying the truth condition of the root, but the implicated meaning induced by a stereotypical use of the verbal concept in the root. Consider (42) - (44):

(42) "我们后来又买了一些。"杨越接口道，"不，不是买，是人家半
买半送给咱们的。" (BCC)
"Women houlai you mai le yixie." Yang Yue jiekou dao, "Bu,
bu shi mai, shi renjia banmai-bansong gei zanmen de."

we later again buy ASP some Yang Yue add say not not buy is

they half-buy-half-get-free to us PRT

"We bought some more later." Yang Yue added, "No, it was not buying; They sold it to us at a very low price for the sake of friendship."

(43) 汤骥伟根本不是在喝酒,而是在灌酒,也不怎么吃菜。 (BCC)

Tang Jiwei genben bu shi zai he jiu, er shi zai guan jiu, ye bu zenme chi cai.

Tang Jiwei at. all not ASP drink wine but ASP infuse wine even seldom eat dish

Tang Jiwei wasn't drinking at all—he was infusing. Throughout the dinner, he didn't eat much food.

(44) 小蓉敲开门,见三个人都坐在地板上。不是坐,是半躺。(BCC)

Xiaorong qiaokai men, jian san ge ren dou zuo zai diban shang. Bu shi zuo, shi ban tang.

Xiaorong knock-open door see three-CL people all sit at floor- at not sit are half lying

Xiaorong got the door open and saw three people sitting on the floor. Indeed, they were not sitting; they were half lying.

Similar to (39) - (41), each of the three sentences disputes a more specific or intensified interpretation of the root, which is derived from the conventional understanding of the verbal concept involved. In (42), the negation does not refute the act of purchasing itself; it challenges the notion that this was a standard transaction. In (43), the denial does not question whether the man was consuming alcohol; rather, it contests the characterization of his actions as typical drinking. Similarly, in (44), the focus of the denial is not on whether the individuals were seated, but on whether their posture could be described as simply sitting.

Unlike typical cases, metaphorical categorical identifying denials utilize metaphorical categorization in the corrective clause. Here, the speaker aims to depict the same situation metaphorically, emphasizing attributes that are not typically associated with the subject. Consider (45) - (47):

(45) 这女人她素来是那么顽强的！这不是一个女人，而是一头公
牛。(BCC)

Zhe nüren ta sulai shi name wanqiang de! Zhe bu shi yi ge nüren, er shi yi tou gongniu.

this woman she always is so tenacious PRT this not one-CL woman but one-CL bull.

This woman has always been so tenacious! She is not a woman, but a bull.

(46) "……没有城管城市还不知道该乱成什么样呢。""这不是城
管，是土匪，以前没有城管时不一样很好吗？"(BCC)

"…… meiyou chengguan chengshi hai bu zhidao gai luan-cheng shenme yang ne." "Zhe bu shi chengguan, shi tufei, yiqian meiyou chengguan shi bu yiyang hen hao ma?"

without city. inspectors city yet not know will chaotic-become what state PRT this not city. inspectors is bandit the-same no city. inspectors when not the-same PRT

"...I don't know how chaotic the city will be if there are no city inspectors." "They are not city inspectors; they are bandits. Wasn't our lives as good as usual when there were no city inspectors?"

(47) 对他来说，演讲不是演讲，而是战争。他在台上不是坐着，不
是站着，也不是走着，而是在来回地奔跑。(BCC)

Dui ta lai shuo, yanjiang bu shi yanjiang, er shi zhanzheng. Ta zai tai shang bu shi zuozhe, bu shi zhanzhe, ye bu shi zouzhe, er shi zai laihui de benpao.

for. him speech not speech but war he on stage-on not sit-ASP not stand-ASP also not walk-ASP but ASP back-and-forth-PRT run

For him, the speech is not a speech, but a war. He was not

sitting, standing, or walking , but running back and forth on the stage.

All the sentences above undergo metaphorical reinterpretation. In (45), the negation does not serve to dispute the person's gender. Instead, it emphasizes a distinctive trait (i. e. tenacity) that diverges from the conventional female stereotype. In (46), the negation isn't to refute their roles as city inspectors; rather, it criticizes their failure to fulfill the expected duties of city inspectors, who are supposed to enforce laws judiciously. A similar interpretation applies to (47).

5.2.2.2 Facet Identifying Denials

Different from categorical identifying denials, facet identifying denials do not involve category judgment but rather focus on specific aspects of the comprehensive knowledge surrounding a concept. These aspects can metaphorically be considered various "facets" of the same concept. Typically, the proposition at the root can be enhanced by incorporating the term *benshen* ("oneself"), suggesting a deeper or more personal aspect of the concept. Facet identifying denials are categorized into canonical and metonymic identifying denials.

In a canonical facet identifying denial, the root proposition can be stereotypically specified into a stronger proposition, denoting a particular aspect of the overall concept. By contrast, the corrective proposition represents a different aspect of knowledge about the same entity. Consider (48) - (50):

(48) 有人说,这座城市是浮躁的,其实浮躁的并不是城市,而是城市里的人。①

You ren shuo, zhe zuo chengshi shi fuzao de, qishi fuzao de bing bu shi chengshi, er shi chengshi li de ren.

have people say this-CL city is impetuous PRT actually impetuous GEN actually not city but city in GEN people

Some people say that the city is impetuous. In fact, what is

---

① https://www.ximalaya.com/diantai/5791/357620.

impetuous is not the city, but people in the city.

(49) 我听过这种论调, 也考虑了很久, 我要的不是他这个人, 而是他的心。(BCC)

Wo tingguo zhe zhong lundiao, ye kaolüle hen jiu, wo yao de bu shi ta zhe ge ren, er shi ta de xin.

I hear-ASP this-CL argument and consider ASP very long I want GEN not he this CL person but he GEN heart.

I have heard this argument before and considered it for a long time. What I want is not the man himself, but his heart.

(50) 有时候你会禁不住感叹:电脑真是一个最聪明的笨蛋! 其实, 不是电脑, 而是电脑软件的设计还没有足够聪明。(BCC)

Youshihou ni hui jinbuzhu gantan: diannao zhenshi yi ge zui congming de bendan! Qishi bu shi diannao, er shi diannao ruanjian de sheji hai meiyou zugou congming.

sometimes you will cannot.help sign computer really one-CL most smart GEN idiot actually not computer but computer software GEN design yet not enough smart

Sometimes you can't help but sigh, "The computer is really the smartest idiot!" In fact, it's not the computer itself that is stupid, but the design of computer software. They are not smart enough yet.

Each sentence contains a root proposition that can be stereotypically enriched into a more specific proposition which denotes a certain aspect of the original concept. It is the enriched proposition, rather than the root proposition, that is the real target of negation. To arrive at a precise interpretation of (48), the address is required to interpret the concept *chengshi* ("city") as the physical atmosphere of a city, rather than PEOPLE living in it. Similarly, the phrase *zhe ge ren* ("this person") in (49) will be interpreted as the physical characteristics of the man, rather than his moral value. And in (50), the concept *diannao* ("computer") actually denotes the hardware of computer, rather than software.

Metonymic facet identifying denials, also known as "metonymic negations" according to Wen and Shen (2012) and Wei (2019), involve metonymic relationships between the propositions in the root and the corrective statements. Typically formatted as "V *de bu shi* X, *er shi* Y", where X usually represents a concrete entity and Y an abstract one. Generally, this type of denials are used to express that the event described in the root should not be understood in a stereotypical manner, but in the way described in the corrective clause. Consider (51) - (54):

(51) 哥抽的不是烟, 而是寂寞! [1]

Ge chou de bu shi yan, er shi jimo!

brother smoke GEN not cigarette but loneliness

Brother is not smoking cigarettes; I am smoking loneliness!

(52) 我们买的不是汽车, 而是面子! [2]

Women mai de bu shi qiche, er shi mianzi!

we buy GEN not car but dignity

We are not buying a car; we are buying dignity.

(53) 哥拍的不是电影, 而是票房。[3]

Ge pai de bu shi dianying, er shi piaofang.

brother make DE not movie but box.office

I am not making a movie; I am making the box of office.

(54) 华为卖的不是手机, 是骨气! [4]

Huawei mai de bu shi shouji, shi guqi!

Huawei sell DE not telephone BE guts

What Huawei company sell are not mobile phones, but guts.

These sentences do not challenge the truth of the root proposition, but

---

[1] https://tieba.baidu.com/p/3150622229?red_tag=3551212985.

[2] http://news.bitauto.com/hao/wenzhang/333469.

[3] http://bbs.tianya.cn/post-free-1771855-1.shtml.

[4] https://www.sohu.com/a/316587729_120153173.

instead address specific stereotypical interpretations associated with it. For instance, in (51) the assertion is that smoking serves not as a hobby or social activity, but as a means to combat loneliness, a motivation less commonly associated with smoking. Similarly, in (52), the denial does not question the act of buying, but challenges the conventional motive of transportation, redirecting focus to the social prestige that owning a certain car may signify. A similar approach is applied to the interpretations of (53) and (54).

5.2.2.3 Relational Identifying Denials

A relational identifying denial involves denying a default relationship between two entities in the root proposition. The implicated meaning of the root (i. e. the stronger proposition) is induced by exemplifying a relation in the root in a stereotypical manner. Very often, in the corrective clause, the relation between the two participants is arranged in a reverse order. Relational identifying denials can be divided into two types in terms of whether the relation is a static or dynamic one: static relational identifying denials and dynamic relational-identifying denials.

Static relational identifying denials refute either a tangible or conceptual spatial relationship between two entities at the core of the negation. The implied meaning arises from the presupposition that typical spatial relationships exist between the entities. These relationships in both the root and the corrective statements are typically depicted in stark contrast. Consider (55) - (57):

(55) 电视剧每播放十五分钟就要插播一次广告。显然,这已不是电视剧插播广告,而是在广告中插播电视剧。①

Dianshiju mei bofang shiwu fenzhong jiu yao chabo yi ci guanggao. Xianran, zhe yi bu shi dianshiju chabo guanggao, er shi zai guanggao zhong chabo dianshiju.

TV shows every play fifteen minute then will insert one-CLF commercial apparently this already not TV show insert commercial but in advertisement-in insert TV shows

---

① https://www.sohu.com/a/26900207_160337.

Every fifteen minutes of a TV series is interspersed with commercials. Apparently, this is not inserting commercials into a TV show, but inserting a TV show into a commercial.

(56) 这些市场上猪肉的平均掺水率达30.24%,最高掺水率竟达 54%。这种分割猪肉已不是掺水的肉,而是掺肉的水。 (BCC)

Zhexie shichang shang zhurou de pingjun chanshui lü da 30.24%, zuigao chanshui lü jing da 54%. Zhe zhong fen'ge zhurou yi bu shi chanshui de rou, er shi chanrou de shui.

these markets-in pork GEN average doping rate reach 30.24% highest doping rate even reach 54% this-CL adulterated pork already not doping GEN pork but meat-injected GEN water

The average doping rate of pork in these markets is 30.24%, with the highest doping rate reaching 54%. This splitting of pork is no longer water-injected meat, but meat-injected water.

(57) 校地里大部分都是长满茂密树木的森林,这已经不是说学校 里有森林,而是森林里有学校了。(BCC)

Xiaodi li dabufen dou shi zhangman maomi shumu de senlin, zhe yijing bu shi shuo xuexiao li you senlin, er shi senlin li you xuexiao le.

school land-in most all is grow-full dense trees GEN forest this already not say school-in have forest but forest-in have school PRT

Most of the school land is covered with dense trees. There is not a forest in the school, but a school in the forest.

Each of them involves denying a stronger proposition arising from specifying the spatial relationship represented in the root. In (55), the fact that commercial advertisements are often inserted into TV shows is not being denied. Instead, the target of negation is a stereotypical situation where the time length of advertisements is much shorter than that of TV shows. The negation in (56) is used to deny a stereotypical situation in which the proportion of meat and injected water is tolerable. The sentence in (57) can be analyzed in the same way.

In a dynamic relational identifying denial, the root proposition encapsulates a transitive relationship between two entities, as opposed to a spatial one. The denial targets a more emphatic assertion of the root that typically conforms to a stereotype. Similar to spatial instances, the transitive relationship is frequently depicted in reverse. Such denials do not refute the existence of the transitive relationship itself but challenge the conventional interpretation of this relationship as presented in the root. Consider (58) - (60):

(58) 遛狗一小时比走了8公里都累,这真的不是人遛狗,而是狗遛人啊！(BCC)

Liu gou yi xiaoshi bi zoule 8 gongli dou lei, zhe zhende bu shi ren liu gou, er shi gou liu ren a!

walk dog one-hour than walk-ASP 8 kilometer even tired this really not man walk dog but dog walk man PRT

I felt more tired after walking my dog for an hour alone than walking 8km. It's really not a man walking dogs; it's a dog walking a man!

(59) 你如果就读于全美排名前10位中的任何一家商学院,都不会为未来的工作发愁。毕业后,不是你找工作,而是工作找你。(BCC)

Ni ruguo jiudu yu quanmei paiming qian 10 wei zhong de renhe yi jia shangxueyuan, dou bu hui wei weilai de gongzuo fachou. Biye hou, bu shi ni zhao gongzuo, er shi gongzuo zhao ni.

if you study in whole America rank top 10-CL in GEN any one-CL business school all not will about job worry graduate after not you look.for job but job look.for you

If you are studying in any of the top 10 business schools in the United States, you will not worry about your future work. After graduation, you do not have to look for a job; jobs will look for you.

(60) 创作更像是一种注定的命运,决定了作家的精神走向。所以说，不是歌德创造了《浮士德》，而是《浮士德》创造了歌德。
(BCC)

Chuangzuo geng xiang shi yi zhong zhuding de mingyun, juedingle zuojia de jingshen zouxiang. Suoyishuo, bu shi Gede chuangzaole 《Fushide》, er shi 《Fushide》 chuangzaole Gede.

creation more like is one-CL doomed GEN fate determine ASP writer GEN spirit direction therefore not Goethe create ASP Faust but Faust create ASP Goethe

Creation is more like a doomed fate, which determines the direction of the writer's spirit. Therefore, it is not Goethe who created Faust, but Goethe who created Faust.

The negation in (58) is not to dispute the act of walking the dog but challenges the notion that walking dogs is merely a leisure activity, a common stereotype. The corrective clause inverts the transitive relationship, yielding a humorous and ironic effect. Similarly, the negation in (59) does not suggest that students in the top business schools do not have to look for jobs after graduation. Instead, it is intended to deny that their job hunting activities are stereotypical ones. Like (58), the transitive relationship is also reversed in the corrective clause, creating a strong rhetoric effect. The same is true to (60). Similar to cases of denials in (55) - (57), the corrective clauses of the three denials represent the same situations to create a sharp contrast between the stereotypical situation and the described situation.

5.2.2.4 Identity Identifying Denials

This category of denials are designated as such because they clarify the identity of individuals or entities, distinguishing whether they are recognized or anonymous. In identity identifying denials, the negation specifically targets an implicature concerning the identity of a person. For instance, when the sentence "Mary did not really meet a man at the bar" is used, it does not imply that Mary met a woman instead. Rather, it refutes the more specific assumption that she met an unrelated man, challenging the listener's expectations based on social norms or stereotypes. Horn (1989) describes this as a classic example of an "R-based implicature", which stems from the R-principle advising to "say no more than you need to". Consider (61) - (63):

(61) "昨天我看到你在给一个女孩子买首饰哦!""不是女孩子,是我表妹。"(BCC)

　　"Zuotian wo kandao ni zai gei yi ge nühaizi mai shoushi o!"

　　"Bu shi nühaizi, shi wo biaomei."

　　yesterday I see you ASP for one-CL girl buy jewelry PRT not girl is my cousin

　　"Oh, I saw you buying jewelry for a girl yesterday!" "It's not a girl; it's my cousin."

(62) 法官注视着被告说:"你被控强暴一位女士,你还有什么可说的?"被告站起来答辩:"那不是什么女士,她是我妻子。"①

　　Faguan zhushizhe beigao suo: "Ni bei kong qiangbao yi wei nüshi, ni hai you shenme ke shuo de?" Beigao zhan qilai dabian: "Na bu shi shenme nüshi, ta shi wo qizi."

　　judge look-at-ASP defendant say you BEI accuse rape one-CL lady you still have what can say GEN defendant stand-up reply that not so-called woman she is my wife

　　The judge looked at the defendant and said, "You are accused of raping a woman. Do you have anything to say?" The defendant stood up and replied, "That's not a lady, she's my wife."

(63) 小朋友看着路边执勤的交警,大声喊警察叔叔,只有他一个人不出声。老师问他为什么不一起喊,他说那不是警察叔叔,是我爸爸。(BCC)

　　Xiaopengyou kanzhe lubian zhiqin de jiaojing, dasheng han jingcha shushu, zhi you ta yi ge ren bu chusheng. Laoshi wen ta weishenme bu yiqi han, ta shuo na bu shi jingcha shushu,

---

① https://www.hahamx.cn/joke/2631014.

shi wo baba.

Children look-ASP roadside on-duty GEN traffic. police loudly shout policeman uncle only he one-CL person not speak teacher ask him why not together shout he say that not police uncle be my father

The children saw the traffic policeman on duty at the roadside and then shouted at him loudly, "Uncle policeman!" Only the boy was silent. The teacher asked him the reason. He said that the man was not "uncle policeman" but his father.

The negation in (61) is not used to deny that the person they are talking about is a girl, but to deny the "R-implicature" (i.e. a stereotypically specified proposition) that the girl is not the person's family member. In (62) the judge's utterance can induce the implicature that the raped lady was not the speaker's wife. The negation is also used to deny this implicature rather than the truth condition of the root proposition. Similarly, in (63) the speaker does not suggest that the man is his dad; rather, the negation attaches to the implicature that the man is an unknown person.

5.2.2.5 Sequential Identifying Denials

Sequential identifying denials target a stronger, temporally enriched proposition of the root, typically presented in a stereotypical sequence. In sequential identifying denials, both the initial and the corrective propositions relate the same sequence of events, but the negation often lacks explicit markers of temporal order. This absence may lead to an implicature, induced by "conjunction buttressing", where the listener infers a temporal or causal sequence (Levinson, 2000). The speaker's intent is not to dispute the occurrence of the events but to challenge this inferred sequence, thus rejecting a temporally specific interpretation of the root proposition. Consider (64) - (66):

(64) 甲：咱们父母那一辈人和咱们的生活方式有什么不一样的，不都是恋爱，结婚生孩子吗？

乙：这可不一样，咱们是先恋爱，后结婚，父母那一辈是先结婚，后恋爱。

Jia: Zanmen fumu na yi bei ren he zanmen de shenghuo fangshi you shenme bu yiyang de, bu dou shi lian'ai, jiehun sheng haizi ma?

Yi: Zhe ke bu yiyang, zanmen shi xian lian'ai, hou jiehun, fumu na yi bei shi xian jiehun, hou lian'ai.

A: we parents that generation with we GEN life way have what not the-same PRT not all is date marry give-birth baby QM

B: this really not the-same we are first date then marry parent that generation are first marry then date

A: What is the difference in life style between our parents and us? Isn't all about dating, getting married, and having children?

B: No, our generation usually dates first and then gets married. But the generation of our parents generally got married first and then dated.

(65) 现在企业需要"做强做大"，而不是"做大做强"。没有"做强"就急着"做大"，是不理性的行为。①

Xianzai qiye xuyao "zuoqiang-zuoda", er bu shi "zuoda-zuoqiang". Meiyou "zuoqiang" jiu jizhe "zuoda", shi bu lixing de xingwei.

nowadays company need get strong get big but not get big get strong" not get strong then eager get big is not rational GEN deed

Nowadays, enterprises need to "become strong and then big", not "big and then strong". Rushing to "become big" without first becoming strong is irrational behavior.

(66) 中国足球伤透了国人的心，所幸我们没有放弃希望。我们不是屡战屡败，而是屡败屡战。②

---

① http://www.people.cn/404/error.html.

② http://www.ballq.cn/bqweb/article/314/.

Zhongguo zuqiu shangtoule guoren de xin, suoxing women meiyou fangqi xiwang. Women bu shi lüzhan-lübai, er shi lübai-lüzhan.

Chinese footbal hurt-badly-ASP Chinese GEN heart fortunately we not give-up hope we not every-time fight every-time lose but every.time lose every-time fight

Chinese football has deeply hurt the hearts of the people, but fortunately, we have not given up hope. We are not repeatedly fighting and losing; instead, we are losing and continuing to fight.

In (64), the negation can be understood in both temporal and atemporal contexts. The events are presented side by side in the negative and corrective clauses without clear temporal connectors, yet our understanding of typical life stages suggests a temporal interpretation. In (65), the phrase *zuoda-zuoqiang* ("getting bigger and stronger") typically outlines two primary development objectives for a company. Here, the negation suggests a specific sequence—first becoming big, then strong—contrasted by the corrective clause advocating for gaining strength before size. Similarly, in (66), the negation emphasizes a sequence of repeated efforts and failures, highlighting resilience rather than a simple cycle of defeat.

5.2.3 Positioning Denials

Positioning denials are instances of metalinguistic negation where the physical or psychological perspectives depicted in the original statement are altered or inverted. These denials challenge the validity of the perspectives or viewpoints initially presented. They are employed to shift the perspective from which a situation is perceived and described. There are five distinct types of positioning denials, each characterized by its method of manipulating these viewpoints: relativistic, causative, deictic, structural, and evaluative positioning denials.

5.2.3.1 Relativistic Positioning Denials

Relativistic positioning denials involve the negation of a term and its replacement with an antonym in the corrective clause, such as *shu/ying* ("win/lose"), *kuai/man* ("fast/slow"), *qiangda/ruoxiao* ("strong/weak"). Although the propositions in both the negative and corrective clauses typically describe the same factual situation, they present contrasting viewpoints, thereby leading to divergent interpretations and implications. Consider (67) - (69):

(67) 如果你走了几步笨棋，以致使他容易地取胜，他就笑着说："嗯，这不是我赢的，而是你输的……"①

Ruguo ni zoule ji bu benqi, yizhi shi ta rongyi de qusheng, ta jiu xiaozhe shuo: "En, zhe bu shi wo ying de, er shi ni shu de…"

if you move-ASP several-CL dumb chess so cause him easily PRT win he then smile-ASP say en this not I win PRT but you lose PRT

If you make a few unwise moves, allowing him to win easily, he will then smile and say, "Well, it's not that I won, but that you lost..."

(68) 钱老师原来是省田径队的短跑运动员，小偷遇到他只好自认倒霉。他则在旁边憨憨一笑，"不是我跑得快，是小偷跑得太慢了！"(BCC)

Qian laoshi yuanlai shi sheng tianjing dui de duanpao yundongyuan, xiaotou yudao ta zhi hao zi ren daomei. Ta ze zai pangbian hanhan yi xiao, "Bu shi wo pao de kuai, shi xiaotou pao de tai man le!"

Qian teacher turn-out is provincial track-and-field team GEN sprint athlete thief meet he have-to accept bad-luck he simply beside nearby humble smile not I run-PRT fast is thief run-PRT too slow PRT

---

① http://book.sbkk8.com/gushihui/lieningdegushi/196524.html.

He turned out to be a sprinter of the provincial track and field team. And the thief had to accept the bad luck. Smiling humbly beside him, Mr. Qian said, "I did not run fast; the thief ran too slowly!"

(69) 联邦德国外长在会上强调"强化北约的欧洲支柱"的必要性时说:"在大西洋联盟内不是美国太强大,而是欧洲太赢弱。"(BCC)

Lianbang Deguo waizhang zai hui shang qiangdiao "qianghua Beiyue de Ouzhou zhizhu" de biyaoxing shi shuo: "Zai Daxiyang Lianmeng nei bu shi Meiguo tai qiangda, er shi Ouzhpou tai leiruo."

Federal. Republic Germany foreign-minister at conference-at emphasize strengthen NATO GEN Europe pillar GEN necessity when say in Atlantic Alliance inside not America too strong but Europe too weak

At the meeting, German Federal Foreign Minister stressed the necessity to "strengthen the European pillar of NATO", and said, "In the Atlantic Alliance, it is not that the United States is too strong, but that Europe is too weak."

In each example, the root and the corrective statements refer to the same scenario, yet they embody starkly different perspectives. In (67), the speaker is not admitting defeat but is suggesting a shift in perspective regarding the game's outcome. In (68), the narrative starts from the teacher's viewpoint and transitions to that of the thief in the corrective clause. Similarly, in (69), the discussion shifts from America's perceived strength to Europe's weakness, highlighting how different perspectives can provide alternative interpretations of the same situation.

5.2.3.2 Causative Positioning Denials

Causative positioning denials strategically attribute causation or responsibility for events to specific agents or factors. These denials selectively emphasize different aspects of an event in the root and the corrective propositions, thereby shifting the listener's focus and challenging the assignment of responsibility to certain entities. Causative positioning denials are categorized into two distinct forms: canonical causative positioning denials and illocutionary causative positioning denials.

Canonical causative positioning denials utilize negation to pinpoint responsibility on the agents causing the event. Consider (70) - (72):

(70) 真正污染环境的不是垃圾,而是乱丢垃圾的人。(BCC)

Zhenzheng wuran huanjing de bu shi laji, er shi luandiu laji de ren.

really pollute environment GEN not rubbish but litter rubbish GEN people

It is not garbage that really pollutes the environment, but people who litter the garbage.

(71) 这些人反对禁枪的另一个所谓理由是"杀人的不是枪,而是人"。因此,是人的问题,而不是枪的问题。(BCC)

Zhexie ren fandui jin qiang de ling yi ge suowei liyou shi "sha ren de bu shi qiang, er shi ren". Yinci, shi ren de wenti, er bu shi qiang de wenti.

these people oppose ban gun GEN another one-CL reason is kill people GEN not gun but people therefore is people GEN issue but not gun GEN issue

Another so-called reason why these people oppose the ban on guns is that "It is not the gun that kills people, but the gunman". Therefore, it is not an issue about guns, but an issue about people.

(72) 威力大的不是飞刀,而是使用飞刀的人,这个道理冷月当然也明白。(BCC)

Weili da de bu shi feidao, er shi shiyong feidao de ren, zhe ge daoli Leng Yue dangran ye mingbai.

power big GEN not flying knife but use flying knife GEN person this-CL truth Leng Yue definitely also understand

It is not the flying knife that is powerful, but the person who uses it. Leng Yue definitely understood this point.

In (70), the negation does not challenge the fact that rubbish can pollute the environment. Instead, it questions the fairness of attributing pollution solely to garbage itself, suggesting that the real cause lies with the people who improperly dispose of it. Similarly, in (71), the negation does not imply that guns are inherently non-lethal. Rather, it is strategically used to redirect the focus from the guns to the individuals who operate them, thereby shifting the responsibility for violence to the users rather than the weapons themselves. The logic in (72) follows a similar pattern; it emphasizes that the true danger does not reside in the flying knife, but in the person who wields it. This shift in focus underscores the importance of human agency and responsibility in each scenario.

Causative positioning denials not only shift attention but also subtly redirect blame or responsibility to abstract entities that may not have a direct causal connection to the event. This rhetorical strategy effectively diverts the responsibility from individuals or entities that are directly involved, thereby diluting their perceived role in causing the event. By focusing on broader, often more intangible forces, these denials provide a way to mitigate direct blame or accountability. Consider (73) - (75):

(73) 出色的效益引来长沙市工商局领导们到店考察。"听说有的百货店被你们逼得要炸楼了。""不是我们逼的,是战局逼的。我们也快被逼得睡不着觉了。" (BCC)

Chuse de xiaoyi yinlai Changsha Shi gongshangju lingdaomen dao dian kaocha. "Tingshuo youde baihuodian bei nimen bi de yao za lou le." "Bu shi women bi de, shi zhanju bi de. Women ye kuai bei bi de shuibuzhao jiao le."

outstanding GEN efficiency attract Changsha city industry commerce bureau leaders come store inspect it-is-heard some stores PSV you force PRT will explode building PRT not we force-PRT but battle force-PRT we also soon PSV force-PRT

can-not-fall-asleep

The outstanding efficiency attracted leaders from the Industry and Commerce Bureau of Changsha to visit the store. "I heard that some stores were forced by your company to go bankrupt." "It's not us that forced them to do that; it's the commercial battle. We are also in great pressure."

(74) 很多公司不是输给对手，而是输给了钱。无论多出色的团队，如果出现资金流断，公司就必死无疑。(BCC)

Hen duo gongsi bu shi shu gei duishou, er shi shu gei le qian. Wulun duo chuse de tuandui, ruguo chuxian zijin liu duan, gongsi jiu bisi wuyi.

many company not lose to opponents but lose to ASP money

no-matter how good GEN team if exist capital cut-off flow

company then dead-as-a-doornail

Many companies are not losing to rivals, but money. No matter how good the team is, if the capital flow is cut off, the company will be dead as a doornail.

(75) 很多人得病而死亡，其实不是死于疾病，而是死于无知。[①]

Hen duo ren debing er siwang, qishi bu shi si yu jibing, er shi si yu wuzhi.

many people get-sick and die but not die of disease but die of ignorance

Many people get sick and die. In fact, they die not of disease, but ignorance.

Unlike typical causative positioning denials, each of the three examples (73) - (75) involves attributing causation or responsibility to an abstract entity or concept rather than the actual direct cause of the event. This approach assigns the status of

---

① https://www.jianshu.com/p/d58cbc3490f5/.

CAUSER to an abstract entity, which indirectly influences the outcome. This method of attribution serves to obscure the direct causes and shifts the focus to broader, less tangible forces, thereby reshaping the narrative around responsibility and causation.

Illocutionary causative positioning denials, termed "metapragmatic negation" by Ran (2013), serve to execute illocutionary acts such as blaming, criticizing, abusing, or threatening. In such denials, the initial negation articulates the performative intent of the speaker, while the subsequent corrective clause provides justification for the speech act. These denials are strategically used by the speaker to mitigate or avoid the unwelcoming effects on the interpersonal relationship. Consider (76) - (78):

(76) 不是我恭维你，你实在比我想象中聪明得多。(BCC)

Bu shi wo gongwei ni, ni shizai bi wo xiangxiang zhong congming de duo.

not I flatter you you really than I thought-in smart PRT more

I don't mean to flatter you, but you are much smarter than I thought you were.

(77) 不是我批评你，你这人虚荣心太强，在班上你就盛气凌人。(BCC)

Bu shi wo piping ni, ni zhe ren xurongxin tai qiang, zai ban shang ni jiu shengqi-lingren.

not I criticize you you this person vanity so strong in class-in you just domineering

I am not criticizing you, but you are too vain, and you are domineering in class.

(78) 不是我狠心，而是你实在太让人失望。我若放过你，也无法对我身边这些人交代。(BCC)

Bu shi wo henxin, er shi ni shizai tai rang ren shiwang. Wo ruo fangguo ni, ye wufa dui wo shenbian zhexie ren jiaodai.

not I cruel but you really so disappointing I if let-go you, also cannot for I around these people explain

I am not cruel, but you are so disappointing. If I let you go, I will not be able to explain to these people around me.

The negation in (76) is employed by the speaker to redirect the interlocutor's focus from the act of praise to the underlying reason for it. Similarly, in (77), the negation serves to shift the listener's attention away from the act of criticism to the behaviors that prompted it. Likewise, the negation in (78) is not used to refute the speaker's actions; instead, it aims to refocus the addressee's attention from the act itself to the motivations behind it. This strategic use of negation helps manage the interpersonal dynamics by emphasizing the reasons for these actions rather than the actions themselves.

5.2.3.3 Deictic Positioning Denials

Deictic positioning denials involve shifts in personal or social deictic expressions. In these denials, both the root and the corrective components contain referential expressions that are truth-functionally equivalent but carry different implications. The focus of the negation is not on the truth of the root proposition but rather on the appropriateness of the deictic choices made. Deictic positioning denials can be categorized into two types: diverging deictic positioning denials and converging deictic positioning denials, based on how they manipulate social distance with the addressee.

Diverging deictic positioning denials involve shifting deictic expressions to address an individual, aiming to emphasize or increase the relational distance between the speaker and the addressed individual. In such denials, the speaker rejects an inappropriate use of referential or addressing terms, often to show respect or deference to the referred individuals. Through these denials, the relational distance between the speaker and the referred individual is made more salient. Consider (79) - (81):

(79) 孙茂才哈哈一笑, 道:"致庸兄, 不, 我该叫你乔东家了! 乔东家, 我听说贵府有难……" (BCC)

*Sun Maocai haha yi xiao, dao: "Zhiyong xiong, bu, wo gai jiao
ni Qiao dongjia le! Qiao dongjia, wo tingshuo guifu you nan …"*

Sun Maocai laugh say Zhiyong Brother not I should call you
Qiao Master ASP Qiao Boss I hear your-family have trouble

Sun Maocai laughed heartily and said, "Brother Zhiyong, no, I
should call you Master Qiao now! Master Qiao, I heard that
your household is facing troubles..."

(80) 紫薇深吸了一口气:"侍卫快马奔来,传递皇阿玛……不,不是
'皇阿玛',是'皇上'的命令,仍然要杀掉我们!" (BCC)

*Ziwei shen xile yi kou qi: "Shiwei kuaima benlai, chuandi
huang'ama … bu, bu shi 'huangama', shi 'huangshang' de
mingling, rengran yao shadiao women!"*

Ziwei deep take-ASP one-CL breathe guard gallop run-come
pass-on lord-father not not lord. father is Emperor GEN order
still will kill us

Ziwei took a deep breath: "The guards came running fast,
announcing the order of our Lord Father ... no, not 'Lord
Father', but "the Emperor" that we still have to be killed!"

(81) 当您说要整垮赵师父……不,是姓赵的那小子时,我一度怀疑
您办不到,没想到真让您给整垮了! (BCC)

*Dang nin shuo yao zhengkua Zhao shifu … bu, shi xing Zhao
de na xiaozi shi, wo yidu huaiyi nin banbudao, meixiangdao
zhen rang nin gei zhengkua le!*

when you say will fix-up Zhao Master not is surname Zhao
GEN that guy when I once doubt you do-not-succeed unexpectedly
really let you PSV fix.up ASP

When you said you would fix up Master Zhao ... no, the brat
Zhao, I once doubted if you could succeed. To my surprise,
you finally make it.

In (79), the negation is used to deny the appropriateness of using the addressing term *Zhiyong xiong* ("Brother Zhiyong") to refer to his interlocutor, which expresses the intimacy of their personal relationships. In the corrective clause, it is replaced by the addressee honorific *Qiao dongjia* ("Master Qiao") to show his deference towards the addressee. In (80), the target of negation is the appropriateness of using the referent honorific *huang'ama* ("the Lord Father") to refer to the king. This term is rectified in the corrective clause by *huangshang* ("the Emperor") in order to emphasize his supreme status. The same is true of (81).

In contrast to diverging deictic positioning denials, converging deictic denials aim to reject an inappropriate use of referential or addressing terms to decrease the relational distance. These denials involve a shift in deixis that reflects the speaker's intention to strengthen relational ties with the referred individuals, thereby minimizing their relational distance. Consider (82) - (84):

(82) 政委回头望着老洪和王强说:"这是山里来的冯老大爷!"显然
这称呼使老人很不高兴,他纠正说:"不,同志! 不要叫大爷,
咱们都是同志呀!" (BCC)
Zhengwei huitou wangzhe Lao Hong he Wang Qiang shuo:
"Zhe shi shan li lai de Feng laodaye!" Xianran zhe chenghu
shi laoren hen bu gaoxing, ta jiuzheng shuo: "Bu, tongzhi! bu
yao jiao daye, zanmen dou shi tongzhi ya!"
commissar turn-around look-ASP Lao Hong and Wang Qiang
say this is mountain-in come GEN Feng Uncle apparently this
appellation make old-man very not happy, he correct say not
comrade don't call uncle we all is comrade PRT
The political commissar looked back at Old Hong and Wang
Qiang and said, "This is Master Feng from the mountains!"
Apparently this appellation upset the old man, who corrected,
"No, comrade! Don't call me Master. We're all comrades!"

(83) 他抓住小宋的肩膀用力摇晃着:"宋秘书,不,宋大哥,我爸一

定是搞错了,你跟我过去把事情弄明白。"①

Ta zhuazhu xiao Song de jianbang yongli yaohuangzhe: "Song mishu, bu, Song dage, wo ba yiding shi gaocuole, ni gen wo guoqu ba shiqing nong mingbai."

he grab little Song GEN shoulder hard shake shuo Song Secretary not Song Brother my father must be confuse ASP you follow I go-over BA matter make-clear

He grabbed Xiao Song's shoulders and shook them hard, "Secretary Song, no, Big Brother Song, my father must have made a mistake, you should go with me to set things straight."

(84) "我的名字是玛丽。"她说。"玛丽小姐。""不,是玛丽。""啊,玛丽……" (BCC)

"Wo de mingzi shi Mali." Ta shuo. "Mali xiaojie." "Bu, shi Mali." "A, Mali…"

my GEN name am Mary she say Mary Miss not is Mary ah Mary

"My name is Mary," she said. "Miss Mary." "No, it's Mary." "Ah, Mary…"

Each of the examples in (82) - (84) employs different addressing terms for the same individual. However, unlike diverging cases, these terms are not used to emphasize or increase social distance but rather to foster a closer psychological connection between the speaker and the addressee. This shift in deixis serves to align the speaker more closely with the addressee, promoting a sense of unity and equality.

5.2.3.4 Structural Positioning Denials

Structural positioning denials refer to cases of denials in which the speaker is rejecting a viewpoint from which certain aspects of the structure of an entity are brought into prominence. These denials can either be based on individuality or

---

① http://www.bjkgjlu.com/96903zch/73612877.html.

dynamicity. An individuality-based positioning denial is used to deny the appropriateness of characterizing the subject as a whole or its constitutive parts. Structural positioning denials can be used to emphasize either unity or multiplicity, depending on the speaker's communicative purpose. The following examples illustrate MN that are used to emphasize unity rather than multiplicity. Consider (85) - (88):

(85) 比赛中大家要团结协作，因为你们的对手不是一个个球员，而是一支配合默契的球队。(BCC)

Bisai zhong dajia yao tuanjie xiezuo, yinwei nimen de duishou bu shi yi gege qiuyuan, er shi yi zhi peihe moqi de qiudui.

match in you must unite cooperate because you GEN opponent not one-CL-CL player but one-CL cooperate tacit GEN team

We need to work together in the game, because your opponents are not individual players, but a team with tacit cooperation.

(86) "物流是一片森林，而非一棵棵树木"，这句话反映了物流的系统性。①

"Wuliu shi yi pian senlin, er fei yi keke shumu", zhe ju hua fanyingle wuliu de xitongxing.

Logistics shi one-CL forest but not one-CL-CL tree this-CL utterance reflect-ASP logistics GEN systematization

"Logistics is a forest, not a tree." This sentence reflects the systematization of logistics.

(87) "……教师集体和学生集体要建立密切的联系。"教师集体和儿童集体并不是两个集体，而是一个集体，而且是一个教育集体。②

" …jiaoshi jiti he xuesheng jiti yao jianli miqie de lianxi." Jiaoshi jiti he ertong jiti bing bu shi liang ge jiti, er shi yi ge jiti, erqie shi yi ge jiaoyu jiti.

① https://www.asklib.com/view/0488eec77413.html.

② http://www.doczj.com/doc/d3e315c0aa00b52acfc7ca31.html.

teacher group and children group should establish close GEN

tie teacher group and children group actually not two-CL

group not one-CL group and are one-CL education group

The teachers' group and the students' group need to establish

close ties. They are not two groups, but one. More specifically,

they belong to the same educational group.

(88) 著名语文教育家于漪认为：“我们进行的是母语教学，语言与

文化不是两个东西，而是一个东西，一个整体。”①

Zhuming yuwen jiaoyujia Yu Yi renwei: "Women jinxing de shi

muyu jiaoxue, yuyan yu wenhua bu shi liang ge dongxi, er shi

yi ge dongxi, yi ge zhengti."

famous language educator YU Yi hold we conduct GEN is

native-language teaching language and culture not two-CL

thing but one-CL thing, one-CL whole

According to Yu Yi, a famous language educator, "We are

teaching the native language. Language and culture are not

two things, but two components of one thing. The two form a

unified whole."

In the negative clause of (85), the phrase *yi gege qiuyuan* ("individual
player") encodes the players as distinct individuals, while the phrase *qiudui* ("a
team") represents the players as a united whole. Through negation, the speaker of
shows his/her refusal to characterize the football players as unorganized
individuals. Similarly, (86) also relates to where we situate ourselves when
describing the forest, the metaphorical source of logistics. (87) is used to express
that teachers and students should not be categorized as two distinct groups; rather,
they should be described as an inseparable whole in the corrective sentence.
Likewise, in (88) the speaker refuses to characterize language and culture as two
distinct entities.

---

① http://club.kdnet.net/dispbbs.asp?id=10810651&boardid=2.

Structural positioning denials can sometimes focus on emphasizing individuality rather than unity. In these instances, the speaker opts to describe the constituents not as a cohesive unit but as distinct and separate individuals. This approach highlights the heterogeneity and independence of the elements within the structure, rather than their collective identity. Consider (89):

(89) 他们上床并排躺着。这一夜, 他们无法相拥互慰。这一夜, 他
     们不是一对, 而是两个人。(BCC)
     Tamen shang chuan bingpai tanzhe. Zhe yi ye, tamen wufa xiang-
     yong-huwei. Zhe yi ye, tamen bu shi yi dui, er shi liang ge ren.
     they get-on bed side-by-side lay-ASP this one night they
     cannot each-other hug each-other comfort this one night they
     not one-couple but two-CL person
     They went to bed and lay side by side. This night, they could
     not hold and comfort each other. At this night, they were not a
     couple, but two individuals.

In (89), the speaker deliberately chooses not to depict the man and woman as a unified couple, but rather as two independent individuals. This choice underscores the dissonance and emotional distance between them during that particular night. The use of negation here serves to emphasize their individuality, reflecting a moment of separation in their relationship, rather than suggesting that they are not a couple in a broader sense.

Dynamicity-based positioning denials focus on the characterization of a state of affairs as either a static condition or an ongoing process, depending on the speaker's communicative intent. Rather than disputing the factual nature of the subject, the speaker challenges the appropriateness of viewing it as merely a final stage or a complete event. Dynamicity-based positioning denials emphasize the fluid and evolving nature of certain conditions or events, suggesting that they should be perceived as processes rather than fixed states. Consider (90) - (92):

(90) 成熟不是一个结果，而是一个过程。 (BCC)

Chengshu bu shi yi ge jieguo, er shi yi ge guocheng.

maturity not one-CL result, but one-CL process

Maturity is not a result, but a process.

(91) 民主不是一个状态，而是一个过程。 (BCC)

Minzhu bu shi yi ge zhuangtai, er shi yi ge guocheng.

maturity not one-CL state, but one-CL process

Democracy is not a state, but a process.

(92) 改革不是一个事件，而是一个过程。(BCC)

Gaige bu shi yi ge shijian, er shi yi ge guocheng.

revolution not one-CL event, but one-CL process

Revolution is not an event, but a process.

In Chinese, terms such as *chengshu* ("mature/maturity") can function both as an adjective, indicating a state where a plant's fruit is ripe or a person exhibits adult characteristics, and as a verb, describing the act of becoming mature. In (90), the speaker clarifies that maturity should not be seen merely as an endpoint but as an ongoing journey. Similarly, the term *minzhu* ("democratic/democracy") typically describes a societal state governed by democratic principles. However, in (91), the speaker emphasizes that democracy is better understood as a continual process of development and adaptation. This perspective is also applied in (92) with the term *gaige* ("revolution"), highlighting that revolution is not merely an isolated event but a progressive sequence of changes. These examples illustrate the dynamic and evolving nature of these concepts, advocating for a perspective that recognizes their continual development over time.

Dynamicity-based positioning denials can also be utilized to emphasize the final state of a process rather than its ongoing nature. This approach is particularly relevant when the speaker intends to highlight the outcome or result of an action, challenging the typical perception of the action as a continuous process. Consider (93) - (94):

(93) 赚钱不是一个过程,而是结果,是你做好一件事顺带的结果。[1]

Zhuan qian bu shi yi ge guocheng, er shi jieguo, shi ni zuohao

yi jian shi shundai de jieguo.

make money not one-CL process but result is you do-well one-CL thing incidental GEN result

Making money is not a process, but a result. It is the incidental byproduct of doing one thing well.

(94) 创业本身不是一个过程,而是一个结果,是目标追逐的结果回馈。[2]

Chuangye benshen bu shi yi ge guocheng, er shi yi ge jieguo,

shi mubiao zhuizhu de jieguo huikui.

entrepreneurship itself not one-CL process but one-CL result is goal pursuit GEN result reward

Entrepreneurship is not a process, but a result. It is the reward of goal pursuit.

In (93) and (94), the common understanding of the verbs *zhuanqian* ("making money") and *chuangye* ("entrepreneurship") as processes is explicitly rejected. Instead, the focus is shifted to the outcomes. In (93), making money is described not as an ongoing process but as a result, specifically as an incidental outcome of performing a task well. Similarly, in (94), entrepreneurship is reframed not as a continuous journey but as the final result of pursuing specific goals. This perspective emphasizes the importance of the outcomes and rewards that culminate from these activities, suggesting a shift from viewing these actions as merely processes to recognizing them as achievements or endpoints.

5.2.3.5 Evaluative Positioning Denials

Evaluative positioning denials refer to cases of MN in which the root and the rectification contain lexical items with contrary or different evaluative connotations. They can be classified into the category of positioning denials because both

---

[1] https://www.wdzj.com/hjzs/ptsj/20180211/548874-1.html.

[2] https://www.sohu.com/a/117800768_465948.

propositions in root and rectification have equal semantic or informational strengths. Like other types of positioning denials, their interpretation requires the addressee to shift his/her perspective of viewing the same state of affairs. Evaluative positioning denials can be further divided into derogating evaluative positioning denials, praising evaluative positioning denials, and neutralizing evaluative positioning denials.

In the case of praising evaluative positioning denials, the negated lexical item in the root often has a negative or neutral connotation, while its counterpart in the rectification carries a positive connotation. This type of negation is employed by the speaker to challenge a negative appraisal of a situation and to recast it in a more favorable light. Consider (95) - (97):

(95) 上次我的话讲错了, 你不是野心勃勃, 而是雄心勃勃! (BCC)

Shangci wo de hua jiangcuole, ni bu shi yexin-bobo, er shi xiongxin-bobo!

last-time I GEN words speak wrong PRT you not ambitious but enterprising

I was wrong last time. You're not aggressive; you're enterprising!

(96) "他呢? 难道这个孩子也去送死吗?"乌兰巴日的胸膛高高挺了起来:"我们不是去送死, 是去捐躯。"(BCC)

"Ta ne? Nandao zhe ge haizi ye qu song si ma?" Wulan Bari de xiongtang gaogao tingle qilai: "Women bu shi qu songsi, shi qu juanqu."

he QM how-can-it-be this-CL kid also go court death Wulan Bari GEN chest high rise-ASP-up we not go court death is go donate life

"What about him? Is this boy going to die too?" Ulan Bari's chest rose high, "We are not going to die; we are going to donate our lives."

(97) 陈晚荣这个经历过贫寒的人没有这想法, 摇头道:"马大哥, 您这不是抠, 是节约, 我很佩服。"(BCC)

Chen Wanrong zhe ge jingliguo pinhan de ren meiyou zhe

xiangfa, yao tou dao: "Ma dage, nin zhe bu shi kou, shi

jieyue, wo hen peifu."

Chen Wanrong this-CL experience-ASP poverty GEN person

not this thought shake head say Ma Brother you this not stingy

is thrifty I very appreciate

Chen Wanrong, a person who has experienced poverty, did not

have this idea. He shook his head and said, "Brother Ma, you

are not stingy, but thrifty. I appreciate it very much."

In each sentence, the propositions expressed by the root and the corrective clause describe the same state of affairs but contain lexical items with different connotations. In (95), the expression *yexin-bobo* ("ambitious") carries negative connotation, whereas the expression *xiongxin-bobo* ("enterprising") carries positive one. The speakers intend to deny the negative evaluation expressed of the roots and re-evaluate the same situation positively. The same is true of the other two examples.

In a derogating evaluative positioning denial, the root of negation contains lexical items with negative or neutral connotations, while the corrective clause contains ones with positive connotations. The speaker does not intend to deny the truth condition of the root proposition, but to redescribe it in a derogatory manner. Consider (98) - (100):

(98) 阿胖子坐下来问道：“今天倒清闲，居然想到这里来吃酒？”“不
是清闲，是无聊。”(BCC)

Apangzi zuo xialai wendao: "Jintian dao qingxian, juran xiang

dao zheli lai chi jiu?" "Bu shi qingxian, shi wuliao."

fatty sit down ask today rather idle unexpectedly want to here

come drink wine not idle is boring

Fatty sat down and asked, "Today you are so idle, even

coming here for a drink?" "I am not idle, but boring."

(99) 文学界的假古典派仍然在抄袭中讨生活，他们不是强大，而是
顽固。①

*Wenxue jie de jia gudianpai rengran zai chaoxi zhong tao
shenghuo, tamen bu shi qiangda, er shi wangu.*

Literary world GEN pseudo classicists still in plagiarize-in
make living they not strong but stubborn

The pseudo-classicists in the literary world are still making a
living by plagiarism. They are not strong, but stubborn.

(100) 就算咱们没有攻城器械，他又能守住？依我看，他不是勇敢，
是鲁莽。(BCC)

*Jiu suan zanmen meiyou gong cheng qixie, ta you neng shou-
zhu? Yi wo kan, ta bu shi yonggan, er shi lumang.*

Even-if we not siege equipment he then can hold In-my-
opinion he not brave but reckless

Even if we do not have siege equipment, can he hold? In my
opinion, he is not brave, but reckless.

The negation in (98) is not intended to deny the truth condition of the root
proposition, but the inappropriateness of using the term *qingxian* ("idle"), because
the latter carries positive connotations. The same is true of the expressions
qiangda ("strong") in (99) and *yonggan* ("brave") in (100). All of them are
replaced by the lexical items that carry contrasting, derogatory evaluation of the
situation at hand.

In addition to derogating evaluative positioning denials and praising
evaluative positioning denials, there is another type of denials which can be
termed as "neutralizing evaluative positioning denials". In a neutralizing
evaluative positioning denial, the root proposition contains lexical items with
either positive or negative connotations. It is corrected by another proposition that
contains lexical items with neutral connotations. The speaker of a neutralizing

---

① https://book.douban.com/subject/1782585/discussion/1085069/.

evaluative positioning denial intends to neutralize the positive or negative connotations carried by certain lexical items. Consider (101) - (102):

(101) "······竟然要我去当见不得光的间谍！一下子两种人都感染上了！""不是间谍，是情报工作人员啊，即情报员。"(BCC)

"···*jingran yao wo qu dang jianbude guang de jiandie! Yi xia-zi liang zhong ren dou ganranshang le!*" "*Bu shi jiandie, shi qingbao gongzuo renyuan a, ji qingbaoyuan.*"

even ask I go become in.disrepute GEN spy suddenly *two-CL* person all infected ASP not spy is intelligence worker PRT namely intelligence agent

"...even asking me to be a spy in disrepute! Both kinds of people are infected at once!" "They are not spies, but intelligence workers, or intelligence officers."

(102) (元稹的作品)在情节设置及作者与人物的交流方面······其"假"不是"虚假"，而是"虚构"。[①]

(*Yuan Zhen de zuopin*) *zai qingjie shezhi ji zuozhe yu renwu de jiaoliu fangmian* ··· *qi "jia" bu shi "xujia", er shi "xugou".*

Yuan Zhen GEN works in plot setting and author and character GEN communication aspect its fake not fakeness but fictive

The plot setting and communication between the author and the characters in Yuan Zhen's works are not real. However, it is not "fake", but "fictive".

The root proposition of negation in each example contains a lexical item with negative connotations. The negation in (101) is meant to deny the negative (or neutral) connotation expressed by the term *jiandie* ("spy"). Likewise, *xujia* ("fake") in (102) conveys negative connotations. All of them involve denying

---

① http://www.1-123.com/Article/Y/yuan/yuanshen/41662.html.

negative evaluation of the states of affairs expressed in the root and re-evaluate the same states of affairs in a neutral way.

5.2.4 Formal Denials

Formal denials, also referred to as "metalinguistic implicature denials" by Davis (2016), focus on the formal aspects of linguistic expressions rather than the state of affairs they describe. These denials aim to correct the formal realizations— specifically the phonology, collocation, or style—of lexical items used in the root statement, rather than their semantic content. Such denials are crucial for maintaining linguistic accuracy and clarity in communication.

5.2.4.1 Phonological Denials

Phonological denials are MN in the sense that phonological realizations are not part of a logic form of a proposition. What is denied is not the truth condition of the root proposition, but the appropriateness of phonological representations for some lexical items. The speaker disputes an inappropriate phonological realization in the root and then rectifies it in the corrective sentence. Consider (103) - (105):

> (103) "你这是污蔑, 赤 guǒguǒ 的污蔑!"龚平纠正道:"不是赤 guǒ-
> guǒ,是赤 luǒluǒ……连这个字都认错。"(BCC)
>
> *"Ni zhe shi wumie, chiguǒguǒ de wumie!" Gong Ping jiuzheng*
> *dao: "Bu shi chiguǒguǒ, shi chiluǒluǒ ⋯ lian zhe ge zi dou*
> *rencuo."*
>
> you this is slander sheer GEN slander Gong Ping corrected
> say not sheer lian this-CL character even mistake"
>
> "You are slandering, sheer (*chiguǒguǒ* in Chinese) slandering!"
> Gong Ping corrected, "It's not *chiguǒguǒ*; it's *chiluǒluǒ* ...
> How can you be so illiterate? "
>
> (104) 作为一个重庆人,我想请电视上那位专家先去扫扫盲,我们
> 吃的是涪(fú)陵榨菜,不是péi陵榨菜。①

---

① https://quanmin.baidu.com/sv?source=share-h5&vid=4826140079774580729.

Zuowei yi ge Chongqing ren, wo xiang qing dianshi shang nawei zhuanjia xian qu saosao mang, women chi de shi Fúling zhacai, bu shi Péiling zhacai.

as one-CL Chongqing person I want ask TV-on that-CL expert first go eliminate illiteracy we eat GEN is Fuling pickles not Fuling pickles

As a Chongqing native, I would like to ask the expert on TV to improve his Chinese first. What we eat is *Fuling* pickles, not *Peiling* pickles.

(105) 什么鬼主播，你小学毕业了吗？是大腹便（pián）便（pián），不是大腹 biànbiàn。连这个词都不认识！ ①

Shenme gui zhubo, ni xiaoxue biye le ma? Shi da fu piánpián, bu shi da fu biànbiàn. Lian zhe ge ci dou bu renshi!

what fucking anchor you elementary school graduate ASP QM be pot-bellied, not pot-bellied even this-CL word even not know

What a fucking anchor. Have you graduated from elementary school? It's *dafupianpian*, not *dafubianbian*. You don't even know this word!

The root in each sentence contains a lexical item with the wrong phonological representation. In (103), the negation is used to correct the wrong pronunciation of the term *chiluoluo* ("sheer"). The target of negation in (104) is the mispronunciation of the place name *Fuling*, a city famous for pickles. And the negation in (105) is intended to reject the mispronounced idiom *da fu pianpian* ("pot-bellied"). None of them is used to deny the truth condition of the root since the phonological realization of a word is not considered as part of the meaning of the lexical items.

5.2.4.2 Collocation Denials

① https://www.ximalaya.com/403/.

Collocation denials are a type of MN where the propositions expressed by the root and the rectification are truth-functionally equivalent but differ in the collocation of lexical items. Collocation denials challenges the appropriateness of specific word combinations in the root, aiming to rectify or suggest a more suitable collocation that better fits the context or conforms to linguistic norms. Consider (106) - (107):

(106) 甲:看看这张照片,想当年你爸爸也是一个帅哥。

乙:您不是一个帅哥,而是一枚帅哥。①

Jia: Kankan zhe zhang zhaopian, xiangdangnian ni baba ye shi yi ge shuaige.

Yi: Nin bu shi yi ge shuaige, er shi yi mei shuaige.

A: look this-CL photo in-the-past your dad also is one-CL handsome-guy

B: you not one-CL handsome-guy but one-CL handsom-.guy

A: Look at this photo, I used to be *yegeshuaige* ("a handsome guy") when I was young.

B: Not *ye ge shuaige* ("a handsome guy"), but *yi mei shuaige* ("a handsome guy").

(107) 养猫的人肯定发现了这个秘密:你家的猫咪根本不是一只猫,而是一条猫,一坨猫,一滩猫。抱起来后变成一条,睡觉时变成一滩,蜷缩在窗台上就变成了一坨。②

Yang mao de ren kending faxianle zhe ge mimi: ni jia de maomi genben bu shi yi zhi mao, er shi yi tiao mao, yi tuo mao, yi tan mao. Bao qilai hou biancheng yi tiao, shuijiao shi biancheng yi tan, quansuo zai chuangtai shang jiu bianchengle yi tuo.

keep cat GEN person must discover-ASP this-CL secret you

---

① https://zhidao.baidu.com/question/207820688325434005.html.

② https://new.qq.com/omn/20180412/20180412A0GHK3.html.

family GEN cat at.all not one-CL cat but one-CL cat one-CL cat one-CL cat hug-up after become one-CL sleep when become one-CL curl-up on windowsill-on simply become-ASP one-CL

People who have cats must have discovered this secret: your cat is not "a cat" at all, but "a strip of cat", and "a puddle of cat", and "a pile of cat". It becomes a "strip" when you pick it up, a "pool" when it sleeps, and a "pile" when it curls up on the windowsill.

The two denials are used to dispute the appropriateness of the collocations in the root, rather than the existence of the entities encoded in it. In (106), *mei* ("buddle") is a highly popular classifier among young people in China in recent years. The construction "Number +*mei*+Noun" is often used to describe people or animals that are lovely and cute. Similarly, the lexical items *tiao* ("strip"), *tuo* ("pile") and *tan* ("pool") in (107) are not conventional classifiers of the noun *mao* ("cat"). These highly novel collocations are used in this context to create a playful jokey effect.

5.2.4.3 Stylistic Denials

Stylistic denials are a form of MN used to address the inappropriate use of lexical items based on stylistic factors such as genre, register, and style. In cases of register denials, the propositions expressed by both the root and the rectification remain truth-functionally equivalent but differ in their degrees of formality. These denials are particularly effective in contexts where the speaker wishes to adjust the stylistic presentation of the statement to better align with the expected linguistic norms or to convey a certain level of propriety or decorum. Consider (108) - (110):

(108) 当翻译将馆长的解说译成"这尊雕像非常真实"时,江主席立即
纠正说:"不,应该说是'栩栩如生'!" (BCC)
Dang fanyi jiang guanzhang de jieshuo yicheng "zhe zun

diaoxiang feichang zhenshi" shi, Jiang Zhuxi liji jiuzheng shuo: "Bu, yinggai shuo shi 'xuxu-rusheng'!"

when translator make curator GEN explanation translate as this-CL statue very real when Jiang chairman immediately correct say not should say is lifelike

When the translator translated the curator's explanation as "this statue looks like a real one", Chairman Jiang immediately corrected, "No, you should use the word 'lifelike'!"

(109) "你说话能不能别那么粗俗……""哦，不是屁股，是臀部，臀部。"林微皱着眉头说。(BCC)

"Ni shuo hua neng bu neng bie name cusu…" "O, bu shi pigu, shi tunbu, tunbu." Lin Wei zhouzhe meitou shuo.

you speak can not can stop so vulgarly oh, not ass is bottom bottom Lin Wei frown-ASP eyebrow speak

"Can you talk less vulgarly..." "Well, not ass, but bottom, bottom." Lin Wei frowned.

(110) 爷爷说："噢，你放伏假了。""不是伏假，是暑假。"我回答。"都一样。把烟口袋给爷爷拿来……" (BCC)

Yeye shuo: "O, ni fang fujia le." "Bu shi fujia, shi shujia." Wo huida. "Dou yiyang. Ba yan koudai gei yeye nalai…"

grandpa say oh, you on dog.days holiday ASP not dog.days holiday is summer holiday I answer both same BA cigarette pocket for grandpa bring

Grandpa said, "Oh, you're on dog days holiday." "Not dog days holiday, but summer holiday." I replied. "There is no difference between them ... bring the cigarette pocket for me..."

The examples in (108) - (110) illustrate how stylistic denials operate by challenging the degree of formality of the lexical items used in the root statements. Each example demonstrates a shift from a less formal to a more formal expression, or vice versa, to match the expected stylistic level of the discourse. This shift is not about disputing the factual accuracy of the statements but rather about ensuring that the language used is appropriate for the context, reflecting considerations of the speaker's literacy, social status, or aesthetic preference. These stylistic adjustments are crucial for effective communication, as they help maintain the social dynamics in various communicative situations.

5.3 Summary

In this chapter, we have proposed a comprehensive classification of MN based on its representational effects, utilizing authentic data collected from modern Chinese usage. We suggest that MN in modern Chinese can be categorized into four primary types: strengthening denials, identifying denials, positioning denials, and formal denials. Each category encompasses various subspecies, which have been detailed and exemplified through relevant examples. This classification system not only incorporates the semantic categories of MN previously discussed in the literature but also expands to cover a broader array of MN types that have not been extensively explored before. By doing so, it provides a more inclusive framework that captures the nuanced ways in which MN is used in linguistic practice.

Chapter 6

A Cognitive Linguistic Account of Strengthening Denials

This chapter will present an account of the cognitive activities underlying the meaning representations of strengthening denials, which consist of scalar strengthening denials, granular strengthening denials, partonomic strengthening denials, epistemic strengthening denials, and directional strengthening denials. Based on the ICA model of MN developed in Chapter 3, it will address in turn how the five types of strengthening denials are conceptually motivated by intersubjective adjustment of alternate construals of the same situation. Our discussion will draw on studies of a number of construal operations including scale, scope/attention, level of specificity, epistemic ground, and action chain.

6.1 Meaning Construction of Scalar Strengthening Denials

This section examines the cognitive mechanisms behind scalar strengthening denials. These denials arise from the intersubjective coordination between two alternate scalar construals, which lead to variations in semantic intensity or informational content. The cognitive processes underlying different types of scalar strengthening denials are diverse and context-dependent.

6.1.1 Scale as Image Schema and Strengthening Operation

The notion of scale is pivotal in both pragmatics and cognitive linguistics.

Pragmatists examine how scales facilitate pragmatic inferences, while cognitive linguists view scales primarily as image schemas, derived from our physical and perceptual experiences. These schemas provide a foundational structure that extends to abstract reasoning. Johnson (1987) remarks, "Scalarity appears to pervade all aspects of human experience, even in contexts devoid of precise quantitative assessment." Croft and Cruse (2004) describe scale as a construal phenomenon that introduces a gradable dimension to any domain, regardless of its intrinsic measurability. Lakoff (1993) conceptualizes scales through the metaphor "Linear scales are paths", where the path's beginning corresponds to the scale's lower end, and progression along the path represents an increase in quantity. He (1993) emphasizes that the logic governing paths mirrors that of linear scales:

> Path inference: Suppose a person travels from A to C, and now is at the intermediate point B, he/she has covered all the distance from A to B, but not any distance between B and C.
>
> Linear scale inference: Suppose one has exactly $50 in the bank account, he/she has $40, $30 at disposal, but not any larger amount than $50, say $60 or $70.

Ruiz de mendoza and Galera (2014) propose two opposing cognitive operations based on the scale image schema: strengthening and mitigating. The two cognitive operations function to position scalar concepts either at the upper or lower points of the scale. A scalar concept can be strengthened or mitigated both explicitly and implicitly. Linguistic systems provide us with a variety of lexical and constructional expressions that are used to intensify or mitigate the semantic or informational value of a concept. For example, lexical intensifiers such as *very, really, greatly, extremely, highly* can be used to upscale the meaning of gradable adjectives, while the resultative construction "to death" can emphasize one's emotional reaction to an event. A scalar concept can also be strengthened inferentially. A semantic or informationally weak concept (or proposition) can be dismissed by the speaker and replaced by another semantic or informational stronger concept (or proposition) in a scale implicitly.

Strengthening operations often interact with other cognitive operations such as contrasting operation and domain mapping (Ruiz de Mendoza & Galera, 2014; Peña & Ruiz de Mendoza, 2017). For example, the meaning effect of hyperbole is created by the combination of strengthening operation and contrasting operation. As discussed in the following section, strengthening operation, sometimes in combination with cognitive operations such as contrasting and domain mapping, plays an important role in the intersubjective coordination process giving rise to scalar strengthening denials.

6.1.2 Adjustment of Scalar Construals and Scalar Strengthening Denials

Scale can be viewed as a matter of construal in another way: during a communicative event, different participants may have their unique scalar construals of the same situation due to differences in knowledge or communication objectives. This introduces considerable flexibility in determining where a particular property should be positioned on a scale. For instance, consider a scenario where a man loves a woman. The default construal would be to place this concept towards the higher end of the emotional scale by stating, "The man loves the woman". However, the man might downplay his feelings and simply state that he "likes" her. These utterances hold true because, in truth-conditional semantics, "love" entails "like". Nevertheless, such a statement can generate an implied meaning—termed "scalar implicature" in neo-Gricean terms—that "The man merely likes the woman, not to the extent of love".

When the speaker realizes that the construal of a situation in an utterance or unspoken thought does not meet his/her expected value, he/she will dispute the appropriateness of the concept, and replace it with another concept higher in the same scale. Scalar strengthening denials are the linguistic manifestations of the intersubjective coordination between different scalar construals of the same situation. In a scalar strengthening denial, the speaker invites the addressee to jointly attend to a particular scalar construal of a situation, rather than the object of conceptualization, and to update their common ground by suggesting another construal that gives rise to a semantic and informational stronger proposition.[①] The latter process is what Ruiz de Mendoza and Galera (2014) call strengthening operations, as discussed in the last section. Consider (1):

(1) 似乎大部分父母都会做这一道菜，不是大部分，是全部。

(BCC)

Sihu dabufen fumu dou hui zuo zhe yi dao cai, bu shi dabufen, shi quanbu.

seem most parents all know cook this one-CL dish not majority be all

It seems that most parents know how to make this dish. Not most, but all.

In (1), the initial statement and its correction represent alternate construals of the number of parents who can cook the dish. The initial phrase, indicated by *dabufen* ("most"), fails to meet the speaker's expectation for informational strength. Consequently, the speaker invites the addressee to reconsider the appropriateness of this construal. The subsequent correction involves a strengthening operation that escalates the concept on the scale of certainty to a higher point, specifically to *quanbu* ("all"). This differs from a denial such as "Most parents do not know how to make this dish", where the existence of the state of affairs is contested, rather than the scale of the construal being adjusted.

As discussed in Chapter 5, canonical scalar strengthening denials are based on true scales (i. e. Horn scales), which are characterized by "unilateral entailment" relations between lexical items in a contrast set. On our view, the linear unilateral entailment relation between lexical items in a scale is deeply

---

① As outlined in Chapter 3, the coordination of alternate construals of the same situation by a single speaker is identified as a unique instance of intersubjectivity adjustment. For clarity and simplicity in this and subsequent discussions, this particular case will not receive separate consideration.

grounded in our experience of the world. In line with Lakoff (1991), we argue that Horn scales, and non-entailment scales, are conceptualized in terms of the metaphor "Linear scales are paths". The generation of "scalar implicature" also follows the logic of path inference. Figure 6.1 illustrates the path inference in Lakoff (1991), and Figure 6.2 represents the scale inference based on the contrast set <all, most, some>:

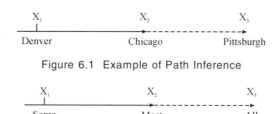

Figure 6.1 Example of Path Inference

Figure 6.2 Example of Scalar Inference

According to Lakoff, being at point X_2 on a path (location B) implies that you have already passed position X_1 (location A) and have not yet reached point X_3 (location C). The logic of scalar inferences based on this path inference is as follows: if you have X_{n+1} on a scale you also have X_n, but not vice versa. For example, if most parents can cook the dish, then some of them can definitely cook it, but not all parents can cook it. The logic of path inference is followed by scalar inferences based on prototypical Horn scales, such as adjective scales <beautiful, pretty, attractive>, adverb scales <always, usually, often, sometimes>, cardinal numbers scales <n, ... 6, 5, 4, 3, 2, 1> (Huang, 2014).

Intersubjective coordination also contributes to the creation of the garden-path effect. Scalar cases of MN are often seen as typical garden-path utterances, designed to mislead the interlocutor. In a normal negation environment, what is subject to negation is the lower-bound meaning of the negated lexical item. In order to deliberately mislead the hearer's inference, the speaker may represent such an expectation of the addressee. The garden-path effect of this sentence results from the violation of this expectation. In (1), the default interpretation of the negative clause is that fewer parents can cook the dish. It is made a contrast with the real situation that all parents can cook the dish. As a consequence, the default interpretation will be canceled out, thereby creating a playful effect.

As we have already noted previously, in addition to true scales, there are a wide array of pragmatic scales which can give rise to strengthening denials.[①] Unlike Horn scales, these scales are more dependent on our socially or culturally shared knowledge of the world. On our view, these contrast sets are formed on the basis of cognitive models. For example, the contrast set <*tiaobo, chaisan*> "*alienate, separate*" is related to our cognitive model of marriage, specifically the knowledge about the extent of damage that can be done to the couple's marriage; <*bingzhong, bingwei*> ("seriously ill, critically ill") pertains to the cognitive model of illness, specifically our knowledge of the severity of illness; and <*gongpo, xiaomie*> ("breached, eliminated") rests on the cognitive model of fighting a battle, specifically the intensity of attacks on enemy forces.

Like canonical scalar strengthening denials, the root and the rectification in a non-canonical scalar strengthening denial represent alternative construals of the same situation on the scale image schema. The speaker performs similar strengthening operation to replace the lexical item in the root with a concept on an upper point of the scale. Compared with standard Horn scales, the non-literal meaning (Q-implicature) is more dependent on our social and cultural knowledge. Let us consider (2), repeated from (5) in Chapter 5:

(2) 支援还没有到, 两个小时内所有的防线都被攻破, 不是被攻破, 而是被消灭! (BCC)

Zhiyuan hai meiyou dao, liang ge xiaoshi nei suoyou de fangxian dou bei gongpo, bu shi bei gongpo, er shi bei xiaomie.

support yet not arrive two-CL hour in all defense all PSV breach but PSV breach but PSV eliminated

The support had not yet arrived. Within two hours, all the

---

① MN based on true scales (i.e. scalar implicature denials) can be further divided into literal and hyperbolic cases. For a detailed discussion of the two types of MN, see Long and Lu (2019).

defense lines had been breached. Actually, it had not been breached; it had been eliminated.

The root and the rectification in this example represent two different construals on the scale of battle severity. The contrast between these scalar concepts activates our knowledge of military conflict. Through the strengthening operation, the severity of the battle is escalated on the scale. The interpretation of these denials also involves contrasting the expected and the actual scenarios. For instance, encountering the negative clause in (2), we might infer a less severe situation than a breach. The corrective clause then overturns this expectation, emphasizing a stronger information strength between the root and the rectification. The greater this asymmetry, the more potent the rhetorical impact of the denial.

The derivation process for metaphorical strengthening denials is notably more complex than for non-metaphorical cases, primarily due to the involvement of cross-domain mapping. In a single-metaphorical case, the propositions at the root and in the rectification typically represent two interpretations of the same situation by two conceptualizers: literal and metaphorical ones. The speaker directs the addressee's attention towards the literal interpretation rather than the object of conceptualization, due to its failure to meet the expected informational strength. Metaphor serves to perform a strengthening operation, which can disproportionately amplify a gradable concept along its underlying scale. Consider (3), repeated from (9) in Chapter 5:

(3) 中国的高铁速度好快啊,高铁司机不是在开火车,而是在开火箭。(BCC)

Zhongguo de gaotie sudu hao kuai a, gaotie siji bu shi zai kai huoche, er shi zai kai huojian.

China GEN high-speed railway speed so quick INT high-speed railway driver not ASP drive train but ASP drive rocket

China's high-speed railway is so fast. The drivers are not driving trains, but rockets.

This sentence exemplifies the intersubjective coordination between the literal and metaphorical interpretations of the speed of a high-speed railway. The addressee's focus is drawn not to the act of driving itself, but to the metaphorical conceptualization of this event. This sentence as a whole prompts the mappings between two mental spaces, which can be captured in Figure 6.3:

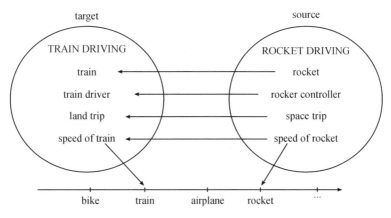

Figure 6.3 Cross-domain Mappings in (3)

As Figure 6.3 shows, there are a set of cognitive operations at work in the meaning construction of the expression. The utilized aspects of the source domain of rocket driving and the target domain of train driving are brought together in a conceptual metaphor through a set of detailed mappings between some of the element: *rocket* is metaphorically mapped to *train*, *train driver* onto *rocket controller*, *land trip* onto *space trip*, and the *speed of train* onto the *speed of rocket*. Triggered by the rectification of the denial, we focus our attention on the speed of the two vehicles and the speed scale of vehicles is evoked. The addressee makes a contrast between different speeds of the two vehicles and further prompts a strengthening operation of the train speed along the scale of vehicles.

Double-metaphorical denials involve intersubjective adjustment between two alternative metaphorical construals of the same situation. The speaker invites the addressee to consider and abandon the metaphorical construal represented in the negative clause because it does not meet the speaker's expected informational strength. By doing so, it explicitly expresses that another rhetorically stronger metaphor is needed for the same situation. The meaning construction of a double-metaphorical denial also involves strengthening operations based on cross-domain mappings. What makes it different from single-metaphorical ones is that, meaning construction of the latter ones involves more than one source domain.

6.2　Meaning Construction of Granular Strengthening Denials

In this section, we will discuss the meaning construction of granular strengthening denials by relating them to the construal operations of "level of specificity" in cognitive grammar. It will be argued that the granular strengthening denials, including qualitative and qualitative cases, are derived from intersubjective adjustment of different levels of specificity on which a particular situation is construed.

6.2.1　Levels of Specificity

According to Langacker (2008), human beings have the capacity of conceptualizing entities at various degrees of specificity. The same situation can be described with either a highly specific expression or expressions of less specificity. The former case represents a fine-grained construal, providing more precise and detailed information about the entity, whereas the latter case represents a coarse-grained construal, providing gross features and global organization. This aspect of construal can be either qualitative or quantitative, giving rise to two types of construal operations, namely qualitative scalar adjustment and quantitative scalar adjustment (Croft & Cruse, 2004). In order to avoid confusion with the cognitive operation on image schema of scale discussed above, we refer to the two types of level of specificity as qualitative specificity and qualitative specificity respectively.

Qualitative specificity and quantitative specificity are two different aspects of quantification, both of which have to do with the amount of information a speaker provides. Qualitative specificity pertains to our ability to describe entities at different levels of categorization, which is cognitively more prominent for the speaker. For example, a rabbit can either be categorized as an animal schematically or be elaborated to a different degree, such as *domestic rabbit, pet rabbit, angora, English angora, black English angora*, and so on. In (4), these expressions form a hierarchy that is ordered from the most schematic to the most detailed ones (from left to right):

(4) Rabbit→domestic rabbit→pet rabbit→angora→English angora→...

Within cognitive psychology, there has also been considerable effort devoted to the study of levels of categorization. It is found that between the most inclusive and least inclusive levels, there is a level of inclusiveness at which there is a cluster of common attributes for a category (Rosch, 1978). This level of inclusiveness is termed the basic level. Categories at the higher level are termed as superordinate categories, encoding more schematic information, while categories at the lower level are subordinate categories, providing more specific information. The reason why the basic level is more salient than other levels is related to the principle of cognitive economy (Rosch, 1978; Geeraerts, 1988). That is, categories at the basic level provide "the largest amount of information about an item can be obtained with the least cognitive effort" (Ungerer & Schmid, 2006). Therefore, categorizing entities at the basic level is the default and unmarked construal of the entities, while using categories at the superordinate and subordinate levels often convey the speaker's particular communicative purposes. As Kleinke (2010) points out, as the marked realization of the cognitive principle of "level of categorization", subordinate-level categorization provides extra amount of information that may induce the implicature concerning the speaker's attitude towards the entities being described.

While qualitative specificity involves conceptualization at different levels of categorization, quantitative specificity refers to the flexibility of construing a measurable concept at various degrees of fineness. For example, we can describe the height of the Mount Everest in different degrees of specification, as in (5), where each expression is schematic with respect to that follows:

(5) high→over 8000m→about 8848m→8848.43m

The leftwards expression in the linearly ordered set is more informative than the rightwards ones. Like the subordinate level items discussed above, if a speaker deliberately violates the principle of cognitive economy and gives a more specific construal of a certain entity, an inference may be triggered in the hearer about the speaker's attitude.

6.2.2 Intersubjective Adjustment of Specificity and Granular Strengthening Denials

Having discussed the cognitive principle of specificity, we shall now proceed to present a cognitive linguistic account of the meaning construction of granular strengthening denials. Based on the ICA model, we propose that granular strengthening denials involve intersubjective adjustment of alternate construal at different levels of specificity between two conceptualizers. When categorizing entities in real communication, we do this according to our communicative needs in the context. That is, a situation will be characterized at the level of specificity that suits his/her communicative purposes optimally. When referring to a particular entity, the speaker may find that the interlocutor's choice of level of categorization provides less information than needed. To give a more precise picture of the entity, the speaker is likely to adjust the construal of the interlocutor and conceptualize it at the lower level of categorization. A qualitative granular strengthening denial reflects the intersubjective coordination of two alternate construals at different levels of specificity. Given the distinct functions of the basic-level and subordinate-level categorization, the former is often placed by the latter in a qualitative granular strengthening denial. Consider (6), repeated from (15) in Chapter 5:

(6) 当同事说他工作起来"像一只狼"的时候,他说:"不是一只狼,是一只饿狼。"(BCC)

Dang tongshi shuo ta gongzuo qilai "xiang yi zhi lang" de shihou, ta shuo: "Bu shi yi zhi lang, shi yi zhi e lang."

when colleague say he work ASP as-if one-CL wolf GEN time

he say not one-CL wolf is one-CL hungry wolf

When his colleagues said he worked "like a wolf", he said, "Not a wolf, but a hungry wolf."

The negated proposition and the corrective proposition represent alternate ways of metaphorically conceptualizing the same person at different levels of categorization. The former conceptualizes it at the basic level, as indicated by the lexical item *lang* ("wolf"), whilst the latter describes it at the subordinate level. This MN utterance has the function of instructing the addressee to abandon the basic level of categorization and opt for the subordinate one. The latter conveys the speaker's specific interpretation of the man's working attitude. The intersubjective adjustment of alternate construals can be illustrated in Figure 6.4[①].

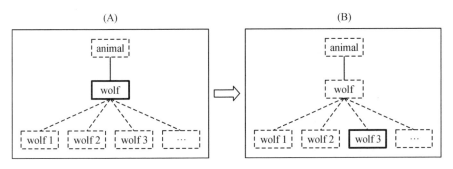

Figure 6.4 Example of Intersubjective Adjustment of Levels of Categorization

Diagram (A) models the first speaker's construal of the animal using the basic level item *lang*, whilst diagram (B) represents the second speaker's construal of the same animal at the subordinate level by adding an adjective *e* ("hungry").

---

① Figure 6.4 and others like this in the following discussion only preserve the central components of the overall model in Figure 3.8.

Given the former construal provides "the most natural access to the world" (Ungerer & Schmid, 1996), it is more naturally used to categorize the man's behavior than lexical items at superordinate or subordinate levels. This way of construal is disputed and replaced by an alternate way of construal which provides further information about the extent of devotion to the job. Consequently, the common ground between the speaker and his colleagues is updated by the extra information provided by the adjective e. The same analysis can also be applied to (7), repeated from (14) in Chapter 5:

(7) "你们汉人有那么多女人,还要女人干什么?"莲柔一听就糊涂了。
"注意,不是女人,而是美女⋯⋯它们之间是有差别的。" (BCC)

Nimen hanren you name duo nüren, hai yao nüren gan shenme?"
Lian rou yi ting jiu hutu le. "Zhuyi, bu shi nüren, er shi
meinü ⋯ tamen zhijian shi you chabie de."

you han. Chinese have so many woman still want women do what
Lian Rou when hear soon confused PRT attention not women
but beautiful women they between are have difference PRT
"Why do you Han People still need women since you already have so many?" Lianrou was confused. "Notice, not women, but beautiful women ... there is a big difference between the two concepts."

The category structure of human beings can be well illustrated in the following way: the notion HUMAN occupies the superordinate level of the category, woman—the basic level while pretty woman is located on the subordinate level of the category structure. In a similar way to (6), this denial represents the intersubjective coordination of alternate construals of the same situation at different levels of categorization. Although not all the cases of qualitative strengthening denials involve rejecting the basic-level construal, they are derived from denying the appropriateness of the choice of level of categorization and are manifestations of the speaker's adjustment of the addressee's construal at different levels of categorization. When interpreting the denial, the addressee might find it confusing at the first pass. However, the oddity can easily be resolved by evoking a schema-instance relation in the mind.

Quantitative granular strengthening denials involve the operation of quantitative specifying, or more specifically, adjustment of different degrees of specificity along a quantitative parameter. When quantifying a certain entity, the amount of information a communicative participant provides may more or less match the specificity expected by his interlocutor due to his/her unwillingness to be more precise or inability of being more precise. If the interlocutor's quantification of the related entity fails to meet the speaker's expectation, the latter is likely to re-construe it at a higher degree of quantification. Therefore, similar to cases of qualitative strengthening denials, quantitative cases result from intersujective adjustment of coarse-grained construal into a fine-grained construal of the same entity. Consider (8), repeated from (20) in Chapter 5:

(8) "十年了。"他叹息着。她知道他说的日子是从那个春夜后开始计算的,她远比他记得更清楚,不是十年,是十年一个月零三天。(BCC)

"Shi nian le." Ta tanxizhe. Ta zhidao ta shuo de rizi shi cong na ge chun ye hou kaishi jisuan de, ta yuan bi ta ji de geng qingchu, bu shi shi nian, shi shi nian yi ge yue ling san tian.

ten-year ASP he sign-ASP he know he say GEN days is from that-CL spring night after start count PRT she far than he remember PRT more clear not ten-year is ten-year one-CL month plus three-day

"Ten years," He sighed. She realized that the days had been calculated since that spring night. And she remembered it far better than he did—not ten years, but ten years plus one month and three days.

The propositions in the negative clause and the corrective clause represent two different ways of conceptualizing the time since they separated. Underlying the negated proposition is the coarse-grained view taken by the first speaker, who describes the period with the approximate expression *shi nian* ("ten years"). The way of construal seems perfectly normal and acceptable. However, it does not include information about the months and days. The MN in this example manifests the second speaker's adjusting alternate granular construals at the intersubjective level. The intersubjective process can be modeled in Figure 6.5.

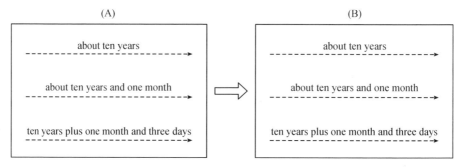

Figure 6.5 Example of Intersubjective Adjustment of Degree of Precision

There is a broad range of expressions a speaker can use to denote the length of time in this context, arranging along the length parameter, as illustrated in Figure 6.5. The expressions at the higher levels of specificity are successively schematic than ones at the lower levels. Diagram (A) diagrams a coarse-grained way of conceptualizing the length of time since they departed, i.e. (about) ten years, while diagram (B) illustrates a more precise characterization of the same period, i.e. ten years plus one month and three days. The speaker is actually disputing the coarse-grained way of construal in the man's utterance and replaces it with a fine-grained construal in the corrective clause. The fine-grained view of the same period provides extra information about the exact number of years. It can convey to the man that the women cherished their relationship with the man very much, thereby updating the common ground about their relationship.

6.3　Meaning Construction of Partonomic Strengthening Denials

As already mentioned in Chapter 5, partonomic strengthening denials are marked by the existence of "part/whole" relations between lexical items in the negative and corrective clause. Such a relation is treated as an image schema in cognitive grammar. This section concerns how partonomic strengthening denials can be explained in terms of intersubjective adjustment of attention and focus that are associated with the "part/whole" schema.

6.3.1 "Part/Whole" Schema and Scope of Attention

Within cognitive linguistics, "part/whole" relations are treated as one of our most basic image schemas (Johnson, 1987; Lakoff, 1987). Like the image schema of scale, such a schema is derived from our bodily experience. It is also widely accepted that "part/whole" relations lie at the core of metonymy and metonymic reasoning (Gibbs, 1994; Kövecses & Radden, 1998). According to Lakoff (1987), the structural elements of the "part/whole" schema include a whole, parts, and a configuration. He characterizes the basic logic of this schema as follows:

The "part/whole" schema is "asymmetric: If A is part of B, then B is not a part of A. It is irreflexive: A is not a part of A. Moreover, it cannot be the case that the whole exists, while no parts of it exist. However, all the parts can exist, but still not constitute a whole...".

When conceptualizing a situation, a speaker can either characterize the situation as a whole or focus our attention on a particular part of the situation. In the latter case, what is focused is surrounded by a scope of attention (Chafe, 1994). Langacker (2008) characterizes scope as "the extent of an expression's 'coverage' in the domains accesses: which portions of these domains it actually evokes and utilizes as the basis for its meaning".

Langacker also makes an important distinction between maximal scope and immediate scope. Maximal scope refers to the full extent of coverage, and the immediate scope refers to a particular region in the maximal scope which is directly relevant for the purpose at hand. The concepts of the body parts are used as an illustration. As we know, the concepts elbow, arm, and body constitute a conceptual hierarchy. As one part of the body, the concept of elbow is most directly related to the concept of arm, but only indirectly related to the concept body. It is because that an elbow is the most immediate part of an arm, which in turn the immediate part of the body. For this reason, we can see body serves as the maximal scope of elbow, while arm is the immediate scope of the concept. The distinctions between maximal and immediate scope are quite significant in hierarchies consisting of successive "part/whole" relations.

6.3.2 Intersubjective Adjustment of Attention, Scope and Partonomic Strengthening Denials

In actual linguistic usage events, different communicative participants may focus on different portions of a "part/whole" hierarchy, depending on their communicative purposes. Consequently, one participant may have to adjust the attention of others in order to jointly attend to certain aspects of an object of conceptualization in a particular way. We want to argue that the meaning construction of partonomic strengthening denials involves intersubjective adjustment of attention and scope between subjects of conceptualization.

Canonical partonomic strengthening denials are motivated by the asymmetrical arrangement of focus and scope when conceptualizing the same situation, thus giving rise to different propositions denoting different portions of the same situation or entity. The negative clause is a linguistic reflection of the speaker's invitation of the addressee to consider and abandon the focus of attention because its coverage is fairly restricted. Subsequently, the corrective clause prompts the activity of expanding the coverage of the focus, which changes part of the previous scope into focus. Consider (9):

(9) 她的六只肢体已基本退化,展现在我面前的是一个圆滚滚的,
不是胳膊圆滚滚,而是整个身躯圆滚滚的女王,大小有普通蚁
人的上百倍。(BCC)

Ta de liu zhi zhiti yi jiben tuihua, zhanxian zai wo mian qian de

shi yi ge yuangungun de, bu shi gebo yuangungun, er shi zheng

ge shenqu yuangungun de nüwang, daxiao you putong yiren de

shang bai bei.

she GEN six-CL limb already largely degraded display in my

face front GEN is one-CL round GEN not arm round but whole-

CL body round GEN queen size have ordinary ant person GEN

over hundred times

Her six limbs had largely been degraded. In front of me was

not a queen with a round arm, but a queen with a round body,

which is a hundred times the size of an ordinary ant-man.

This sentence is taken from the scientific novel *Nanke Xin Meng* (*New
Dreams of Nanke*). In the previous discourse, the speaker had expected to see an
ant woman with just fat arms. However, it turned out later that the whole body of
the ant woman was fat. In the negative clause, the arm of the ant queen is the
focus of attention, while in the corrective clause the whole body becomes the new
focus of attention. The negation reflects the speaker's intersubjective adjustment of
focus and scope on the conceptual structure of body, which can be modeled in
Figure 6.6.

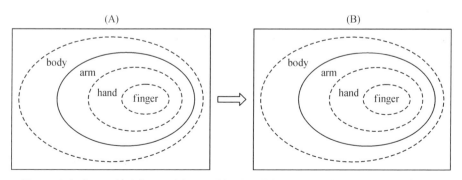

Figure 6.6 Canonical Case of Intersubjective Adjustment of Attention and Scope

The heavy-line circle in Figure 6.6 represents the concept designated by the negative clause. The dotted correspondence lines symbolize the body and its parts that are not brought foregrounded. Each term incorporates in its matrix the essential content of all the terms that precede it in the hierarchy. Diagram (A) illustrates the potential focus of one's attention (i. e. the arm) due to his/her previous knowledge of the ant woman. This way of construal becomes the target of argumentation and is replaced by the speaker's focus of attention through zooming out. This can be illustrated in diagram (B). The whole body, which is both the immediate scope of arm and the maximal scope of other body parts, is foregrounded and becomes the new focus of attention. Consequently, the common ground between the subjects of conceptualization is updated by shifting one's attention and scope.

While the above example which contains body-part terms affords the clearest example, the same analysis can also be applied to partonomic strengthening denials based on "part/whole" relations in other domains of experience. Consider (10):

(10) 如果稍加润色，它完全称得上是经典，不是网文圈里的经典，而是整个小说圈里的经典。(BCC)

Ruguo shao jia runse, ta wanquan chengdeshang shi jingdian, bu shi wangwen quan li de jingdian, er shi zheng ge xiaoshuo quan li de jingdian.

if minor to touch. up it completely qualified is internet literature circle-in GEN classic but entire-CL novel circle-in GEN classic

With a few touch-ups, it would be completely qualified as a classic, not just in the circle of network literature, but the circle of fiction as a whole.

In this sentence, the circle of network literature and the circle of novel are of abstract "part/whole" relation since network literature is just a sub-field of novel in general. The negation is cognitively motivated by inadequate windowing of attention represented by the root proposition.

Metonymic partonomic strenghtening denials are also associated with asymmetry of attention and scope between different subjects of conceptualization when conceptualizing the same situation. However, they differ from canonical cases in that the partonomic relations are established through part for whole metonymy. Metonymy is a cognitive and linguistic process through which one entity "provides access to" another related entity (Littlemore, 2015). Part for whole metonymy is one of metonymic relations that have been identified in the cognitive linguistic literature (Radden & Kövecses, 1999). Metonymy can serve a wide range of communicative functions, including textual cohesion, humour, irony, euphemism, and vagueness (Deignan et al., 2013; Panther & Thornburg, 2007; Ruiz de Mendoza & Otal Campo, 2002). One of its key functions is to create a hyperbolic meaning effect. As Littlemore (2015) points out, many hyperbolic expressions rely on WHOLE FOR PART metonymies, or "domain reduction" (Ruiz de Mendoza & Diez Velasco, 2002). For example, suppose someone finds that the trunk of your car is empty, and says "Your car is so empty". In this sentence, *your car* stands metonymically for "the trunk of your car". According to Littlemore (2015), the rhetorical strength of metonymic hyperboles is derived from the fact that both the vehicle and its referent can be evoked in the interpretation of metonymy.

Metonymic partonomic strenghtening denials are also motivated by the asymmetry of focus and scope arrangement represented by the roots and rectifications. Different from canonical cases, the root of negation affords explicit afford access (or domain expansion) to the corrective clause through part for whole metonymy. Consider (11), repeated from (26) in Chapter 5:

(11) 那场足球赛已经不是两支球队在场上的对决，而是两个城市
之间的对决。当时就感觉，没有别的，就是为青岛而战。
Na chang zuqiu sai yijing bu shi liang zhi qiudui zai chang shang
de duijue, er shi liang ge chengshi zhijian de duijue. Dangshi

jiu ganjue, meiyou bie de, jiu shi wei Qingdao er zhan.

that-CL football match already not two-CL team on field-on
GEN showdown but two-CL city between GEN showdown
then just feel not other simply is for Qingdao to fight

That football competition was no longer a showdown between
two teams on the field, but between two cities. At that time, I
have no choice but to fight for the honor of Qingdao.

The negation in (11) is derived from the process in which the speaker invites
the addressee to consider and abandon the windowing of attention on the football
team, and to expand the focus of attention to the city that the football team
represents. Arguably, this process is supported by the part for whole metonymy
(or domain expansion), as illustrated in Figure 6.7.

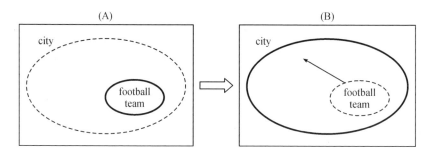

Figure 6.7 Metonymic Case of Intersubjective Adjustment of Attention and Scope

The heavy line represents the football team of Qingdao city, which is the
focus of the conceptualizer's attention in the negative clause. The dotted line in
diagram (A) represents the concept of Qingdao city, which is the maximal scope
of various hierarchical organizations in the city. Through part for whole
metonymy (i.e. domain expansion), the previous dotted line becomes a heavy line
in diagram (B), indicating that the maximal scope in diagram (A) is brought into
focus. The expanded coverage indicates that the two football teams are not just
competing for themselves, but for the cities they represent respectively.

6.4 Meaning Construction of Epistemic Strengthening Denials

In this section, the meaning construction of epistemic strengthening denials will be discussed. Drawing on the epistemic models in cognitive grammar, it will be argued that epistemic strengthening denials, including validity and predictability cases, are manifestations of intersubjective adjustment of epistemic grounds.

6.4.1 Cognitive Model of Epistemic Ground

There has been much discussion in cognitive linguistics surrounding the notion of epistemic modality (Langacker, 1991; Lyons, 1977; Nuyts, 2001; Traugott, 1989). Among them, Langacker (1991) develops some epistemic models in order to provide a cognitive account of the modals (and tense). One of the epistemic models, which he calls the "elaborated epistemic model" is particularly useful to account for validity strengthening denials concerning present and past here. This model can be illustrated in Figure 6.8.

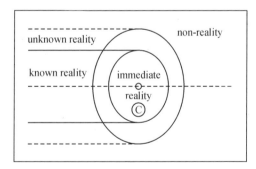

Figure 6.8 The Elaborated Epistemic Model

In Figure 6.8, the cylinder represents the reality that is ever-evolving along the axis, as indicated by the arrow. The leading edge of the expanding structure, indicated by the face of the cylinder, is termed immediate reality. It is a portion of current reality accepted by the conceptualizer (indicated by C) as true. Reality can either be known or unknown. The known reality is what is accepted by a particular conceptualizer (indicated by the small solid circle) as being real. It is surrendered by a much larger region of the unknown reality, which contains situations whose reality is uncertain and has not been accepted by the conceptualizer as true.

Another epistemic model proposed by Langacker is called the dynamic evolutionary model. It incorporates the important components of the elaborate epistemic model and some force-dynamic concepts with an attempt to give a unified account of the epistemic modals. The central aspects of this model are diagrammed in Figure 6.9.

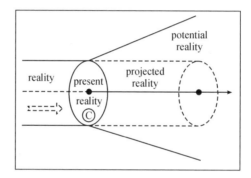

Figure 6.9 The Dynamic Evolutionary Model

The dashed arrow indicates that reality has evolutionary momentum which tends to carry in certain directions of the future. If the momentum of an event is believed to be sufficient enough to reach the expected points, this is termed potential reality. By contrast, if an event does not have sufficient momentum for the speaker to project it as evolving along the path, it only constitutes a projected reality. This epistemic model can be used in accounting for the cognitive grounding of predictability strengthening denials.

6.4.2 Intersubjective Adjustment of Epistemic Ground and Epistemic Strengthening Denials

Due to different knowledge, beliefs, and attitudes, individuals may have alternate epistemic construals of the same situation. Consequently, they may produce propositions with different epistemic statuses. Sometimes, the epistemic status of a particular proposition in the previous utterance or unspoken thought may fail to meet the speaker's expectation. On this occasion, the speaker may modify the epistemic ground by denying the epistemically weaker expressions and replacing them with an epistemically stronger one. In an epistemic strengthening denial, the propositions in the root and the rectification represent different epistemic grounds on which a particular situation is conceptualized. These denials arise from the intersubjective adjustment of epistemic asymmetry between the speaker and the hearer about the same state of affairs. Validity strengthening denials are manifestations of the cognitive process in which the speaker seeks shared epistemic ground with the interlocutor. Consider (12), repeated from (29) in Chapter 5:

(12) 不几天,野战医院来告状……人家挺客气,用了"据说"和"牵" 这样两个词。"不是'据说'。"工兵不领情:"实实在在全是我们 扛走的。不信我领你去看看。" (BCC)

Bu ji tian, yezhan yiyuan lai gaozhuang ⋯ renjia ting keqi, yong le "jushuo" he "qian" zheyang liang ge ci. "Bu shi 'jushuo'." Gongbing bu lingqing: "Shishizaizai quan shi women kangzou de. Bu xin wo ling ni qu kankan. "

not few-days field hospital come complain they quite polite use PRT It-is-said. and pull such two-CL words not it-is-said sappers not appreciate truly all is we carry-away PRT not believe I lead you go have-a-look

In just a few days, the field hospital came to complain ... They were quite polite and described the event with the expression "it is said" and "pull". "Not 'it is said'." The engineers didn't appreciate their kindness and said, "It was really us who carried them away. If you don't believe me, I will show you where they are. "

The propositions expressed by the root and the rectification represent two different ways of conceptualizing the same situation. The former expresses the speaker's construal of the event as unknown reality, whereas the latter construes it as known reality. This negation reflects the speaker's invitation of the addressee to consider and abandon the epistemically weaker construal and to choose an epistemically stronger one. The intersubjective adjustment activity can be modeled in Figure 6.10.

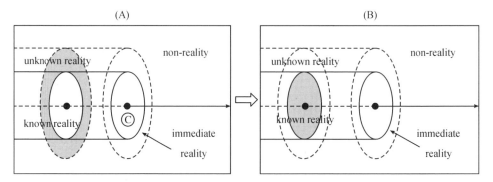

Figure 6.10 Example of Interusbjective Adjustment of Known and Unknown Reality

Diagram (A) shows the way of construal in the root proposition. The smallest solid circle in this part represents the first conceptualizer of the situation (i. e. someone from the field hospital). The epistemic *jushuo* ("it is said") locates the designated event at some point of unknown reality which lies on the left of immediate reality, indicating the event happening in the past. By contrast, diagram (B) shows the way of construal in the corrective clause. The smallest circle in diagram (B) represents the second conceptualizer, i.e. the speaker of (12). Given his acknowledgment of their deed, the designated event falls within the realm of known reality at the same point of time. Hence, the common ground is established through cognitive coordination of the unknown reality and known reality between different subjects of conceptualization.

The meaning construction process of predictability strengthening denials could be captured by the dynamic evolutionary model discussed above. These denials have their roots in the asymmetry of epistemic distances that are designated by the epistemic expressions in the root and the rectification. When conceptualizing a future event, the speaker and the hearer often have different assurance of the future event due to their differences in knowledge, beliefs, and attitudes. Predictability strengthening denials are manifestations of the speaker's dispelling of the hearer's predictive uncertainty to establish common ground with his/her conversation partner. In a similar fashion to validity strengthening denials, this type of MN involves manipulating the epistemic distance through the use of stronger epistemic expressions to describe the same events. Consider (13), repeated from (33) in Chapter 5:

(13) 黛娜忽然用十分苦涩的声音问:"鹰,如果我们……离开这
里——"这时他忍不住道:"不是如果,我们一定可以离开这
里!" (BCC)

Daina huran yong shifen kuse de shengyin wen: "Ying, ruguo,
women … likai zheli——" Zheshi ta renbuzhu dao: "Bu shi
ruguo, women yiding keyi likai zheli!"

Daina suddenly use very bitter GEN voice ask Ying if we
leave here then he can-not-help say not if we definitely can
leave here

Daina suddenly asked in a very bitter voice, "Eagle, if we ...
get out of here..." Then he couldn't help but said, "Not 'if',
we can definitely leave here!"

As was seen previously, the epistemic item *ruguo* ("if") is semantically weaker than *yiding* ("definitely"). According to Langacker's dynamic evolutionary model, the former situates the designated event to some point in the realm of potential reality that is non-immediate to the ground. By contrast, the expression *yiding* situates the designated event in the realm of projected reality. The intersubjective adjustment of projected and potential reality can be modeled in Figure 6.11.

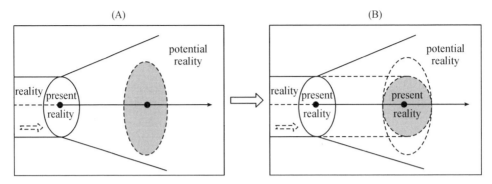

Figure 6.11 Example of Intersubjective Adjustment of Potential and Projected Reality

Diagram (A) represents the mental space which contains the way of construal of the first speaker. The expression *ruguo* situates the leaving event in the realm of potential reality, as indicated by the shadowed circle. By contrast, diagram (B) represents the mental space that contains the speaker's epistemic construal of the same event. As shown in Figure 6.11, the same event is situated in the projected reality, as indicated by the shadowed circle of the same size as the present reality. In the intersubjective coordination, the addressee is invited by the speaker to consider and abandon a positive epistemic stance towards the weak epistemic construal of the leaving event, and to accept a stronger one. Consequently, the common epistemic ground between the speaker and the addressee is updated through this intersubjective adjustment activity.

6.5 Meaning Construction of Directional Strengthening Denials

In this section, the meaning construction of directional strengthening denials will be addressed. It will begin with the introduction of the study of construal operations concerning action chain schema, and then discuss the intersubjective adjustment activities underlying this type of denials.

6.5.1 Asymmetrical and Reciprocal Action Chain Schema

Action chain schema is an abstract cognitive structure derived from repeated patterns of forceful interactions that involving the transmission of energy from one participant to the next (sometimes via an instrument). This ubiquitous image schema is also termed as the "billiard ball" model in Langacker (1991). It underlies the prototypical transitive clause encoding the physical interaction between different participants (Langacker, 1991). In the prototypical transitive clause, the agent, patient, and instrument are respectively encoded as the subject, direct object, and indirect object. The prototypical action chain can be represented by Figure 6.12.

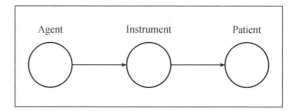

Figure 6.12 Prototypical Action Chain

In the action chain, the circles represent the participants of the action and the arrows represent the transfer of energy from the initiator of the action (the agent) to the object that undergoes the action (the patient) through an energy transmitter, the instrument. Obviously, the prototypical action chain is "asymmetrical" in the sense that the energy flow is unidirectional. There is a variant of the prototypical image schema which represents a bidirectional flow of energy, the reciprocal action chain (Hart, 2013, 2014, 2015). In the reciprocal action chain, the two participants can not be ascribed to the status of agent and patient. Each participant is both the initiator and receiver of the energy. The reciprocal action chain can be illustrated in Figure 6.13.

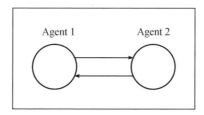

Figure 6.13 Reciprocal Action Chain

According to Hart, the same event can be construed in terms of either an "asymmetrical" or a "reciprocal" action chain, thus producing a different ideological vested meaning effect. The alternate construals of an action chain are also useful in accounting for the meaning mechanisms of directional strengthening denials.

6.5.2 Intersubjective Adjustment of Direction of Action Chain and Directional Strengthening Denials

As discussed above, the same event, especially one involving the mutual transmission of energy between two entities, can be conceived as either an asymmetrical action chain or a reciprocal action chain. In an actual usage event, communicative participants may construe the same action chain differently in terms of directionality. The alternative conceptualizations invoked by the two ways of construal may carry significant meaning consequences. Specifically, characterizing a bidirectional action chain as a unidirectional one may play down the agency of one participant in the event. Thus, it may fail to meet one's expectation of informational strength. On such occasions, a speaker can adjust the asymmetrical way of construing an action chain and replace it with the reciprocal one to realize a certain communicative purpose. It can be argued that directional strengthening denials are manifestations of the intersubjective coordination between asymmetrical and reciprocal construal of an action chain. Consider (14):

(14) 深夜是人们心里最脆弱的时候, 在这样的时刻, 不是我陪伴着你, 而是我们互相陪伴着。 (BCC)

Shenye shi renmen xin li zui cuiruo de shihou, zai zheyang de shike, bu shi wo peibanzhe ni, er shi women huxiang peibanzhe.

late night is people heart inside most vuluerable GEN time at such GEN time not I accompany-ASP you but we mutual accompany-ASP

Late night is the most vulnerable time in people's hearts. In such moments, it is not that I accompany you, but we accompany each other.

In this example, the propositions in the root and the rectification respectively represent the asymmetrical and reciprocal construal of an action chain. The negation is motivated by the inappropriateness of recruiting the asymmetrical action chain when conceptualizing the same situation. The intersubjective adjustment process can be modeled in Figure 6.14.

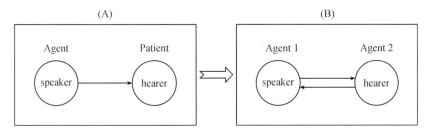

Figure 6.14 Intersubjective Adjustment of Asymmetrical and Reciprocal Action Chain

Diagram (A) illustrates the asymmetrical action chain represented in the root proposition. The even is construed in terms of a unidirectional flow of energy from the agent (the speaker) to the patient (the hearer) (not via an instrument). By contrast, diagram (B) illustrates the reciprocal action chain represented in the corrective proposition. The same event is construed in terms of a bidirectional flow of energy so that both participants assume the status of agent. The negative clause prompts the addressee to consider and abandon the asymmetrical construal represented in the root and replaces it with the reciprocal one. The former construal is rejected because the source of energy is attributed to only the speaker and no transmission of energy from the hearer to the speaker. It may induce the implicature that the addressee is only the receiver of the speaker's companion, but without the ability to provide his/her companion to the speaker. The intersubjective adjustment of alternate construal effects an updating of the common ground with respect to their relationship.

6.6 Summary

Based on the conceptual framework developed in the previous chapter, this chapter presents a cognitive linguistic account of the cognitive processes underlying the meaning representations of strengthening denials. Four categories of strengthening denials are investigated, namely scalar strengthening denials, granular strengthening denials, partonomic strengthening denials, epistemic strengthening denials, and directional strengthening denials. It is found that strengthening denials are generated through the intersubjective adjustment of alternate construals of the same situation which can give rise to different propositions varying in semantic or informational strength. The above five categories of strengthening denials are derived from different cognitive coordination activities between subjects of conceptualization: (1) Strengthening denials are derived from intersubjective adjustment of alternate scalar construals of the same state of affairs; (2) Granular strengthening denials involve the cognitive adjustment of different levels of specificity on which a state of affairs is characterized; (3) Partonomic strengthening denials result from cognitive coordination of one's attention and scope on the "part/whole" schema; (4) Epistemic strengthening denials pertain to the activity of coordinating different modal ground between different conceptualizers; (5) Directional strengthening denials arise from shifting the symmetrical into reciprocal action chain. The point of a strengthening denial, in broad terms, is that the speaker invites the addressee to consider and abandon a semantic or informational weak construal in some specific way. Subsequently, the common ground is updated by suggesting another construal of the same situation that can create a strengthening representational effect.

Chapter 7

A Cognitive Linguistic Account of Identifying Denials

This chapter is concerned with the meaning construction mechanisms of identifying denials, namely categorical identifying denials, facet identifying denials, relational identifying denials, identity identifying denials, and sequential identifying denials. Based on the ICA model developed in Chapter 3, we will present an analysis of identifying denials in terms of the cognitive coordination between the two conceptualizers. We attempt to show how the five types of identifying denials are generated through the intersubjective adjustment of default or marked construals of the same situation based on cognitive principles such as prototypicality, cognitive domain, "trajector/landmark" alignment, epistemic ground, and mental scanning.

7.1 Meaning Construction of Categorical Identifying Denials

This section deals with the cognitive processes that give rise to categorical identifying denials. Based on a discussion of the prototypical model of category structure, it will show how category identifying denials are derived from intersubjective categorical adjustment that is closely related to the typicality effects exhibited by graded categories.

7.1.1 The Prototypicality of Category

Categorization is a central cognitive ability for us to know the world and build our conceptual system. In Croft and Cruse (2004), it is classified as an important construal operation. The classic model of category structure holds that category membership is defined according to a set of necessary and sufficient conditions. Contrary to this view, cognitive linguists hold that semantic structure is encyclopedic in nature. This means that words themselves do not encode neatly packaged bundles of meaning, but serve as "prompt" or "points of access" to the rich encyclopedia knowledge associated with a particular concept and conceptual domains (Langacker, 1987; Evans & Green, 2006). The pioneering research carried out by Rosch and her colleagues (Rosch, 1975, 1978; Rosch & Mervis, 1975) reveals that members in a category do not enjoy equal status, but exhibit prototype or typicality effects. For example, table or chair is generally treated as "better" members of the category furniture than other members (like carpet).

A central assumption of the prototypical model of category is that, a prototype or higher-degree member tends to receive more attention from language users than other category members. Given the degree of category membership, on hearing an expression, one is more likely to interpret it as the prototype or higher-degree members of the category it represents, rather than a peripheral or lower-degree one (Talmy, 2000). For instance, when a Chinese adult hears the word *pet*, he/she is more likely to have a dog or a cat in mind than a lizard or a mouse. Consequently, a speaker can use the lexical item to denote the prototype member of a particular category without arousing much confusion. Another important claim is that categories tend to have fuzzy boundaries. Due to the absence of a number of shared features, it is not always straightforward to determine whether a particular entity can be judged as a member of a given category.

Following the observations made by Rosch and her colleagues, Lakoff (1987) develops the theory of ICMs that might plausibly explain sources of typicality effects. He argues that typicality effects can be generated in a range of ways: mismatches with ICMs, cluster models, and metonymy. For example, the concept mother is structured by a cluster model which consists of a number of cognitive models such as the birth model, the genetic model, the nurturance model, the marital model, and the genealogical model. The typicality effect is created when one of the cognitive models is considered as a primary one in a particular context, while other cognitive models are rendered secondary.

7.1.2 Intersubjective Adjustment of Category Boundaries and Categorical Identifying Denials

As we have seen, canonical cases of categorical identifying denials are used to deny stereotypically exemplified concepts denoted by a lexical item in the negative scope. From a cognitive linguistic view, the stronger proposition is generated by the typicality effect of category. As Croft and Cruse (2004) points out, different communicative participants often have different views on which category a certain entity should belong to. The latter case makes it possible for non-truth-conditional negation to be derived. Here we argue that categorical identifying denials involve the intersubjective coordination activity: the speaker invites the interlocutor to consider and abandon a particular judgment of categorical boundary and then proposes an alternative categorization. Consider (1), repeated from (39) in Chapter 5:

(1) 巴黎一向是灯红酒绿，洋溢着欢乐的花都，可波德莱尔偏偏写了一本《巴黎的忧郁》，况且竟不是诗，而是什么"散文诗"。①

Bali yixiang shi denghong-jiulü, yangyizhe huanle de huadu, ke Bode Laier pianpian xie le yi ben 《Bali de Youyu》, kuangqie jing bu shi shi, er shi shenme "sanwen shi".

Paris always is flamboyant brim-ASP joyful GEN flower.city but Baudelaire just wrote ASP one-CL Paris GEN sulk moreover not poem but so-called prose peom

Paris has been well known as a flower city, which is

---

① http://www.miaoqiyuan.cn/cyjl.m/show-zzjm.html.

flamboyant and brimming with joy. However, it was written by Baudelaire in a collection of poems entitled *Le Spleen de Paris*. What is more, they are not actually poems, but so-called "prose poems".

According to Lakoff (1987), the typicality effect of the category poetry is created by typical members of the category. As we know, the category of poetry embraces all varieties of poems, from major types of poems such as sonnet, Ballad, Limericks and Rhymes, to less known types such as free verse, prose poetry, the idyll, senryu, doggerel, and enjambment. The former ones constitute the prototypical center of the category poetry because they share a bundle of salient features such as line breaks, rhythms, figures of speech, internal rhyme, assonance, and so on. Prose poetry is a peripheral category member because it shares fewer salient features of poetry. For example, the line breaks of poetry are not apparent, which makes them read likes prose. The relation of the two categories can be illustrated in Figure 7.1.

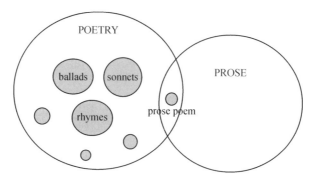

Figure 7.1 Boundaries of the Category of Poetry and the Category of Prose

The bigger circles represent prototypical members in the category of poetry such as ballads, sonnets, rhymes. Prose poem, represented by a smaller circle, is less prototypical and lies in the boundary between the category of poetry and the category of prose. In this usage event, the speaker invites the addressee to consider and abandon the way of categorizing Baudelaire's work as poems because of its peripheral or lower-degree status. In this way, the speaker conveys to the addressee the negative attitudes towards the writer's literary work. In other words, the common ground between the speaker and the addressee is updated through the intersubjective adjustment of categorical boundaries.

Category identifying denials can also be derived from the typicality effects that are generated by cluster models, which are cognitive models consisting of a number of converging ICMs. Sometimes a woman who does not give birth to a child may be judged atypical with respect to the social stereotype for mothers. The denials in (2) - (3) are derived from the typicality effect, which is generated by viewing the birth model as the primary model:

> (2) 她觉察到我们的表情有点异样, 补充道:"她是父亲的夫人, 不
>   是我的妈妈。"(BCC)
>   *Ta juechadao women de biaoqing you dian yiyang, buchong
>   dao: "Ta shi fuqin de furen, bu shi wode mama."*
>   she sense-ASP our GEN expression a-little strange add say she
>   is father GEN wife not my mother
>   She sensed that we were looking a little strange and added,
>   "She's simply my father's wife, not my mother."
> (3) 我们不敢相信这句话是真的。妈妈重复说:"我不是你们的妈
>   妈, 我没有生过你们。" (BCC)
>   *Women bu gan xiangxin zhe ju hua shi zhende. Mama chongfu
>   shuo: "Wo bu shi nimen de mama, wo meiyou shengguo nimen."*
>   we not dare believe this-CL words is real mother repeat say I
>   not your GEN mother I not give-birth-ASP you
>   We couldn't believe this was true. Mom repeated, "I'm not your
>   mother, because I never gave birth to you."

According to Lakoff (1987), the phenomena whereby a typical example of an individual ICM stands for the category as a whole is based on metonymy. For example, there is a metonymic relation between the concept *mother* and the more specialized concept *genetic mother*. As Panther and Thornburg (2003) note, the stereotypically enriched meaning constituent is a GCI which is induced on the basis of Levinson (2000)'s I-heuristic: "What is expressed simply is stereotypically exemplified."[①] They also propose that metonymic links can be regarded as natural inference schemas for people to work out GCI. Therefore, it could be argued that metonymy also has a role to play in the meaning construction of categorical identifying denials. Consider (4):

(4) 确定她丈夫是否还在人间,需要花这么多时间吗? 不是丈夫, 是前夫,他纠正自己。(BCC)

Queding ta zhangfu shifou hai zai renjian, xuyao hua zheme duo shijian ma? Bu shi zhangfu, shi qianfu, ta jiuzheng ziji.

confirm her husband whether still in world require take so much time QM not husband is ex-husband he correct self

Does it take so much time to confirm if her husband is still alive? Not my husband, but my ex-husband, he corrected himself.

According to Levinson's I-heuristic, the use of the semantically general expression implicates a semantically specific interpretation. Therefore, the use of *zhangfu* ("husband") in the sentence induces the GCI that the man in the context is her current husband. The whole for part metonymy serves as a natural schema in the derivation of the GCI.

The same analysis is also applicable to other examples of action or activity denials in Chapter 5. In the same way, they are derived from typicality effects of categories. The speaker intends to mean that the action or activity in the context diverges from prototypical ones. What is denied an erroneous, default assumption held by the hearer or a third party. For example, the denial in (42) is associated with a prototypical situation of buying in which a consumer pays corresponding fees to the seller based on the actual price of the goods. Through intersubjective categorical judgment, the speaker also dispels the wrong

---

① "I" stands for "Informativeness".

assumption held by the addressee, thereby updating their common ground. Category identifying denials can also be rectified metaphorically. Consider (5), repeated from (45) in Chapter 5:

(5) 这女人她素来是那么顽强的！这不是一个女人，而是一头公
牛。(BCC)

Zhe nüren ta sulai shi name wanqiang de! Zhe bu shi yi ge
nüren, er shi yi tou gongniu.

this woman she always is so tenacious PRT this not one-CL
woman but one-CL bull.

This woman has always been so tenacious! She is not a woman,
but a bull.

The domain of animals constitutes a productive source domain in linguistic communication. It is often the case that human beings are understood in terms of certain properties of animals. In (5), the speaker intends to attribute the bull's remarkable character (i.e. toughness) to the woman in the context. On our view, the negation is tied to the cognitive coordination between the speaker and the addressee: the speaker firstly invites the addressee to consider and abandon the default way of construing her as a woman because her behavior is not consistent with the stereotypical image of a woman. Subsequently, the woman is reconstrued as a bull so as to highlight her toughness. The metaphorical mapping process can be captured in Figure 7.2.

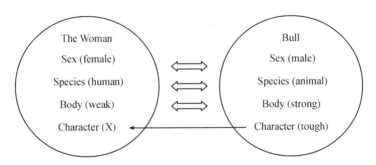

Figure 7.2 Cross-domain Mapping in "The Woman Is a Bull" Metaphor

In the interpretation of the rectification, our world knowledge concerning how a bull generally behaves in front of enemies will be mapped onto the woman (indicated by the arrow line), allowing us to understand the woman's character through that of the bull. However, the elements which are related to sex, species, physical strengthen are not selected for mapping but intended to make a sharp contrast with the former (indicated by the double-headed arrows).

It is worth noting that the typicality effects in metaphorical cases of categorical identifying denials are not obvious as they are in metaphorical strengthening denials. In the terminology of Davis (2016), the former cases involve denying the so-called "strengthening implicature" (i. e. a stereotypical exemplified entity or situation), while the target of denial in the latter is the "limiting implicature" (i. e. just). Both of them evoke the ICM of the concept. However, in the former, the speaker intends to profile a property that is central to the ICM, while in the latter he/she intends to profile a property that is contradictory to that of the ICM, or not shared in the ICM. What's more, what is denied in a strengthening denial is not restricted to the prototypical cases, but virtually the whole category. And the rectification is used to strengthen the central property of the category. By contrast, what is denied in an identifying denial is just the existence of property in the context.

7.2 Meaning Construction of Facet Identifying Denials

This section is intended to give a cognitive-linguistic interpretation of facet identifying denials. Following a discussion of the organization of our encyclopedic knowledge, it will be argued that the meaning representation of a facet identifying denial results from intersubjective adjustment of different domain profiles concerning the same entity.

7.2.1 Organization of Encyclopedic Knowledge in Domains

In cognitive grammar, our encyclopedic knowledge is seen as being organized in "domains". According to Langacker (1987), "Domains are cognitive entities: mental experiences, representational spaces, concepts, or conceptual complexes." Very much like frame in fillmore's frame semantics, domains serve as background information against which a linguistic expression can be understood and used in language. For example, lexical concepts like *small forward*, *power guard*, and *shooting guard* belong to the domain of football match. One would find it difficult to understand and use them if he/she does not have the knowledge of football matches.

A single expression is usually structured by a set of conceptual domains. The combination of domains underlying the concept is called domain matrix. For example, the expression *book* denotes a lexical concept that presuppose a range of domains, such as *shape, space, tome, text, function, size* and other domains pertaining to *prize, storage,* or *history.* Langacker (2008) argues that domains are ranked in terms of different degrees of centrality in a complex domain matrix. Central domains are much more likely to be evoked than peripheral ones because they are central for the understanding of an expression's meaning. For example, the domain of [economical status] is ranked high in the domain matrix of the concept beggar. Therefore, it has a higher likelihood of activation compared with other domains associated with other aspects of information, such as their political views, education, and language. By contrast, peripheral domains are less important for understanding and use of a particular expression. They are only accessed in particular situations when they happen to be relevant.

Domains activation is subject to the influence of various contextual factors. For example, *a beautiful book*, *a profound book*, and *an old book* can be used to describe the same object. However, the adjectives respectively activate [tome] domain, [text] domain and [history] domain. Moreover, contextual factors can obviously focus attention on a domain that might otherwise not be accessed at all or only at a lower level of activation (Langacker, 2008). Consider (6):

(6)《美的历程》是一部小书, 篇幅不过十几万字。《美的历程》又是
一部大书, 它考察了数千年中华民族艺术的发展。(BCC)
《*Mei de Licheng*》 *shi yi bu xiao shu, pianfu bu guo shiji wan*

zi. 《Mei de Licheng》 you shi yi bu da shu, ta kaochale shu qian nian Zhonghua Minzu yishu de fazhan.

beauty GEN journey is one-CL small book length just ten over ten-thousand word beauty GEN journey yet is one-CL big book it examine-ASP several thousand year Chinese nation art GEN development

The Journey of Beauty is a small book with no more than a hundred thousand words. It is also a big book because it examines the artistic development of Chinese art for thousands of years.

Normally, the adjectives *xiao* ("small") and *da* ("big") added before the noun *shu* ("book") evoke the [size] domain. However, this default activation is suppressed by the linguistic context in which the significance of the book is expressed. The linguistic context evokes the metaphor "important is big" (as in the sentence "This is a big deal"), through which the [text] domain becomes the focus of attention.

7.2.2 Intersubjective Adjustment of Domain Activation and Facet Identifying Denials

The division of conceptual content of an expression and the set of domains associated with it sheds light on the cognitive underpinning of facet identifying denials discussed here. Given the variable activation of domains, in actual usage events, different participants may have asymmetrical profiling of domains concerning the same concept. In order to gain a shared apprehension of the situation, the speaker may adjust the domains being activated in the addressee's utterance or thought. On our view, canonical facet identifying denials are derived from the intersubjective adjustment of domain profiles in the same domain matrix. Specifically, when the speaker realizes the "mismatch" of domain profiles between the two participants, he/she will invite the addressee to consider and abandon the domain activated, and deliberately profile another domain in the domain matrix. Consider (7), repeated from (48) in Chapter 5:

(7) 有人说,这座城市是浮躁的,其实浮躁的并不是城市,而是城市
    里的人。[1]

You ren shuo, zhe zuo chengshi shi fuzao de, qishi fuzao de

bing bu shi chengshi, er shi chengshi li de ren.

have people say this-CL city is impetuous PRT actually

impetuous GEN actually not city but city in GEN people

Some people say that the city is impetuous. In fact, what is

impetuous is not the city, but people in the city.

The domain activated in the proposition expressed in the root is [physical environment], rather than [people] living in the city. What the speaker is actually denying is the contextually salient concept profile in the domain matrix of city, rather than the whole conceptual content denoted by it. By doing so, the speaker intends to reject the potential assumption that the impetuous state of the city should be attributed to non-human factors.

Similarly, there are also a set of domains underlying our conceptualization of human beings, which include [living entities], [physical objects], [volitional agent] and so on (Croft, 2007). More often, only one particular domain is activated when an expression denoting human beings is used on a given occasion. This also provides us with two options when denying a certain proposition: one can either deny the existence of a certain person or the domains activated on a given occasion. A speaker may invite the addressee to consider and abandon the domain activated in actual utterance or unspoken thought. This is the case in (8), repeated from (49) in Chapter 5:

(8) 我听过这种论调,也考虑了很久,我要的不是他这个人,而是他
    的心。(BCC)

---

[1] https://www.ximalaya.com/diantai/5791/357620.

Wo tingguo zhe zhong lundiao, ye kaolüle hen jiu, wo yao de bu shi ta zhe ge ren, er shi ta de xin.

I hear-ASP this-CL argument and consider ASP very long I want GEN not he this CL person but he GEN heart.

I have heard this argument before and considered it for a long time. What I want is not the man himself, but his heart.

The negation is not intended to deny the propositional content descriptively understood, but a pragmatically enriched proposition, i.e. what I intend to get is the man's physical companion. The enriched proposition is derived from the activation of the domain [physical object] from the domain matrix of human beings.

As discussed in the above section, domain activation interacts dynamically with contextual factors. A domain activated in a particular usage event may become inactive in another context of usage. This property is also reflected in facet identifying denials. Compare (9):

(9) 他爱的不是她这个人,而是她的美色,但此时她的美色已经失去魅力了。(BCC)

Ta ai de bu shi ta zhe ge ren, er shi ta de meise, dan cishi ta de meise yjing shiqu meili le.

he love GEN not her this-CL person but her beauty but now she GEN beauty already lose charm ASP

What he loves is not the woman herself, but her beauty. However, her beauty has lost its charm at present.

In the same way as (9), this example also contains the phrase *zhe ge ren* ("the person") in the negative scopes. However, in this context, a different domain is activated in the domain matrix of human beings, namely the domain of [personality] or [mind]. By contrast, in the rectification the activated domain is the [appearance] domain, which is also one of the central domains in the domain matrix. However, in the negative clause it is backgrounded.

A speaker may profile the properties of different aspects in the same utterance, by adding different modifiers to the same concept. MN can be derived by modifying the same entity in different ways to profile different aspects of the same entity. In (10), the adjective *xiao* ("small") activates the [tome] domain, while the adjective *da* ("big") activates the [content] domain.

(10) 读旧书题跋时那种轻松的情绪消失了。这时，我觉得自己最初的印象改变了，这并不是一本"小书"，其实应该如实地说是一本"大书"。(BCC)

Du jiushu tiba shi na zhong qingsong de qingxu xiaoshi le. Zheshi, wo jue de ziji zuichu de yinxiang gaibianle, zhe bing bu shi yi ben "xiao shu", qishi yinggai rushi de shuo shi yi ben "da shu".

read old book inscription when that-CL relax GEN mood disappear ASP then I feel self initial GEN impression change-ASP this just not one-CL small book actually should honest PRT say is one-CL big book

The relaxed mood disappeared when I read the inscriptions in the old book. At that time, I felt that my initial impression has changed. To be honest, this is not a "small book", but a "big book".

As is often the case, the speaker may profile knowledge about the peripheral domains in the domain matrix by suppressing the central domains of the concept. The following examples are used to highlight various domains of less centrality: the domains of [skill], [identity], and [power] respectively. Consider (11) - (13):

(11) 他看上的只是她的手艺，不是她这个人！(BCC)

Ta kanshang de zhi shi ta de shouyi, bu shi ta zhe ge ren!

he value GEN just she GEN craftsmanship not she this-CL person

He was just attracted by her craftsmanship, not the woman

herself.

(12) 我讨厌的不是他这个人，而是他的身份。(BCC)

Wo taoyan de bu shi ta zhe ge ren, er shi ta de shenfen.

I hate GEN not he this-CL person but his identity

What I hate is not the man himself, but his status.

(13) 你看中的不是这个人，而是他手中的权力。(BCC)

Ni kanzhong de bu shi zhe ge ren, er shi ta shou zhong de quanli.

he value GEN not this-CL person but he hand-in GEN power

What attracted you was not the man himself, but the power in

his hands.

Compared with the central domains such as [appearance], [body], [personality] and [mind], the domains of [skill], [identity] and [power] are more peripheral. In (11) - (13), the negation functions to invite the addressee to consider and abandon a canonical construal of the related event in which a central domain of a concept is profiled. Subsequently, in the rectification a peripheral domain will be highlighted. The intersubjective adjustment of domain profiles can be depicted in Figure 7.3.

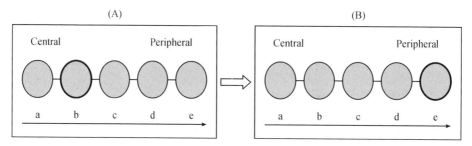

Figure 7.3 Intersubjective Adjustment of Domain Profiles with Different Centrality

Metonymic facet identifying denials are much more complicated in both structure and meaning construction than canonical ones. The verb in the root does not only apply to the abstract noun in the negative scope but also governs the corresponding concrete noun in the corrective clause. For example, (51) in Chapter 5 contains two propositions with the same verb-object structure of *chou* ("smoke") + *N*: *chou yan* ("smoke cigarette") and *chou jimo* ("smoke loneliness"). The first expression describes the dining event in a stereotypical way, while the latter expression is pretty weird and amusing because the noun *jimo* ("loneliness") denotes an abstract entity and is not edible. Arguably, the central rhetorical effect of such a denial is created through the semantic incompatibility between the verb and the noun in the corrective clause.

Wei (2019) accounts for the cognitive motivation of this type of denials from the perspective of pragmatic empathy theory. This construction is viewed as a linguistic manifestation of empathy, a general cognitive ability to transfer people's subjective feelings to objective things for the purpose of conveying strong emotional impact (Kuno, 1987; He, 1991; Ran, 2007). Specifically, pragmatic empathy construes the "action" denoted by the root and the "result" denoted by the rectification as components of a complete event structure, thereby making verb-object collocations easy to interpret. However, it is not clear how the rhetorical effect is created and how the semantic incompatibility between the verb and the noun can be easily resolved.

On our view, metonymic facet identifying denials arise from the intersubjective adjustment of domains in combination with metonymy. Similar to the canonical cases of facet identifying denials, the proposition expressed in the root of negation represents a default consumption about the event described, which is derived from the activation of certain central conceptual domains. By contrast, the proposition in the rectification activates another (often peripheral) domain that is not easily accessed in normal circumstances. Consider (14):

(14) 桂花糕作为中国传统糕点有着悠久的历史。你吃的不是糕点，而是文化! [①]

Guihua gao zuowei Zhongguo chuantong gaodian youzhe youjiu de lishi. Ni chi de bu shi gaodian, er shi wenhua!

Osmanthus cake as Chinese traditional pastry have-ASP long

---

① https://new.qq.com/omn/20181026/20181026A04GPN.html.

GEN history you eat GEN not pastry but culture

As a traditional Chinese cake, Osmanthus cake has a long

history. What you eat is not a cake, but culture!

The speaker in (14) does not intend to say that he/she is eating an Osmanthus cake. Rather, he/she wants to express the idea that you can get a deeper understanding of the related culture through eating it. In the root, suggested by the verb *chi* ("eat"), domains with a high likelihood of being accessed are [material], [shape], and [taste]. The negative clause represents the speaker's invitation of the addressee to consider and abandon the central domain profiles activated by the default assumption that people usually eat Osmanthus cake for its good taste or material. Subsequently, the lexical item *wenhua* ("culture") in the corrective clause cues for the activation of the domain of [function] which contains the cultural background of Osmanthus cake. The intersubjective adjustment activity can be captured in Figure 7.4.

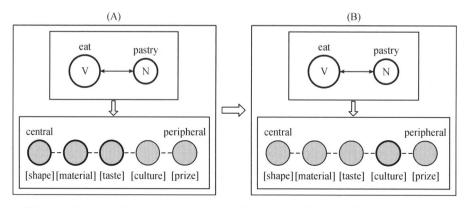

Figure 7.4 Intersubjective Adjustment of Domain Profiles in a Metonymic Denial

The rhetorical effect is arguably derived from mismatches of domains evoked by the verb-object collocations. According to Michaelis (2003), when there is a mismatch between the event structure of the verb and of the construction, the construction will force the verb to acquire a new sense in order to make it conceptually compatible with the noun. This phenomenon is called the constructional coercion. The reason why the rectification is not semantically anomalous lies in the "action for result" metonymy. That is, the verb *chi* metonymically stands for "to understand the culture behind the food through eating it". Consider (15):

(15) 开豪车摆地摊，哥摆的不是摊，是寂寞！ [①]

Kai haoche bai ditan, ge bai de bu shi tan, shi jimo!

drive luxury car set-up stall brother set-up GEN not stall is loneliness

Driving a luxury car to set up a street stall: what I set up is not a stall, but loneliness.

There are two propositions with the same format [*V de shi N*] in the negative clause and the corrective clause. The speaker in (15) does not intend to deny the fact that he/she is setting up a street stall. What is denied is that he/she is setting a street stall with the common purpose of making money. Cued by the verb *bai* ("set up"), the central domains of the concept *ditan* ("street stall") such as [space] and [material] will be activated. Moreover, the domain of [function] will also be activated, giving rise to the default assumption that people set up a street stall for commercial purposes. There are two interpretations of the corrective clause, with minor differences in meaning: (1) the vendor sets up the street stall out of loneliness; (2) the vendor sets up the street stall with the purpose of passing the lonely hours. The former interpretation construes the vending event as a cause, whilst the latter construes it as a result. Whatever is the intended one, the expression *bai jimo* ("set up loneliness") cue for activation of another peripheral domain of [function] that contains the knowledge that vending is a time-consuming activity and could be used to kill time. In a similar fashion to (15), the semantic anomaly could easily be resolved through the metonymy of "action for result" or "result for action", depending on the interpretation adopted.

---

① https://xw.qq.com/cmsid/20200612A0CS6F00?f=newdc.

7.3 Meaning Construction of Relational Identifying Denials

In this section, we will discuss the meaning construction of relational strengthening denials by relating it to the cognitive principle of trajector/landmark alignment. It will be argued that the relational strengthening denials arise from intersubjective adjustment of alternate trajector/landmark alignments.

7.3.1 Trajector/Landmark Alignment

In cognitive grammar, a linguistic expression may profile either a thing or a relationship. Consequently, linguistic structures are classified into nominal predications and relational predications. The former profiles a thing, invoking concepts that are inherently meaningful, such as nouns or noun phrases. The latter profiles the interconnections between the entities, with varying degrees of prominence conferred on them. The notion of trajector (TR) is understood as the most prominent participant in a profiled relationship, while the notion of landmark (LM) is defined as a less prominent and the secondary focus in the relationship. Trajector/landmark alignment in the language is a manifestation of the general attention phenomenon of "figure/ground" organization. Talmy (2000) summarizes a list of typical characteristics of figure and ground, as shown in Table 7.1.

Table 7.1 Typical Characteristics of Figure and Ground

Figure	Ground
Properties inherent in the entities	
(a) more movable	more permanently located
(b) smaller	larger
(c) geometrically simpler	geometrically more complex
Properties related to the perception to the entities vis-à-vis each other	
(d) less immediately perceivable	more immediately perceivable
(e) more salient, once perceived	more backgrounded, once figure is perceived
(f) more dependent	more independent
Properties related to the activation status of the concepts	
(g) more recently on the scene/in current awareness	more familiar
(h) of greater concern/relevance	of lesser concern/relevance

Relational profiles may be further subdivided into two subcategories, which are atemporal or static relationships and temporal or dynamic relationships. The former are encoded by prepositions, word-classes, and non-finite verbs, which can be schematically characterized as state. By contrast, the latter are encoded by finite verbs can be schematically characterized in terms of processes. Compare the sentence "There is a plane (TR) over the town (LM)" with the sentence "A plane (TR) flies over the town (LM)". The former construes the relationship between the two entities as stationary, whereas the latter construes their relationship as evolving through time.

The same relationship, be it static or dynamic, can be construed in alternate ways through different choices of trajector and landmark (Langacker, 2008). Consequently, language users have thus a good deal of freedom in organizing trajector/landmark alignment. Of course, different trajector/landmark arrangements would have impacting consequences on their meanings. According to Talmy (2000), "The entity that functions as the figure of situations attracts focal attention and is the entity whose characteristics and fate are of concern." For example, compare the sentence "The police have arrested a number of demonstrators" with the sentence "The demonstrators have been arrested (by the police)". In the former, the police, as the trajector, is conceptually more salient than the demonstrators, while in the latter, they receive less attention than the demonstrators. The alternative construals invoked by the two sentences may carry significant ideological consequences when they are used in news reports.

7.3.2 Intersubjective Adjustment of Trajector/Landmark Alignment and Relational Identifying Denials

The distinction between a designated relationship and its trajector/landmark alignment creates two possibilities for denials: one can deny either the existence of the relation or the default trajector/landmark alignment represented in the proposition. Given that the same relationship can be construed in alternate ways through different choices of trajector and landmark, participants in a usage event may impose different or converse trajector/landmark alignments of a particular relationship. On our view, relational identifying denials involve adjustment of a default trajector/landmark alignment and a non-default one between two conceptualizers.

Static relation identifying denials are motivated by a speaker's denying of the appropriateness of a stereotypical trajector/landmark alignment. The proposition in the root encapsulates stereotypical information about the static or atemporal relationship between the two entities. The speaker does not intend to deny the existence of the relationship, but the trajector/landmark alignment imposed on this relationship. Consider (16), repeated from (55) in Chapter 5:

(16) 电视剧每播放十五分钟就要插播一次广告。显然,这已不是电视剧插播广告,而是在广告中插播电视剧。①

Dianshiju mei bofang shiwu fenzhong jiu yao chabo yi ci guanggao. Xianran, zhe yi bu shi dianshiju chabo guanggao, er shi zai guanggao zhong chabo dianshiju.

TV shows every play fifteen minute then will insert one-CLF commercial apparently this already not TV show insert commercial but in advertisement-in insert TV shows

Every fifteen minutes of a TV series is interspersed with commercials. Apparently, this is not inserting commercials into a TV show, but inserting a TV show into a commercial.

In (16), the root proposition represents the default assumption that the duration of an advertisement is shorter than that of a TV show. The negative clause has the effect of inviting the addressee to consider and abandon the default trajector/landmark alignment. The rectification contains another proposition that overstates the duration of a TV show and understates that of advertisement. This process can be captured in Figure 7.5.

---

① https://www.sohu.com/a/26900207_160337.

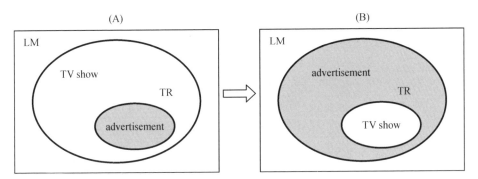

Figure 7.5 Intersubjective Adjustment of Static Trajector/Landmark Alignments

Diagram (A) represents the default figure/ground alignment of the situation concerned. The trajector in the profiled relationship is the "advertisement", which accounts for a very small proportion of the time duration. The landmark is the "TV show", which enjoys a much longer broadcasting time than the advertisements. Diagram (B) represents a hardly conceivable imaginary situation in which the rates of the meat and water are respectively strengthened and mitigated excessively. The landmark that does not initially have the properties of the figure, acquires a higher degree of conceptual prominence. Correspondingly, the figure which is the more prominent part of the profiled relationship is brought into the background. According to Ruiz de Mendoza and Galera (2014) and Peña and Ruiz de Mendoza (2017), the meaning effects of a hyperbolic statement are derived from the creation of a counterfactual scenario, thereby maximizing a scalar value to an abnormal degree. Following this view, it could be argued that the hyperbolic effect of this example is derived from the cross-domain mappings between the two situations and contrasts between the corresponding elements.

In a similar fashion to the static cases, dynamic relation identifying denials involve adjustment of alternate trajector/landmark alignment between two subjects of conceptualization. However, they differ from the former cases because the trajector/landmark alignments being rejected are temporal or dynamic ones. Consider (17), repeated from (58) in Chapter 5:

(17) 遛狗一小时比走了8公里都累,这真的不是人遛狗,而是狗遛

人啊！(BCC)

Liu gou yi xiaoshi bi zoule 8 gongli dou lei, zhe zhende bu shi

ren liu gou, er shi gou liu ren a!

walk dog one-hour than walk-ASP 8 kilometer even tired this

really not man walk dog but dog walk man PRT

I felt more tired after walking my dog for an hour alone than

walking 8km. It's really not a man walking dogs; it's a dog

walking a man!

In the root of negation, the focal participant (TR) is the dog owner, and the agent, and the secondary participant (LM) is the dog, the patient. This is so arranged because the former is generally considered to be more movable, salient, and easily perceived, while the latter is more stable, not easily perceived, and backgrounded once the former is perceived. Through negation, the addressee is invited by the speaker to consider and abandon the default trajector/landmark alignment and to adopt a reversed trajector/landmark alignment. The intersubjective adjustment activity can be captured in Figure 7.6.

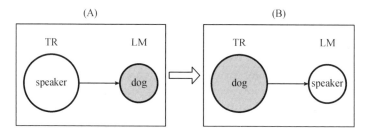

Figure 7.6 Intersubjective Adjustment of Dynamic Trajector/Landmark Alignments

In diagram (A) of Figure 7.6, the speaker is the agent of the action, marked by the bigger circle as TR, while the dog walked is the patient, marked by the smaller circle as TR. By contrast, the positions of the participants are reversed: the original agent becomes the patient and the original patient becomes the agent. Taken together, Figure 7.6 captures the essential point of cognitive coordination of different trajector/landmark alignments between two speakers. Specifically, the speaker leads the addressee to reject the assumption about a stereotypical dog-walking activity, that is, a man is walking leisurely and in absolute control of the dog's direction. Furthermore, knowledge about the real dog-walking event is included in the common ground.

7.4 Meaning Construction of Identity Identifying Denials

In this section, based on a discussion of the concept common ground, a cognitive-linguistic analysis of identity identifying denials will be provided. We attempt to show that the derivation of an identity identifying denial arises from intersubjective adjustment of individual ground concerning one's identity.

7.4.1 Common Ground as Cognitive Principle

As discussed in Chapter 5, an identity identifying denial is used to clarify one's ignorance or pretended ignorance of a person's identity. This is closely linked to the cognitive principle of common ground. In Chapter 3, there has already been some preliminary discussion about this concept. Broadly, common ground refers to the knowledge, beliefs, and attitudes shared by the speaker and hearer as the basis for communication. Croft and Cruse (2004) characterize this concept as a type of construal operation. According to them, the use of definite and indefinite articles represent alternate construals of the same situation. Consider (18):

(18) a. Did you see a hedgehog?
     b. Did you see the hedgehog?

In (18) a, the use of the indefinite article indicates that the animal referred to is unknown to the hearer. By contrast, the use of the indefinite article describes the hedgehog as their shared knowledge.

In actual usage events, the speaker and hearer are constantly engaged in assessing the knowledge and intentions of their interlocutors. Seeking common ground is the key to linguistic communication. As Langacker (2008) points out, it is impossible to understand a linguistic expression if there is no common ground between the interlocutors. The same is true of linguistic production because the content of our expression and the way we organize our expression depend to a significant degree on the assumption of the common ground (Clark, 1996). Thus, this concept is a prerequisite for both linguistic expression and interpretation.

7.4.2 Intersubjective Adjustment of Identity Grounds and Identity Identifying Denials

Given the asymmetry of grounds between different participants in a usage event, they may have alternate construals of the same entity or person. In order to communicate successfully, the speaker and hearer have to engage in cognitive coordination of their individual grounds concerning one's identity. Viewed from the perspective of our ICA model, an identity identifying denial is a manifestation of the speaker's intention to instruct the address to consider and abandon some information about one's identity in their individual ground. Consider (19), which involves an alternation between definite and indefinite articles:

(19) Tai Long: You are just a big fat panda.[①]
Po: I'm a big fat panda. I'm the big fat panda.

This dialogue is taken from the Holywood movie *Kung Fu Panda*. Tai Long wanted to express his disdain for Po's kung fu. The use of the indefinite article *a* indicates that Tai Long regarded Po as an unknown panda. And the adjectives *big* and *fat* help evoke the stereotypical image of a panda who is inactive and clumsy. In contrast to this construal, Po uses the definite article *the* to characterizes his identity as part of the common ground shared by Tai Long and others, indicating his uniqueness and popularity. In (19), the two communicative participants are engaged in the cognitive coordination of individual ground concerning Po's

---

① http://www.bjdcfy.com/qita/gfxmjdtc/2017-12/1094191.html.

identity.

Similar denials can be found in Chinese. Consider (20), repeated from (61) in Chapter 5:

(20) "昨天我看到你在给一个女孩子买首饰哦!""不是女孩子,是我表妹。" (BCC)

"Zuotian wo kandao ni zai gei yi ge nühaizi mai shoushi o!"

"Bu shi nühaizi, shi wo biaomei."

yesterday I see you ASP for one-CL girl buy jewelry PRT not girl is my cousin

"Oh, I saw you buying jewelry for a girl yesterday!" "It's not a girl; it's my cousin."

The expression *yi ge nühaizi* ("a girl") in this context may induce an implicature that the man was dating with the girl, who is not the man's family member. Underlying the negation is the intersubjective adjustment process in which the speaker invites the addressee to consider and abandon this way of construal and to update their common ground concerning the girl's identity.

Of course, identity identifying denials in Chinese (as well as English) can also be generated through other ways. In Chinese, the concept of indefiniteness is not always encoded in terms of formal markings. The example of (21), repeated from (63) in Chapter 5, is the case:

(21) 小朋友看着路边执勤的交警,大声喊警察叔叔,只有他一个人不出声。老师问他为什么不一起喊,他说那不是警察叔叔,是我爸爸。 (BCC)

Xiaopengyou kanzhe lubian zhiqin de jiaojing, dasheng han jingcha shushu, zhi you ta yi ge ren bu chusheng. Laoshi wen ta weishenme bu yiqi han, ta shuo na bu shi jingcha shushu, shi wo baba.

Children look-ASP roadside on-duty GEN traffic.police loudly

shout policeman uncle only he one-CL person not speak
teacher ask him why not together shout he say that not police
uncle be my father

The children saw the traffic policeman on duty at the roadside
and then shouted at him loudly, "Uncle policeman!" Only the
boy was silent. The teacher asked him the reason. He said that
the man was not "uncle policeman" but his father.

The negation in (21) also arises from a mismatch of individual grounds
between the speaker and the addressee. Different from (19) and (20), there is no
use of lexical markings indicating its indefiniteness. Rather, the portion of
meaning is induced by contextual factors. Nevertheless, it also lends to the
intersubjective adjustment analysis.

7.5 Meaning Construction of Sequential Identifying Denials

This section is devoted to an exploration of semantic motivations of
sequential identifying denials. It is argued that the semantic motivation of this
type of denials is a mismatch of mental scanning modes between the propositions
in the root and the rectification, and underlying its semantic representation is the
intersubjective coordination activity happening between two subjects of
conceptualization.

7.5.1 Sequential Scanning and Summary Scanning

The meaning construction of sequencing denials is tied to the notion of
mental scanning. Langacker (1987) makes a distinction between summary scanning
and sequential scanning. Summary scanning refers to a mode of viewing in which
all facts of a complex situation are conceived as a whole or activated
simultaneously. By contrast, sequential scanning is described as a mode of
viewing a complex situation as successive series of components. While in the

former a situation is construed as static, and as a state, in the latter it is construed as dynamic, and as a process.

Closely related to the notions are the distinction of processing time and conceived time (Langacker, 2008). Conceived time is a way of viewing time as an object of conception, while processing time is a way of viewing time as the medium of conception. Langacker points out that "there is a natural tendency for conceived time and processing time to be coaligned". That is, the order in which the events are mentally processed parallels the real order in which events are conceived as occurring. This phenomenon is known as temporal iconicity, such that the order of events in the conceived world is mirrored in language, as in *I came, I saw, I conquered*. Given temporal iconicity as a natural tendency, the events are normally interpreted as occurring successively. Consider his example in (22) a. Without any linguistic markers indicating the sequence, the events tend to be interpreted as happening in the time order.

(22) a. I quit my job, got married, and had a baby.

b. I had a baby, got married, and quit my job—in reverse order, of course.

It is worth emphasizing that such iconicity is only a tendency. We can mentally access events and describe them linguistically in a sequence that diverges from their order of occurrence or even runs directly counter to it, as indicated in (22) b.

7.5.2 Intersubjective Adjustment of Mental Scanning Modes and Sequential Identifying Denials

Given the flexibility of mental processing, different communicative participants in a particular usage event may have their own ways of mental scanning concerning the same sets of events. Sequential identifying denials can be characterized as deriving from the inappropriateness of a particular mode of mental scanning in the previous utterances or one's unspoken thought. When a speaker has one model of mental scanning in mind and the addressee the other, the asymmetry will lead the interlocutors to engage in a cognitive coordination activity. Specifically, the speaker invites the speaker to consider and abandon a particular mode of mental scanning and makes him/her accept another. Consider (23), repeated from (64) in Chapter 5:

(23) 甲:咱们父母那一辈人和咱们的生活方式有什么不一样的,不都是恋爱,结婚生孩子吗?

乙:这可不一样,咱们是先恋爱,后结婚,父母那一辈是先结婚,后恋爱。

Jia: Zanmen fumu na yi bei ren he zanmen de shenghuo fangshi you shenme bu yiyang de, bu dou shi lian'ai, jiehun sheng haizi ma?

Yi: Zhe ke bu yiyang. Zanmen shi xian lian'ai, hou jiehun, fumu na yi bei shi xian jiehun, hou lianai.

A: we parents that generation with we GEN life way have what not the-same PRT not all is date marry give-birth baby QM

B: this really not the-same we are first date then marry parent that generation are first marry then date

A: What is the difference in life style between our parents and us? Isn't all about dating, getting married, and having children?

B: No, our generation usually dates first and then gets married. But the generation of our parents generally got married first and then dated.

Different from (22) a, in the first speaker's utterance, the three events *lian'ai* ("date"), *jiehun* ("marry"), and *sheng haizi* ("give birth to babies") are intended simultaneous ones, rather than successive ones. In Langacker's term, it represents the mode of summary scanning, rather than sequential scanning. It is the reason why the utterance is negated by the second speaker. The use of a negative marker has the function of inviting the first speaker to consider and abandon this mode of mental scanning and entertain the sequential one, as indicated by the connectives. The intersubjective adjustment of mental scanning modes can be illustrated in Figure 7.7.

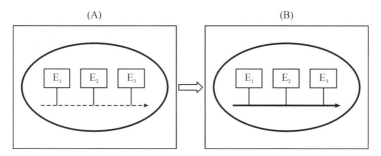

Figure 7.7 Intersubjective Adjustment of Mental Scanning Modes

In Figure 7.7, E_1, E_2, and E_3 represent three events, namely "quitting a job", "getting married" and "having a baby". In diagram (A), the solid circle represents the mode of summary scanning adopted by the first speaker. The dotted line represents a potential but not evoked way of sequential scanning due to temporal iconicity. By contrast, in diagram (B) the solid line represents sequential scanning adopted by the second speaker, as signified by the connectives. Through intersubjective coordination of alternate modes of mental scanning, the speaker makes the address to entertain the thought that the lifestyle of modern young people is quite different from that of their parents.

7.6 Summary

Based on the ICA model, this chapter has discussed the cognitive activities underlying the meaning representations of five types of identifying denials, namely categorical identifying denials, facet identifying denials, relational identifying denials, identity identifying denials, and sequential identifying denials. It is argued that identifying denials are also generated through the intersubjective adjustment of alternate construals of the same situation. The above five categories of identifying denials are derived from different cognitive coordination activities:

(1) Categorical identifying denials involve intersubjective adjustment of categories motivated by prototypicality; (2) Facet identifying denials result from cognitive coordination of clashes of domains profiles related to the same entity; (3) Relational strengthening denials are derived from different (or opposite) trajector/ landmark alignment imposed on the same situation; (4) Identity identifying denials reflect the speaker's attempt to seek common ground about one's identity with the interlocutor; (5) Sequential identifying denials arise from intersubjective coordination of alternate mental scanning modes represented in the root and the rectification. They have the same function of instructing the addressee to consider and abandon a default construal that can give rise to a more specific proposition, and thereby updating the common ground by introducing his/her own construal.

Chapter 8

A Cognitive Linguistic Account of Positioning Denials

In this chapter, we will provide a cognitive linguistic account of the meaning construction of five types of positioning denials, namely relativistic positioning denials, causative positioning denials, deictic positioning denials, structural positioning denials, and evaluative positioning denials. Following the line of argumentation in previous chapters, we intend to show that positioning denials are the linguistic manifestations of intersubjective adjustment of alternate construals with the aim of shifting one's perspective of viewing a state of affairs.

8.1 Meaning Construction of Relativistic Positioning Denials

As discussed in Chapter 5, relativistic positioning denials are characterized as cases of denials that are used to reverse the physical or metaphorical position represented in the root proposition. In order to show how they are cognitively motivated, it is necessary to introduce Langacker's account of viewing arrangement shifting.

8.1.1 Viewing Arrangement

In Langacker's cognitive grammar, viewing arrangement metaphorically refers to the overall relationship between the conceptualizers and the situation being conceptualized. The same situation may be conceptualized in different ways depending on the viewpoints of the conceptualizers or the same conceptualizer on different occasions. The most obvious aspect of perspective is the vantage point. It refers to the actual or imaginary location assumed by a conceptualizer. Normally, a vantage point is the actual location of the speaker and the hearer. For example, the sentences "He went into the forest" and "He came into the forest" presuppose different locations of the speaker: outside the forest and inside the forest, respectively. However, this is just the default arrangement. The vantage point represented in language need not be the speaker's actual position, nor is it limited to space and vision (Langacker, 2008). On the one hand, the same situation can be described from a vantage point other than speaker's. As mentioned in Chapter 3, the speaker may adopt the addressee's viewpoint in uttering "I will come to Chicago tomorrow", when he/she is actually speaking out of Chicago. On the other hand, a vantage point can also be used to describe experience in other domains, in particular, the domain of time. For example, the expressions "the following years" and "years to come" are used to describe temporal concepts.

Another important aspect of viewing arrangement is orientation. It refers to the viewer's position in a given vantage point. From a given vantage point, the same situation can be observed in different orientations. Suppose you are standing at the intersection of two roads, looking forward you will see a road you are not taken, and looking backward you will see a road you have just walked on. The spot you are on will both be a beginning and an ending point depending on your different orientations. Linguistic predications relating to orientation can be based on either the actual orientation of a scene in the field at the time of speaking or else its canonical orientation. (Langacker, 1987)

Describing the same situation from an alternate vantage point or orientation can give rise to truth-conditionally equivalent propositions, and often induce different meaning implications. Although non-canonical construals for vantage points and orientation are much rare, they can offer a novel understanding of the experience and achieve a special rhetorical effect.

8.1.2 Intersubjective Adjustment of Viewing Arrangement and Relativistic Positioning Denials

As discussed in Chapter 5, a relativistic positioning denial is characterized by the relativity of spatial or non-spatial positions represented by the root and rectification. Different from descriptive denials, they are not denying the conceptual content denoted by the root proposition but the presupposed vantage point. Very often, relativistic positioning denials are used to reject a default arrangement. From the perspective of our ICA model, the speaker invites the addressee to consider and abandon the default viewing arrangement represented in the root and introduce another vantage point in order to express his/her own interpretation of the same state of affairs. Consider (1), repeated from (68) in Chapter 5:

(1) 钱老师原来是省田径队的短跑运动员,小偷遇到他只好自认倒霉。他则在旁边憨憨一笑,"不是我跑得快,是小偷跑得太慢了!" (BCC)

Qian laoshi yuanlai shi sheng tianjing dui de duanpao yundongyuan, xiaotou yudao ta zhi hao zi ren daomei. Ta ze zai pangbian hanhan yi xiao, "Bu shi wo pao de kuai, shi xiaotou pao de tai man le!"

Qian teacher turn-out is provincial track-and-field team GEN sprint athlete thief meet he have-to accept bad-luck he simply beside nearby humble smile not I run-PRT fast is thief run-PRT too slow PRT

He turned out to be a sprinter of the provincial track and field team. And the thief had to accept the bad luck. Smiling humbly beside him, Mr. Qian said, "I did not run fast; the thief ran too slowly!"

The speaker in this sentence does not intend to suggest that his running speed is not fast. Rather, the negation is employed to invite the addressee to engage in the cognitive coordination. The rectification has the function of instructing the viewer to take the vantage point of the thief from which the same event is described. The intersubjective adjustment process can be illustrated in Figure 8.1. In Figure 8.1, the circle marked "V" represents the vantage point taken by people who were talking about the running event. Diagram (A) illustrates the conceptualization of the crowd in the context that presupposes the vantage point of the thief. From this vantage point, the teacher's speed becomes the primary focus. By contrast, diagram (B) represents the teacher's construal of the event in which the chasing event is described from his vantage points. Consequently, the thief's speed becomes the focus of attention.

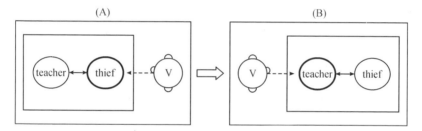

Figure 8.1 Example of Intersubjective Adjustment of Vantage Points

While the default arrangement in (1) is overridden by adopting the vantage point of another participant in the relationship, the non-default arrangement can arise in other ways. According to Langacker (2008), a fictive motion may give rise to non-canonical viewing circumstances. One example he uses to illustrate the point is "The trees are rushing past at 90 miles per hour". The interpretation of the sentence does not involve the actual motion of trees, but an imaginary visual expression. It is found in our data that relativistic positioning denials can also be generated by fictive motion phenomena. Consider (2):

> (2) 搞笑段子:你不是发际线在后退,而是眉毛在下沉。(安慰一名
>   脱发者) [1]

---

[1] https://xw.qq.com/cmsid/20190324B0EDIC00?f=newdc.

Gaoxiao duanzi: Ni bu shi fajixian zai houtui, er shi meimao

zai xiachen. (Anwei yi ming tuofazhe)

funny joke your not hairline ASP recede but eyebrow ASP sink

comfort one-CL loss hair person

Funny joke: Your hairline is not receding; you eyebrow is

sinking. (An utterance used to comfort a hair loss patient)

The speaker in (2) does not intend to suggest that the hairline of the listener

is not receding. Rather, the negation is used to reject the default, literal construal

of the motion event. In our terminology, the speaker invites the addressee to

consider and abandon the default construal in which the vantage point is set on

the eyebrow, and the landmark is the moving event. Further, he/she is instructed

to shift the vantage point to the hairline, which is conceptualized as a fictive

vantage point and an imaginary landmark. This can be illustrated in Figure 8.2.

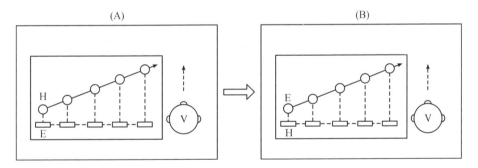

Figure 8.2 Example of Intersubjective Adjustment of Real and Fictive Motion

In Figure 8.2, diagram (A) represents the real description of what happens to

the speaker. The small circle H represents the hairline, which is the trajector of

the moving event, while the small bracket E represents the eyebrow, which is the

landmark. And the solid line represents the real direction of movement of the

hairline relative to the eyebrow (or other stationary parts in the head). While

diagram (A) represents the real description of what happens to the speaker,

diagram (B) represents the non-default viewing arrangement in conceptualizing

the same event. Apprarently, the default arrangement of trajector and landmark in diagram (A) is reversed in diagram (B).

There are cases of relativistic positioning denials derived from shifts of orientations rather than vantage points. Consider (3) - (5):

(3) 婚姻并不是一个故事的结束，而是另一个故事的开始！ (BCC)

Hunyin bing bu shi yi ge gushi de jieshu, er shi ling yi ge gushi de kaishi!

marriage actually not one-CL story GEN end but another-one-CL story GEN beginning

Marriage is not the end of one story, but the beginning of another!

(4) 成交并不是销售工作的结束，而是下一次销售活动的开始。 (BCC)

Chengjiao bing bu shi xiaoshou gongzuo de jieshu, er shi xia yi ci xiaoshou huodong de kaishi.

closing actually not is sale work GEN end but next-one-time sale activity GEN beginning

Closing is not the end of the sales effort, but the beginning of the new sales campaign.

(5) 失恋不是爱情的结束，而是下一个爱情的开始。(BCC)

Shilian bu shi aiqing de jieshu, er shi xia yi ge aiqing de kaishi.

breakup not love GEN end but next-one-CL love GEN beginning

A breakup is not the end of love, but the beginning of the next love.

In each sentence, the speaker and the addressee are engaged in cognitive coordination of orientations. While the root represents a canonical orientation, the rectification represents a non-canonical one. In each case, the end of an event is figuratively reconceptualized as the beginning of another event, leading the addressee to reconsider the state of affairs from a new perspective. This intersubjective adjustment of orientations can be modeled in Figure 8.3.

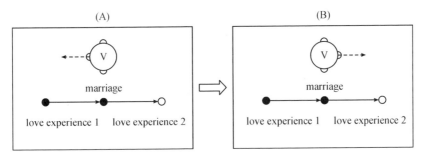

Figure 8.3 Example of Intersubjective Adjustment of Orientations

In Figure 8.3, diagrams (A) and (B) presuppose the orientations in the root and the rectification, respectively. Unlike that of Figure 8.1, the viewer does not shift the position from which the scene is viewed. That is, the vantage point is fixed at the point of marriage, which is at the junction of two different love experiences. Diagram (A) models the orientation conveyed by the root, which construes the point of marriage as an endpoint of the love experience before marriage. Contrary to diagram (A), diagram (B) models the orientation conveyed by the rectification, which construes the point of marriage as a starting point of the love experience after marriage. Figure 8.1 as a whole represents the cognitive coordination of two conversing orientations between two subjects of conceptualization.

8.2　Meaning Construction of Causative Positioning Denials

This section is devoted to exploring how causative positioning denials can be explained in terms of cognitive coordination of alternative construals of an action chain between subjects of conceptualization. We will firstly discuss construal operations concerning action chain profiling, then analyze the meaning construction of two types of causative positioning denials based on the ICA model.

8.2.1 Alternate Profiling of an Action Chain

In Chapter 6, we have already discussed a set of alternate construals concerning the directionality of energy flow in action chain schema: asymmetrical construal and reciprocal construal. It is argued that MN generated by intersubjective adjustment of the two construals can produce a strengthening representational effect. Here, we focus on another somewhat different, but very closely related aspect of action chain profiling that can give rise to positioning representational effect: the conceptual flexibility of profiling different aspects of a given action chain. The language system provides lexical or grammatical means by which certain aspects of a scene can be profiled. Consider (6), which reflects alternate profilings of the same scene:

> (6) a. Jack knocks the door with a hammer.
>
> b. A hammer knocks the door.

The act of knowing the door involves an agent (Jack), a patient (the door) and an instrument (hammer). In (6) a, each aspect of this action chain is profiled: the energy source (Jack), the medium of energy (hammer), and the endpoint of energy (door). On the other hand, in (6) b only the instrument, and the patient are profiled. Nevertheless, the agent is still understood as part of the event of (6) b based on the encyclopedia knowledge that a door generally can not be opened automatically. This phenomenon can be found not only in physical realm but also in various other domains of a cause-effect relation.

8.2.2 Intersubjective Adjustment of Action Chain Profiles and Causative Positioning Denials

The division of the action chain and its profiles makes it possible for a speaker to deny either the existence of an action chain or the appropriateness of profiling certain aspects of the action chain. Given the construal flexibility discussed above, different participants of a usage event may have their own ways of profiling the same action chain. As Langacker (2008) puts it, "When one participant is left unspecified, the other becomes more salient just through the absence of competition. On the other hand, augmenting the salience of one participant diminishes that of others (in relative terms)." Therefore, alternate profiling of an action chain often induces the implicature that the related responsibility or causation should be attributed to the profiled individual or object.

Based on the ICA model, we propose that the intersubjective coordination activity underlies causative positioning denials: the speaker invites the interlocutor to consider and abandon inappropriate profiling of an action chain and subsequently introduces an alternative way of profiling. By doing so, the addressee is instructed to change the original perspective of viewing a particular situation and cancel the related assumptions associated with it. Consequently, their common ground can be updated. Consider (7):

> (7)《孟子》说:"是何异于刺人而杀之,曰:'非我也,兵也!'"意思
> 是,不是我杀你,是武器杀你! 岂不正是这种理论吗? (BCC)
> 《Mengzi》shuo: "Shi he yi yu ci ren er sha zhi, yue:'Fei wo ye,
> bing ye!'" Yisi shi, bu shi wo sha ni, shi wuqi sha ni! Qi bu
> zheng shi zhe zhong lilun ma?
> Mencius-in says this where different from thrust people to kill
> ZHI say not I INT weapon INT meaning is not I kill you is
> weapon kill you how-can-it-be not exactly is this-CL theory QM
> Mencius said, "It is no different from making excuse for killing
> a person by saying 'I did not kill you; the weapon did!'" How
> ridiculous!

In (7), the killer is the source of energy and agent of the killing event. The energy is transferred via the instrumen (the weapon), to the patient (the victim). In the negative clause, the agent and the patient are profiled and the instrument is left implicit. Given the "energy source" status of the agent, profiling an agent can induce the implicature that the killer is the direct causer of the victim's death, thus solely responsible for the assassination. According to the ICA model, the negative clause of this MN utterance has the effect of inviting the addressee to consider and abandon the inappropriate profiling. Subsequently, he/she is oriented to an alternate construal that profiles the INSTRUMENT. The intersubjective adjustment of action chain profiles can be modeled in Figure 8.4.

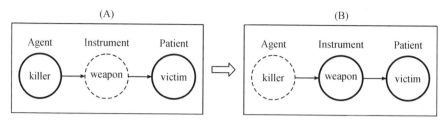

Figure 8.4 Example of Intersubjective Adjustment of Action Chain Profiles

It should be noted that which way of profiling is rejected or selected is highly dependent on the communicative purpose of the speaker. Compare (7) with (8), repeated from (71) in Chapter 5:

(8) 这些人反对禁枪的另一个所谓理由是"杀人的不是枪，而是人"。因此，是人的问题，而不是枪的问题。(BCC)

Zhexie ren fandui jin qiang de ling yi ge suowei liyou shi "sha ren de bu shi qiang, er shi ren". Yinci, shi ren de wenti, er bu shi qiang de wenti.

these people oppose ban gun GEN another one-CL reason is kill people GEN not gun but people therefore is people GEN issue but not gun GEN issue

Another so-called reason why these people oppose the ban on guns is that "It is not the gun that kills people, but the gunman". Therefore, it is not an issue about guns, but an issue about people.

Contrary to (7), the sentence in (8) is intended to attribute the sole responsibility of shooting to the real initiator, i.e. the shooters. For this reason, the speaker invites the addressee to consider and abandon the construal that profiles the instrument and to accept an alternate construal that profiles the agent. In this way, the agent is explicitly specified and becomes the focus of attention. The intersubejctive adjustment process can be modeled in Figure 8.5.

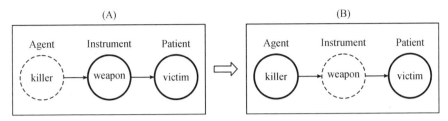

Figure 8.5 Intersubjective Adjustment of Action Chain Profiles in (8)

Causative positioning denials can also be used to foreground an entity that normally does not have the status of the source of energy. Consider (9), repeated from (75) in Chapter 5:

(9) 很多人得病而死亡,其实不是死于疾病,而是死于无知。

Hen duo ren debing er siwang, qishi bu shi si yu jibing, er shi si yu wuzhi.

many people get-sick and die but not die of disease but die of ignorance

Many people get sick and die. In fact, they die not of disease, but ignorance.

In (9), ignorance is deliberately profiled as an upper portion of the action chain and becomes the source of energy. Here, the speaker invites the addressee to focus attention on the appropriateness of regarding the speaker as the initial energy source of the event. Then, he/she is oriented towards another construal in which the upper portion of the action is profiled. The cognitive coordination process can be modeled in Figure 8.6.

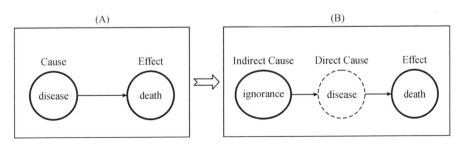

Figure 8.6 Intersubjective Adjustment of Action Chain Profiles in (9)

In diagram (A) of Figure 8.6, the speaker is represented by the round circle A, which is the energy source and initiator of the event. Since there is no other upper portion, the speaker bears the sole responsibility for people's death. By contrast, in diagram (B) the posited upper portion of the energy flow is brought to foreground. Through adjusting the former way of construal, the speaker makes the addressee to realize the potential harm of their ignorance about health.

An illocutionary causative positioning denial (or metapragmatic negation) is considered as a rapport-oriented mitigating device in terms of its interpersonal purposes because it helps to manage interpersonal relationships in interaction (Ran, 2013). However, the previous studies do not examine the underlying cognitive processes that give rise to this mitigating effect. We argue that this type of denials involves intersubjective adjustment of alternate profiles concerning face-threatening speech acts such as "blaming", "criticizing", "abusing" or "threatening". The energy source of the action is what causes the speaker to make this type of speech act. It can be an utterance or behavior of the hearer, or other external factors. Such an action chain can be regarded as an instantiation of the more abstract action chain schema in interpersonal communication. (See Figure 8.7)

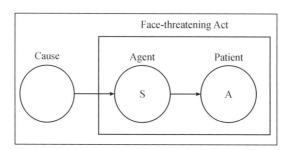

Figure 8.7 Illocutionary Action Chain Underlying Metapragmatic Negation

In Figure 8.7, the circles marked S and A represent the speaker and the addressee, respectively. The small box indicates the face-threatening act done by the speaker to the hearer. In this relationship, the former is the agent, whereas the latter is the patient, the receiver of the speech act. The circle to the left of the bracket represents the supposed cause of the face-threatening act, which assumes the role of "energy source" of the face-threatening act. The possible unwelcome effect of the negative performative force of a face-threatening act can thus be softened by focusing the hearer's attention on the cause of the face-threatening act. In this way, the speaker shifts the perspective from which the event is "viewed". The negation has the function of inviting the addressee to consider the appropriateness of focusing attention on the face-threatening act itself. Let us illustrate the point in the light of (10), repeated from (77) in Chapter 5:

(10) 不是我批评你，你这人虚荣心太强，在班上你就盛气凌人。
(BCC)

Bu shi wo piping ni, ni zhe ren xurongxin tai qiang, zai ban shang ni jiu shengqi-lingren.

not I criticize you you this person vanity so strong in class-in you just domineering

I am not criticizing you, but you are too vain, and you are domineering in class.

In (10), the speaker does not intend to deny his/her performing of blaming speech act. What is done is to instruct the addressee to entertain an inappropriate construal that profiling the face-threatening act. The rectification functions to instruct the addressee to accept an alternate construal that profiles the reason for performing the act, i.e. the implicit "energy source". This process can be shown in Figure 8.8.

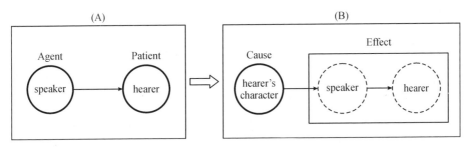

Figure 8.8 Example of Intersubjective Adjustment in Illocutionary Action Chain

As diagram (A) of Figure 8.8 illustrates, in the root proposition both the agent (the speaker) and the patient (the hearer) are profiled. In contrast to diagram (A), in diagram (B) the cause is profiled and the agent and the patient are backgrounded. Through the intersubjective adjustment, the speaker shifts the address's perspective from the speech act of criticizing to the addressee's inappropriate behavior, the upper portion of the energy flow. In this way, the face-threatening effect is mitigated.

8.3 Meaning Construction of Deictic Positioning Denials

This section deals with cognitive processes underlying the meaning representations of deictic positioning denials. By relating the use of deixis to the concept of empathy, we attempt to show how deictic positioning denials receive a semantic account in terms of the intersubjective adjustment of deixis.

8.3.1 Empathy and Deixis

According to Croft and Cruse's (2004) classification, deixis and empathy are different aspects of perspectival construal, and both of them can give rise to alternative construals of the same situation. However, there are some inherent connections between the two concepts. Empathy can be broadly defined as a psychological phenomenon that one person feels into the thought, experience, or emotion of another one. It is a prerequisite for effective communication (Miller & Steinberg, 1975) and constitutes a part of communicative competence (Wilce, 2009). Empathy has also received increasing attention in cognitive-oriented linguistic research (Kuno & Kaburaki, 1977; Kuno, 1987, 2004; Croft & Cruse, 2004; Ran, 2007).

Based on the accommodation theory (Coupland, 1995; Giles & Powesland, 1997; Verschuren, 1999), Ran (2007) proposes another concept that refers to the psychological process opposite to empathy, namely de-empathy. According to him, the purpose of empathy is to shorten the psychological distance between each other in order to achieve the emotional convergence between the two communicators. Contrary to empathy, the pragmatic function of de-empathy is to create or enlarge the social distance between the two parties, thereby alienating the interpersonal relationship between the communicative subjects.

Ran also points out that empathy and de-empathy are the major constraints of functions of personal deixis. He summarizes personal deixis into two categories in terms of the pragmatic functions: pragmatic empathetic deixis and pragmatic de-empathetic deixis. Empathetic deixis is used to shorten the relational distance between the two parties in order to achieve psychological convergence. By contrast, de-empathetic deixis is used to extend the psychological distance between the two parties in order to highlight the psychological divergence. They are manifestations of empathic and de-empathic processes respectively.

8.3.2 Intersubjective Adjustment of Deixis and Deictic Positioning Denials

It is not difficult to find that, for each entity or person, we usually have more than one deixis available. Thus, in a particular usage event, different participants may use different deictic expressions to address the same entity or person, dependent on their social status, personal relations, communicative purpose, or cultural background. When a particular deictic expression used in the context is considered unacceptable, its appropriateness will be disputed. On our view, deixis positioning denials can be characterized as linguistic means used to adjust the psychological distances between the interlocutors. In line with Ran (2007), we argue that the intersubjective adjustment of deixis is achieved through the performance of empathizing or de-empathizing operations.

Let us first consider converging deictic denials. From the perspective of our ICA model, the speaker and the addressee are engaged in the intersubjective adjustment of alternate deixis through the empathizing process, with an aim to shorten the psychological distance between two individuals. Consider (11), repeated from (82) in Chapter 5:

(11) 政委回头望着老洪和王强说:"这是山里来的冯老大爷!"显然
     这称呼使老人很不高兴,他纠正说:"不,同志! 不要叫大爷,

咱们都是同志呀！"（BCC）

Zhengwei huitou wangzhe Lao Hong he Wang Qiang shuo:
"Zhe shi shan li lai de Feng laodaye!" Xianran zhe chenghu
shi laoren hen bu gaoxing, ta jiuzheng shuo: "Bu, tongzhi! bu
yao jiao daye, zanmen dou shi tongzhi ya!"

commissar turn-around look-ASP Lao Hong and Wang Qiang
say this is mountain-in come GEN Feng Uncle apparently this
appellation make old-man very not happy, he correct say not
comrade don't call uncle we all is comrade PRT

The political commissar looked back at Old Hong and Wang
Qiang and said, "This is Master Feng from the mountains!"
Apparently this appellation upset the old man, who corrected,
"No, comrade! Don't call me Master. We're all comrades!"

In (11), *daye* ("uncle") and *tongzhi* ("comrade") represent two different construals of the same person. The former can express the political commissar's respect to the old man, highlighting the psychological distance between them. In order to indicate their common political belief, the old man re-construed himself as the "comrade". The negation used in this example represents the old man's attempt to invite the soldier to reconsider the relationship between them with an aim to shorten their psychological distance. The intersubjective adjustment process can be modeled in Figure 8.9.

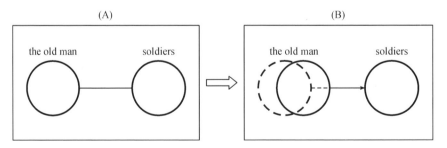

Figure 8.9 Example of Intersubjective Adjustment of Deixis Through Empathy

The two solid circles in diagram (A) of Figure 8.9 represent the speaker (the old man) and the hearers (the soldiers) respectively. And the solid line represents the psychological distance signified by the address honorific *daye* between the speaker and the hearers. In diagram (B) the original deixis position is shifted through empathizing with the soldiers by using the address form *tongzhi*. This empathizing process is indicated by the dotted line moving closer to the soldiers and thereby shortens the distance between them.

In the context of diverging deixis denials, the primary objective is to accentuate the emotional and psychological conflict between the speaker and the addressee. The speaker encourages the addressee to re-evaluate and ultimately reject the inappropriate deixis, which implies a reduced relational distance. This invitation to reassess the deixis is not merely a correction but a strategic move to emphasize disagreement or disapproval, deepening the perceived emotional divide. Unlike converging deixis denials, which aim to reduce social distance and foster agreement, diverging deixis denials facilitate a de-empathizing process. This process effectively widens the psychological and emotional gap, reinforcing the distinction and separation between the communicators. Consider (12):

(12) 小点声……现在皇军，不，鬼子，正在追我呢。从大王庄一直
追到这儿…… (BCC)

Xiaodiansheng ⋯ xianzai huangjun, bu, guizi, zhengzai zhui wo ne. Cong Dawang Zhuang yizhi zhuidao zher ⋯

be-quiet now imperial army not japs ASP chase me INT from Dawangzhuang all-the-time chase to here

Be quiet ... Now the Imperial Army, no, the japs, have been chasing me, from Dawangzhuang to here.

In (12), the speaker is not disputing the fact that he is being pursued by Japanese soldiers. Rather, what he denies is the inappropriate use of the honorific term *huangjun* ("the Imperial Army"), to describe these soldiers. By rejecting this term and its connotations of respect, and substituting it with the derogatory epithet *guizi* ("the japs"), the speaker vividly demonstrates his animosity towards the

Japanese military. This choice of language serves to emphasize his psychological and emotional distance from the Japanese forces. This shift in terminology is not just a linguistic correction but a deliberate intersubjective adjustment that underscores the speaker's de-empathizing process, effectively widening the psychological divide between him and the referenced group. This example illustrates how strategic language use in diverging deixis denials can reinforce social and emotional separation, marking a clear distinction in the speaker's stance and relationship with the subject being discussed.

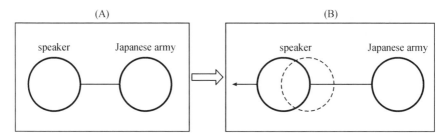

Figure 8.10 Intersubjective Adjustment of Deixis Through De-empathy

The two solid circles in diagram (A) of Figure 8.10 represent the speaker and the referred subject (the Japanese army) respectively. And the solid line represents the psychological distance signified by the address honorific *huangjun* between the speaker and the hearers. In diagram (B), a de-empathizing process is performed, as indicated by the dotted line. The original deixis position is shifted and the corresponding psychological distance is increased with the use of the term *guizi*. It should be noted that the direction of deixis adjustment is also dependent on the communicative goals of the speaker. Compare (12) with (13):

(13) 可是你们是远乡人,又没有良民证,夜里鬼子——不,皇军查店,不但你们吃不消,就是我也犯罪了。(BCC)

Ke shi nimen shi yuanxiangren, you meiyou liangminzheng, ye li guizi——bu, huangjun cha dian, budan nimen chibuxiao, jiu shi wo ye fanzui le.

but you are nonnative and not police-clearance-letter at-night japs not Imperial-Army check hotel not-only you be-in-trouble

even I also guilty PRT

But you are nonnative and do not have police clearance letters.

If the japs … no, the Imperial Army check the shop, not only

will you be in trouble, but I will also be guilty.

Obviously, the deixis adjustment in (12) and (13) are in opposite directions. It is because that the former is derived from an empathizing process, whereas the latter is generated through de-empathizing process. Whichever cognitive process is involved, these sentences are manifestations of intersubjective adjustment of deixis, through manipulating their psychological distances.

8.4 Meaning Construction of Structural Positioning Denials

This section is concerned with the meaning construction of structural positioning denials. We will firstly discuss the construal operations associated with this type of denials, and then present a cognitive analysis of the cognitive activities underlying individuality-based or dynamicity-based positioning denials.

8.4.1 Construal Operations Concerning Individuation and Relationality

Given that structural positioning denials are about the very structure of the entities in a scene and the way in which the structure of an entity or event is characterized, it will be helpful to draw insights from the cognitive linguistic studies of two kinds of constitutive construal: individuality and relationality. The category "individuality" is also known as "plexity" in Talmy's (2000) conceptual structure systems, which has two subcategories: multiplex and uniplex. When a matter or an action is characterized as a set of components, it represents a multiplex construal, or as a homogeneous unit. By contrast, when a matter or an action is describes as a whole unit, it represents a unplex construal. For example,

"I saw a forest and I saw many trees" can be used to represent a uniplex construal and a multiplex construal of the same object, respectively.

Relationality is another constitutive construal that can impose a structure on a scene. Cognitive grammar makes a distinction between nominal predications and relational predications. The latter can be further divided into temporal relational and atemporal relational ones (Langacker, 1987). Temporal relations (process) such as verbs are derived from sequential scanning, whereas atemporal relations such as adjectives result from summary scanning. The same conceptual content can be construed either statically or dynamically, giving rise to different conceptual representations. For example, while the temporal (processual) predication *leave* designates a set of states evolving through time, the static particle *left* designates only the final state of the overall process. Obviously, the alternate construals are represented by different linguistic markings. However, in Chinese, the static construal and the processual construal of a process are generally represented by the same lexical item, without morphological markers. This makes it possible for many unique cases of MN in Chinese which seem rarely occur in English.

8.4.2 Intersubjective Adjustment of Constitutive Construals and Structural Positioning Denials

As discussed earlier, individuality-based positioning denials are used to deny the appropriateness of characterizing the subject as a whole or its constitutive parts. In a uniplex construal, all the individuals are characterized as a whole unit. For this reason, the addressee's attention will be focused on the global features of the scene, rather than the specialty of each individual. Contrary to the multiplex construal, the uniplex construal can generate the assumption that a united and cooperative team will produce competitiveness greater than the sum of its members. If the speaker is dissatisfied with either of them, he/she would invite the addressee to consider and abandon the inappropriate plexity construal and then suggest an alternate one. Consider (14), repeated from (85) in Chapter 5:

(14) 比赛中大家要团结协作,因为你们的对手不是一个个球员,而
是一支配合默契的球队。(BCC)

Bisai zhong dajia yao tuanjie xiezuo, yinwei nimen de duishou

bu shi yi gege qiuyuan, er shi yi zhi peihe moqi de qiudui.

match in you must unite cooperate because you GEN opponent

not one-CL-CL player but one-CL cooperate tacit GEN team

We need to work together in the game, because your opponents

are not individual players, but a team with tacit cooperation.

The denial in (14) is generated by denying an inappropriate construal
concerning individuality of a concept. The phrase *yi gege qiuyuan* ("individual
players") in the negative clause represents a multiplex construal, characterizing
the players as bounded individuals. In contrast to it, the phrase *qiudui* ("a team")
represents a uniplex construal, characterizing the players as relatively homogeneous
collection, without clear boundary. Through adjusting the multiplex construal to a
uniplex one, the speaker shows his/her denial to the real or potential wrong belief
that the opposing team could be defeated without tacit cooperation. The cognitive
coordination process in (14) can be represented in Figure 8.11.

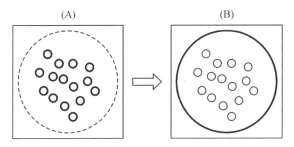

Figure 8.11 Intersubjective Adjustment from a Multiplex to a Uniplex Construal

However, the inverse shifting process might occur if the individuality and
diversity of members of a group should be emphasized. This is the case in (15),
repeated from (86) in Chapter 5:

(15) "物流是一片森林,而非一棵棵树木",这句话反映了物流的系

统性。

"*Wuliu shi yi pian senlin, er fei yi keke shumu*", *zhe ju hua fanyingle wu liu de xitongxing.*

Logistics shi one-CL forest but not one-CL-CL tree this-CL utterance reflect-ASP logistics GEN systematization

"Logistics is a forest, not a tree." This sentence reflects the systematization of logistics.

The denial in (15) is also derived from intersubjective adjustment of a uniplex construal and a multiplex construal, but in a conversing way. The phrase *yi pian senlin* ("a forest") in the negative clause construes the logistics as whole units with distinct parts, while *yi keke shumu* ("individual trees") represents individuals bounded spatiotemporally. Through cognitive coordination, the speaker invites the addressee to abandon the potential wrong belief about logistic business, and places emphasis on the quality of systematicity. It can be diagramed in Figure 8.12.

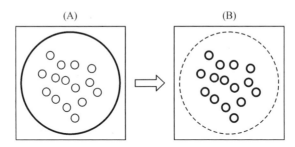

Figure 8.12 Intersubjective Adjustment from a Uniplex Construal to a Multiplex Construal

Similar processes also underlie some cases of MN in which the denoted entities are not generally regarded as a homogeneous category. In order to emphasize their commonplace, the speaker chooses to ignore their heterogeneity of the related categories and construe them as an ad hoc category. Consider (16), repeated from (87) in Chapter 5:

(16) "……教师集体和学生集体要建立密切的联系。"教师集体和儿童集体并不是两个集体，而是一个集体，而且是一个教育集体。

"··· *jiaoshi jiti he xuesheng jiti yao jianli miqie de lianxi.*"
Jiaoshi jiti he ertong jiti bing bu shi liang ge jiti, er shi yi ge
jiti, erqie shi yi ge jiaoyu jiti.

teacher group and children group should establish close GEN
tie teacher group and children group actually not two-CL
group not one-CL group and are one-CL education group
The teachers' group and the students' group need to establish
close ties. They are not two groups, but one. More specifically,
they belong to the same educational group.

In (16), teachers and children are construed as a unified whole in order to
emphasize their interconnection. Similar to the above two sentences, this denial is
also generated by intersubjective adjustment of uniplex/multiplex construals. The
intersubjective adjustment process can be captured in Figure 8.13.

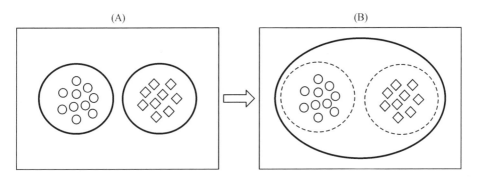

Figure 8.13 Individuality-based Intersubjective Adjustment in (16)

The bold solid circles in diagram (A) of Figure 8.13 represent the construal
of teachers and students as two separate categories, respectively represented by
small circles and diamonds. In diagram (B), the interconnection, represented by
the bold solid circle between the two entities is profiled, and thus the
heterogeneity is backgrounded. Through negation, the speaker shows his/her
denial of the real or potential beliefs about their heterogeneity followed by a
corrective clause that emphasizes their interconnection or homogeneity.

Different from individuality-based cases, dynamicity-based denials are derived from intersubjective adjustment of dynamic/static construals of the same situation, depending on whether a situation can be construed as a dynamic process or the final state. Consider (17):

(17) 分手真的不是一个结果，而是一个过程。给自己一段时间，慢慢地你就不怎么在乎他了。(BCC)

Fenshou zhende bu shi yi ge jieguo, er shi yi ge guocheng. Gei ziji yi duan shijian, manman de ni jiu bu zenme zaihu ta le.

separation really not one-CL result, but one-CL process give self a period time gradually-PRT you simply not so care him ASP

Breaking up is really not an outcome, but a process. Give yourself some time, and gradually you won't care much about him.

The lexical items *jieguo* ("result") and *guocheng* ("process") designate a state and a process respectively. In the root, the concept of *fenshou* ("separate/ separation") is construed as a final state of the human mind. The base for this static construal is a dynamic process, which is left unprofiled. The same state of affairs in the corrective proposition is characterized as continuous series of states evolving through time. This makes the process become a prominent facet. Figure 8.14 captures the intersubjective coordination activity.

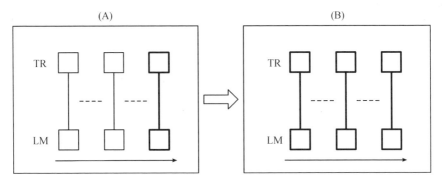

Figure 8.14 Intersubjective Adjustment from a Static Construal to a
Dynamic Construal

Following the notational devices in Langacker (1987), the boxes indicate entities, the line connecting two entities indicate their relationship, and the arrow indicates conceived time. The upper profiled entity in a relationship is the trajector, and the lower one is the landmark. A relationship obtains between the trajector and landmark of a process at every point during its evolution through time; each point defines a separate state within the process (Langacker, 1987). Diagram (A) of Figure 8.14 represents the stative construal, where the last portion of the continuous series of states is profiled, as indicated in bold line. By contrast, diagram (B) represents the processual construal, where the overall process becomes the prominent facets of both concepts.

Conversely, the speaker may invite the addressee to consider and abandon a stative construal and adopt a processual one, whereby the continuous series of states distributed through time is profiled. Through intersubjective adjustment, the addressee is taken to reject the processual construal and choose the static one, thereby canceling out the assumption associated with the former construal. This is the case in (18):

> (18) 赚钱不是一个过程，而是结果，是你做好一件事顺带的结果。①
>
> *Zhuan qian bu shi yi ge guocheng, er shi jieguo, shi ni zuohao yi jian shi shundai de jieguo.*
>
> make money not one-CL process but result is you do well one-CL thing incidentally GEN result
>
> Money making is not a process, but a result. It is the incidental byproduct of doing one thing well.

The denial in (18) is not a DN because earning money is a dynamic process in character. The root of the negation represents the default construal of money-making event, i. e. the processual construal. This default way of construal is rejected and replaced by a stative one by focusing on the final state of the same

---

① https://www.wdzj.com/hjzs/ptsj/20180211/548874-1.html.

event. In this way, human wealth and entrepreneurship are characterized as natural results of a dynamic process. This process can be illustrated in Figure 8.15.

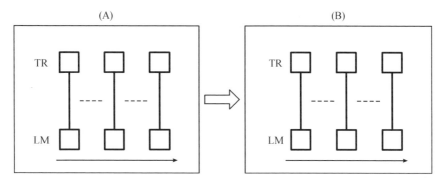

Figure 8.15 Intersubjective Adjustment from a Dynamic Construal to a
Static Construal

Obviously, the adjustment of construals is just in the opposite direction. Diagram (A) of Figure 8.15 represents the processual construal which profiles the overall process of making money, while diagram (B) represents the stative construal, which only profiles the final state of the continuous series of states is profiled.

8.5 Meaning Construction of Evaluative Positioning Denials

In this section, we will discuss the interconnection between frame and evaluative connotation, then show how evaluative positioning denials can be derived from intersubjective adjustment of alternate ways of framing the same situation.

8.5.1 Intersubjective and Intrasubjective Frame-shifting

As already mentioned in the discussion of the cognitive semantic accounts, alternate ways of framing a single situation may give rise to different evaluative connotations of the lexical items. Examples like "Mary is not stingy but thrifty" which lend to the frame-semantic account are actually what are termed as "evaluative positioning denials" in this study. However, the existing accounts pay little attention to the dimension of intersubjective coordination, which is closely tied to the function of linguistic negation in the meaning construction of such phenomenon.

As we have already pointed out in Chapter 3, it is plausible to make a distinction between intrasubjective construal adjustment and intersubjective construal adjustment. It follows that frame-shifting can also be sub-categorized into intrasubjective and intersubjective cases. Intrasubjective frame-shifting involves alternate construals of the same situation within a single discourse participant at a particular usage event. For example, "We will win the battle of environment protection.", "The woman is like an angel." "Sometimes Tom is stingy, and sometimes he is stingy." By contrast, intersubjective frame-shifting concerns adjustment of alternate frames across different subjects of conceptualization, or of the same subject of conceptualization at different times of speaking. The latter is more complex than the former for the reason that the interaction between two mental states is essential for its meaning representation. In the following section, we will show how the intersubjective adjustment of frames gives a more refined explanation of the meaning construction of evaluative positioning denials.

8.5.2 Intersubjective Adjustment of Frames and Evaluative Positioning Denials

An evaluative positioning denial can be characterized as being derived from intersubjective adjustment of alternate framings of a single situation. Consider (19), repeated from (99) in Chapter 5:

(19) 文学界的假古典派仍然在抄袭中讨生活,他们不是强大,而是顽固。

Wenxue jie de jia gudianpai rengran zai chaoxi zhong tao shenghuo, tamen bu shi qiangda, er shi wangu.

Literary world GEN pseudo classicists still in plagiarize-in make living they not strong but stubborn

The pseudo-classicists in the literary world are still making a living by plagiarism. They are not strong, but stubborn.

In (19), the propositions in the root and the rectification denote the same state of affairs, i.e. the pseudo-classicists are tenacious and unwilling to withdraw from the literary world. However, they profile it against different frames: *qiangda* ("strong") describes the behavior of the pseudo-classicists in contrast with *ruoxiao* ("weak"), while *wangu* ("stubborn") describes their behavior in contrast with *biantong* ("flexible"). Therefore, the two alternate ways of framing represent different scales of measurement. This negation prompts for a cognitive process in which the addressee is invited by the speaker to consider and abandon the former scale of measurement and accept the latter. This process can be modeled in Figure 8.16.

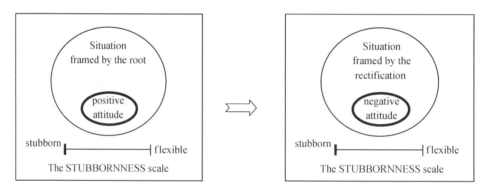

Figure 8.16 Example of Intersubjective Adjustment of Alternate Framings

This analysis shares some essential points with the frame semantic account. However, it gives a more refined explanation of its meaning mechanism by incorporating the intersubjective view of negation. Moreover, by orienting our attention to the intersubjective dimension, it also sheds light on how its "garden-path" effect is created. Given that negating a positive value directs our attention to a value within the negative range, the speaker may entertain the addressee's state of mind in advance, deliberately run counter to what would be predictable, and create a semantic contradiction. The process can be diagrammatically represented in Figure 8.17.

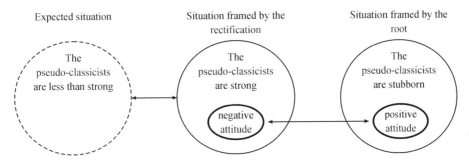

Figure 8.17 Example of the Generation Process of Garden Path Effect

The dotted circle denotes the expected situation activated by the negative clause, which contains the default assumption that the pseudo-classicists are less than strong. This situation is rejected and the related assumption is denied by the following-up clause, which places the value at the much higher point of the stenghth scale. The positive connotation of the lexical item *qiangda* ("strong") may not be profiled in the first interpretation. However, the semantic contradiction cues for the hearer to focus on this meaning aspect and forms a sharp contrast with the negative connotation expressed in the subsequent corrective clause. The same analysis can also be applied to analyzing the garden-path effect of other types of denials.

8.6 Summary

Based on the conceptual framework developed in the previous chapter, this chapter has characterized the meaning construction of positioning denials, including relativistic positioning denials, causative positioning denials, deictic positioning denials, structural positioning denials, and evaluative positioning denials. It is found that strengthening denials are generated through the intersubjective adjustment of alternate construals of the same situation that give rise to propositions of equal semantic or informational strength. The above five categories of strengthening denials are derived from different cognitive coordination activities between subjects of conceptualization: (1) Relativistic positioning denials involve adjustment of viewing arrangement between two conceptualizers; (2) Causative positioning denials are derived from cognitive coordination of alternate action chain profiles; (3) Deictic positioning denial are the linguistic manifestations of deixis adjustment between the interlocutors through empathizing and de-empathizing operation; (4) Structural positioning denials are closely associated with intersubjective adjustment activities on the basis of individuation and relationality; (5) Evaluative positioning denials can be accounted by intersubjective adjustment of alternate ways of framing. Taken together, positioning denials are generated through the following processes: the speaker invites the addressee to consider and abandon a particular perspective, and to update the common ground by suggesting another perspective, thereby creating a positioning representational effect.

Chapter 9

A Cognitive Linguistic Account of Formal Denials

In this chapter, we will offer a cognitive linguistic account of the meaning construction of three types of formal denials, namely phonological denials, collocation denials, and stylistic denials. It will relate formal denials to the construal operation of "schematicity" and the concept of "sanction" in Langacker's cognitive grammar. We propose that the formal denials are the linguistic manifestations of intersubjective adjustment of sanctioning relations encoded in the conventional linguistic units (i. e. sanctioning structures) and the contextual linguistic expressions (i.e. target structures).

9.1 Meaning Construction of Phonological Denials

This section will firstly introduce the concept of "sanction" which is related to the construal operation of schematicity. Then, it will show how a phonological denial can be explained in terms of the adjustment of phonological sanctioning relations between different subjects of conceptualization.

9.1.1 Full Sanction and Partial Sanction

As already discussed in Chapter 6, human beings possess the cognitive ability to conceptualize the same situation at different levels of schematicity. This parameter of construal is also reflected in the relationship between grammatical patterns and specific language expressions. Langacker describes the linguistic expression used to conceptualize a particular situation as target structure, and the conventionalized linguistic unit as sanctioning structure (Langacker, 1987). The target structure represents a symbolic relationship between a specific conceptualization of a state of affairs and some phonological structure or actual vocalization. It is created by language users in a particular context for a specific communicative purpose. By contrast, the sanctioning structure is a more schematic structure representing the abstract commonality of detailed linguistic expressions in different contexts. Given the richness and variety of actual usage events, a conventional unit can give rise to an unlimited number of symbolic realizations with different sanctioning relations.

When a target structure is fully sanctioned by a schema, the sanctioning structure provides a full, or direct sanction to the target structure. That is, the latter fully meets the specifications of the former. For example, suppose the sentence "There is a house" denotes a house with all essential features of a typical house. The conceptual structure of the word "house" in this usage event is fully sanctioned by the conceptual structure of the conventional unit. Following the standard practice in Langacker's cognitive grammar, the linguistic unit *house,* which is the sanctioning structure can be represented as [[HOUSE]/[house]]. It consists of the semantic unit [HOUSE] and the phonological unit [house]. The square bracket in between represents the conventionalized status of the linguistic unit. The target structure can be represented as ((HOUSE')/(house')). The close curves indicate the non-unit status of the words. A solid arrow is used to represent the relation of schematicity between the sanctioning structure and the target structure. Thus, the full sanction relation has the following formulaic representation: ([[TRIANGLE]/[triangle]]→((TRIANGLE')/(triangle'))).

In partial sanction, the specifications of the sanctioning structure and the target structure are not fully compatible. The target exhibits deviant behavior in certain aspects of their semantic or phonological structure. Suppose you encounter a temporary house-like shelter that provides transit accommodations for homeless people in disaster, and you react by uttering "There is a house". The use of the lexical item house is a case of partial sanction. The reason is that the sanctioning structure is only partially schematic for the target: there are a few properties of the house-like shelter which conflict with the specification of the sanctioning structure. The partial sanction relation can be represented by the following representation: ([[TRIANGLE]/[triangle]--->((TRIANGLE')/(triangle'))). In contrast to the solid arrow in full sanction representation, a dotted arrow is used to indicate the target structure is fully compatible with the sanctioning structure.

9.1.2 Intersubjective Adjustment of Phonological Sanctioning Relations and Phonological Denials

The idea that the target structure can be sanctioned in different ways is not restricted to its conceptual structure. Given a variety of phonological realizations of the same conventional units and varying linguistic capacities of language users, different communicative participants may have their own way of instantiating the schema. As we saw in Chapter 5, a phonological denial is used to negate a mispronounced lexical item in the context. The negated lexical item is only partially sanctioned by the conventionalized linguistic unit (i. e. sanctioning structure) because the phonological structure is deviant and ill-formed. For this reason, the lexical item is not judged to be a legitimate member of the category it is supposed to denote. Based on the ICA model, it can be argued that phonological denials involve adjustment of sanctioning relations between two participants. Consider (1), repeated from (104) in Chapter 5:

(1) "你这是污蔑, 赤 guǒguǒ 的污蔑!"龚平纠正道:"不是赤 guǒ-guǒ,是赤 luǒluǒ······连这个字都认错。" (BCC)
   "Ni zhe shi wumie, chiguǒguǒ de wumie!" Gong Ping jiuzheng dao:
   "Bu shi chiguǒguǒ, shi chigluǒluǒ ··· lian zhe ge zi dou rencuo."
   you this is slander sheer GEN slander Gong Ping corrected say not sheer lian this-CL character even mistake"
   "You are slandering, sheer (*chiguǒguǒ* in Chinese) slandering!" Gong Ping corrected, "It's not *chiguǒguǒ*; it's *chiluǒluǒ* ... How

can you be so illiterate? "

The term *chiluoluo*, pronounced [chìluǒluǒ], is a conventional linguistic unit in Chinese. In the root of negation, it is mispronounced as [chìguǒguǒ], probably because the basic part of the character (i. e. root) *guo* ("fruit") is pronounced [guǒ]. While its morphological and grammatical structures are identical to the sanctioning structure, the phonological structure only receives partial sanction because it is not fully compatible with the conventional vocalization of the linguistic unit. For this reason, the lexical item is not judged to be a legitimate member of the category it is supposed to denote. The illegitimacy is made explicit by comparing it with its counterpart in the rectification which is fully sanctioned because the specification of sanctioning and target structure is fully compatible. Thus, the negation in (1) reflects the cognitive coordination process of sanctioning relations between two participants. This process can be illustrated in Figure 9.1.

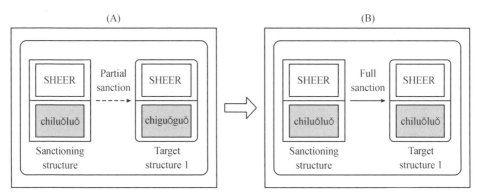

Figure 9.1 Example of Intersubjective Adjustment of Phonological
Sanctioning Relations

Diagram (A) of Figure 9.1 illustrates categorization in which the target structure is only partially sanctioned by the sanctioning structure, indicated by the dotted arrow. While the semantic structure of the target structure and sanctioning structure are fully compatible, their phonological structures are not identical. This relation can be represented as follows: ([[SHEER]/[chiluǒluǒ]] → ((SHEER ')/ (chiguǒguǒ'))). Diagram (B) of Figure 9.1 illustrates categorization in which the target structure is fully sanctioned by the sanctioning structure, indicated by the solid arrow. Both the semantic structure and the phonological structure of the target structure are fully compatible with the sanctioning structure. This relation can be represented as follows: ([[SHEER]/[chiluǒluǒ]] --- > ((SHEER')/(chiluǒluǒ'))). Figure 9.1 as a whole represents the following activity: the speaker invites the addressee to consider and abandon the way of instantiating the conventional unit (because it only receives partial sanction), then he/she introduces an acceptable way of instantiation.

9.2 Meaning Construction of Collocation Denials

In what follows, the meaning construction of collocation denials will be discussed based on the account of linguistic creativity in Langacker's cognitive grammar. It will be shown that collocation denials also reflect the adjustment of different sanctioning relations between two conceptualizers. However, different from phonological denials, a collocation denial pertains to elaborating the semantic structures rather than the phonological structure of a linguistic unit.

9.2.1 Partial Sanction and Generation of Novel Structure

Obviously, language use is not a simple matter of language users making use of the finite set of conventional units stored in their minds. Novel expressions frequently emerge in our daily communication. According to Langacker (1987), schematic patterns sanction both established and novel structures. Language creation which gives rise to novel structures depends more on partial rather than full sanction, and whose sanction comes only from elaboratively distant sources. For example, the word *minzhu-dang* ("democratic party") receives full sanction from the more schematic structure *X+dang*, which is conventionally used for political groups. On the analogy of the conventionally entrenched word, the new formation *xuesheng-dang* ("students") was coined to designate the group of students, especially college students. This expression does not sanction itself because it does not refer to a particular political group. However, it receives indirect sanction from a more abstract schema (i.e. the affixed compound *X+Affix*) and qualifies it as an acceptable lexical item. With frequent use, the originally novel structure becomes progressively entrenched and finally becomes a conventional linguistic unit. This has the result that a new schema has been extracted containing the common sense of the original and new subcases.

There is also a further extension of this group of structures in recent years, such as *aoye-dang* ("people who are used to stay up late"), *pingguo-dang* ("people who use iPhone") and *qiongyou-dang* ("people who like traveling on a budge"). Assuming this formation is created on the analogy of *xuesheng-dang*, it only receives partial sanction from the lexical item because it does not designates a particular social group but people pursuing a particular activity. Such new structures will be judged as legitimate to the degree that they elaborate the remote, more abstract schema *X+dang*. The partial sanction will activate the specifications shared by the two structures and help to establish a schematic structure that consists of these specifications. The new schema is also represented in the form of *X+dang*, but it acquires a new sense, i.e. group of people with common goals or interest.

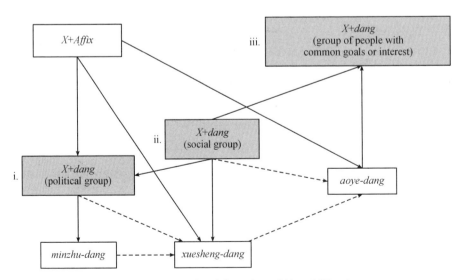

Figure 9.2 Example of Sanction of Novel Structure

9.2.2 Intersubjective Adjustment of Grammatical Sanctioning Relations and Collocation Denials

In a collocation denial, the negated lexical item in the root and its counterpart in the rectification are sanctioned in different ways. While the former is fully sanctioned by the sanctioning structure, the latter (i. e. the novel collocation) is only partially sanctioned when it is originally used. In a collocation denial, the speaker invites the addressee to consider and abandon the full-sanction manner of construing an entity or state of affairs, then introduces a partial-sanction construal which gives rise to a novel structure. Consider (2), repeated from (107) in Chapter 5:

(2) 养猫的人肯定发现了这个秘密:你家的猫咪根本不是一只猫,
  而是一条猫,一坨猫,一滩猫。抱起来后变成一条,睡觉时变成
  一滩,蜷缩在窗台上就变成了一坨。[①]

  Yang mao de ren kending faxianle zhe ge mimi: ni jia de maomi
  genben bu shi yi zhi mao, er shi yi tiao mao, yi tuo mao, yi tan
  mao. Bao qilai hou biancheng yi tiao, shuijiao shi biancheng yi
  tan, quansuo zai chuangtai shang jiu bianchengle yi tuo.

  keep cat GEN person must discover-ASP this-CL secret you
  family GEN cat at. all not one-CL cat but one-CL cat one-CL
  cat one-CL cat hug-up after become one-CL sleep when become
  one-CL curl-up on windowsill-on simply become-ASP one-CL

  People who have cats must have discovered this secret: your cat
  is not "a cat" at all, but "a strip of cat", and "a puddle of cat",
  and "a pile of cat". It becomes a "strip" when you pick it up, a
  "pool" when it sleeps, and a "pile" when it curls up on the
  windowsill.

[①] https://new.qq.com/omn/20180412/20180412A0GHK3.html.

yi zhi mao is a conventional collocation for native speakers of Chinese. The sanction it receives from well-entrenched *Num+CL+N* reinforces its legitimacy as part of the Chinese language. By contrast, the collocations in the corrective clause are highly novel and context-dependent. In other words, they do not sanction themselves. They only receive partial sanctions from *yi zhi mao* and the established schema *Num+tiao+N*. However, these collocations are fully sanctioned by the schema *Num+CL+N* which qualifies them as acceptable in the context. The intersubjective adjustment of different sanctioning relations can be modeled in Figure 9.3.

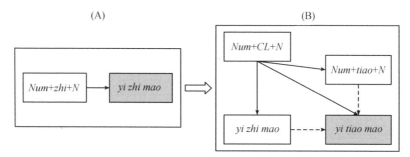

Figure 9.3 Example of Intersubjective Adjustment of Collocational
Sanctioning Relations

Diagram (A) of Figure 9.3 represents the full sanction of the target structure (represented in the shadowed block) received from the schema *Num+CL+N*, marked by the solid arrow. Diagram (B) represents the sanctions received by the novel collocation *yi tiao mao*. The two dotted arrows indicate that this novel collocation is only partially sanctioned by the conventional expression *yi zhi mao* and the schema *Num+tiao+N*. The solid arrow between the target structure and the schema *Num+CL+N* represents the full sanction relation between them, which supports the acceptability of the novel collocation.

As we have discussed, with repeated uses a novel structure will become established in its own right and can become the sanctioning structure for other target structures. On this occasion, the contextual usage of the same lexical item will receive full sanction from the sanctioning structure because it has already become part of the inventory of conventional linguistic units. For example, using the classifier "枚" (*mei*) to modify a person is originally a highly contextual and novel expression, not widely used in modern Chinese. However, in recent years, the novel structure has progressively become a well-entrenched and acceptable structure, which is often used to describe non-adult people who are cute or pretty (Zeng, 2010; Zhang, 2017). Consider (3), repeated from (106) in Chapter 5:

(3) 甲:看看这张照片,想当年你爸爸也是一个帅哥。

乙:您不是一个帅哥,而是一枚帅哥。[①]

Jia: Kankan zhe zhang zhaopian, xiangdangnian ni baba ye shi yi ge shuaige.

Yi: Nin bu shi yi ge shuaige, er shi yi mei shuaige.

A: look this-CL photo in-the-past your dad also is one-CL handsome-guy

B: you not one-CL handsome-guy but one-CL handsom-.guy

A: Look at this photo, I used to be *yegeshuaige* ("a handsome guy") when I was young.

B: Not *ye ge shuaige* ("a handsome guy"), but *yi mei shuaige* ("a handsome guy").

Suppose the conversation occurs in a situation when the novel collocation *yi mei shuaige* ("a handsome guy") is not well entrenched. It only receives partial sanction from both the conventional collocation and the highly entrenched schema *Num+mei+N*. However, the novel structure is still acceptable in modern Chinese syntactically because it receives full sanction from the more abstract and remote schema *Num+CL+N*. With repeated uses, a new schema will be extracted from the shared semantic structures of the two collocations. (See Figure 9.4)

---

① https://zhidao.baidu.com/question/207820688325434005.html.

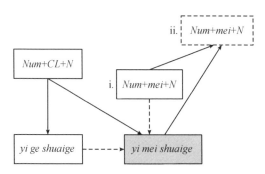

Figure 9.4 Sanction of the Novel Collocation *yi mei shuaige*

As we note, such a collocation has been used repeatedly and has gradually become an acceptable structure. When the same expression is used, it will receive direct sanction from the newly-established linguistic unit. In other words, both the collocation *yi ge shuaige* in the negative clause and *yi mei shuaige* in the corrective clause receives full sanction from their respective sanctioning structures.

9.3 Meaning Construction of Stylistic Denials

In what follows, stylistic denials will be analyzed based on the cognitive grammar view of the discourse genre. It will be argued that a stylistic denial is motivated by the inappropriate elaboration of the register or style schema expected by the speaker. Like phonological denials and collocation denials, a stylistic denial also reflects the intersubjective coordination of different sanctioning relations between the sanctioning structures and the target structures.

9.3.1 Genre as Schema and Its Instantiation

According to Langacker (2008), discourse genre can be characterized in a similar way to the linguistic units at other levels. He (2008) uses the notion of schemata to categorize the necessary knowledge associated with a particular discourse genre:

[o]ur knowledge of a given genre consists of a set of schemata

abstracted from encountered instances. Each schema represents a recurring commonality in regard to some facet of their structure: their global organization, more local structural properties, typical content, specific expressions employed, matters of style and register, etc.

A particular genre schema and its constitutive schemata embody our expectations about the genre and serve as templates in producing and apprehending new instances. Drawing on the notion of sanction, a given genre schema, and its constitutive schemata can be characterized as the sanctioning structures, while particular language expressions or structures used in a particular discourse can be treated as the target structure. A given genre schema imposes restrictions on specific linguistic expressions or structures that are used to elaborate it. For example, an expression typically used in a face-to-face conversation register will not receive sufficient sanction from the schema of a poetic genre due to factors such as rhyme, meter, and a number of lines per stanza.

9.3.2 Intersubjective Adjustment of Genre Schemas and Stylistic Denials

In actual usage events, the register or style of a particular expression may totally match or deviate from the specifications of a genre schema to some degree. In other words, it may receive full, partial or no sanction from the conventionalized genre schema. From the perspective of our ICA model, a stylistic denial manifests the intersubjective coordination of different sanctioning relations between an expected genre schema and its constitutive schemata. Specifically, the speaker invites the addressee to consider and abandon a non-sanction or partial-sanction manner of instantiating an expected genre schema or its constitutive schemata, then introduces a full-sanction one. Consider (4), repeated from (108):

(4) 当翻译将馆长的解说译成"这尊雕像非常真实"时,江主席立即纠
正说:"不,应该说是'栩栩如生'!" (BCC)

Dang fanyi jiang guanzhang de jieshuo yicheng "zhe zun diaoxiang feichang zhenshi" shi, Jiang Zhuxi liji jiuzheng shuo: "Bu, yinggai shuo shi 'xuxu-rusheng' !"

when translator make curator GEN explanation translate as this-CL statue very real when Jiang chairman immediately correct say not should say is lifelike

When the translator translated the curator's explanation as "this statue looks like a real one", Chairman Jiang immediately corrected, "No, you should use the word 'lifelike'!"

The colloquial expression *feichang zhenshi* ("very real") violates the restriction imposed by a museum commentary genre (as well as other literary genres) on the stylistic features (formality) of language. While it is a legitimate elaboration of some spoken-language genres, it does not receive sufficient sanction from the expected genre schema because of the low level of formality. By contrast, the expression *xuxu-rusheng* ("lifelike") is a fairly literary expression, which can well elaborate the museum commentary genre. Therefore, it receives full sanction from the expected genre schema. Likewise, the colloquial expressions *pigu* in (109) and *fujia* in (110) in Chapter 5 are common in conversation compared to formal registers. Denying these expressions reflects the speakers' reluctance to conceptualize them as illegitimate elaborations of the expected formal registers.

9.4 Summary

This chapter has presented a detailed analysis of the meaning construction of three types of formal denials, namely phonological denials, collocation denials, and stylistic denials. All these denials are generated on the basis of the cognitive principle of "schematicity" and different sanctioning relations between the sanctioning structure and the target structure in the root and the rectification. The latter can be understood as alternate construals of the same situation between different individuals. Phonological denials involve intersubjective adjustment of different phonological sanctioning relations, collocation denials result from intersubjective adjustment of different grammatical sanctioning relations, and stylistic denials are based on adjustment of different sanctioning relations between a genre schema and its constitutive schemata. Through adjustment of sanctioning relations between the conventional units and target structure, the speaker and the addressee update their common ground concerning formal features of the expressions being discussed.

Chapter 10

Conclusion

This study represents a usage-based and cognitive-based account of a linguistic phenomenon traditionally studied within the realm of pragmatics, namely metalinguistic negation. Over the past few decades, it has been treated as a pragmatic phenomenon that directly bears upon the classic topics of implicature, presupposition, and pragmatic principles. Researchers working in the field of pragmatics have proposed a few theoretical accounts for the "ambiguity" of negation and derivation mechanisms of MN. A number of pragmatic accounts have been proposed, including the standard accounts, the relevance-theoretical accounts, and the idiomatic account. While these studies are undoubtedly insightful and influential, they rest either explicitly or implicitly on the theoretical assumption that meaning is independent of the users' bodily experience and conceptual system. Most of them adopt the intuition-based approach, as reflected by their use of infelicitous invented examples.

MN has also received much attention from linguists working in the frameworks of cognitive semantics, giving rise to a few accounts such as the frame-denying account, the ICM-denying account, and the dynamic categorization account. Among them, the frame-denying account, proposed by Charles Fillmore, represents pioneering attempts to reveal the conceptual motivations of the marked use of negation. However, like the pragmatic accounts, they have largely been conducted without recourse to intuitive language data. Researchers tend to draw conclusions based on a handful of invented examples, which may not reflect the true picture of the actual use of MN. Yet "linguistic analysis will benefit if it is based on real language used in real contexts" (Meyer, 2002). Needless to say, as new linguistic evidence arises, the existing accounts need to move forward and revise their postulates. Obviously, corpora and other sources of real linguistic data play a role both in testing and developing the existing accounts. Another problem with the existing accounts is that they lack a description of the cognitive underpinning of linguistic negation operators, that is, their function at the conceptual level. Nor do researchers begin to consider the roles of a wider array of cognitive operations than cognitive semantic concepts such as framing and categorization.

In recent years, an experiential view of linguistic negation has been developed within the field of cognitive linguistics. The model of intersubjectivity proposed by Verhagen (2005) provides a novel interpretation of the conventional meaning and conceptual function of linguistic negation, shedding new light on the old dispute of "ambiguity" of linguistic negation in pragmatic studies. Researchers in cognitive grammar have proposed a rich set of construal operations that help us explain the various ways in which the non-truth-conditional aspects of meaning can be derived. These construal operations may equally serve as the cognitive basis for the generation of MN.

Drawing insights from both models, it is proposed that the existing accounts can be revised and updated by considering authentic linguistic data in modern Chinese and various other cognitive processes. Our most important contribution is to provide an explanatorily adequate account of MN in modern Chinese. It has provided an innovative interpretation of the "ambiguity" of negation (i. e. the "conceptual ambiguity" position) in terms of its conventional function at the conceptual level, and developed a new theoretical model (i.e. the intersubjective construal adjustment model). In the meantime, we wish to base this explanatory account on a descriptively adequate account of the phenomenon by adopting the usage-based approach as methodology. In doing so, this study is intended to offer insights on the description and explanation of MN, and inform further attempts on the dialogue between the related theories and disciplines.

10.1 Major Findings

The major findings of the present study can be summarized in the following paragraphs. These findings have, by and large, answered the research questions proposed in Chapter 2.

10.1.1 Cognitive Grounding of the "Ambiguity" of Negation

Based on Langacker's model of construal, we argue that MN should be not characterized as a "semantic ambiguity", or a "pragmatic ambiguity"; rather, it is a matter of "conceptual ambiguity". That is, the "ambiguity" of negation does not purely reside either at the semantic or pragmatic level, but at the conceptual level. It is closely associated with the two-fold nature of conceptualization, which consists of both conceptual content and a particular way of construing that content. This feature makes it possible for a single proposition to be denied in two different ways: A speaker can either object to the conceptual content, including the existence of certain attributes, entities, and the relationships between entities, or simply reject the way of construing this conceptual content. Given its conceptual nature, our view of the "ambiguity" of negation can be termed the "conceptual ambiguity". It is intended as an alternative account to the "semantic ambiguity" and the "pragmatic ambiguity". This view can be treated as another version of "metarepresentational" ambiguity, different from the relevance-theoretical one.

In line with Verhagen's model of intersubjectivity, it is further argued that the negation operators in natural languages should not be considered as merely relating language to the object of conceptualization, with a function of reversing the truth value of a proposition. Rather, they should be characterized as linguistic means of cognitive coordination, with the function of inviting the addressee to consider and abandon a particular epistemic stance towards some idea. In this sense, MN is a linguistic phenomenon that reflects the cognitive coordination of alternative ways of construing the same situation. The integrated model we develop in this study endows researchers with a powerful set of analytical tools capable of dealing with a broader range of MN phenomena than in the previous accounts.

10.1.2 Semantic Patterns of MN in Modern Chinese and Its Classification

Our data analysis focus on three major forms of MN of negative utterances, namely *bu shi X, (er) shi Y, bu* or *bu shi* as discourse marker, and *Y, (er) bu shi X*. Based on a careful examination of data collected from BCC and the internet, this study has presented a comprehensive description of their semantic behavior. In line with Moeschler (2019), MN has been classified in terms with different representational effects (or propositional, cognitive effects), as reflected in the meaning impact of the rectification. Four major types of MN have been identified, namely strengthening denials, identifying denials, positioning denials, and formal denials. Strengthening denials are cases of MN in which the rectification are semantically or informationally stronger than the root, thereby reinforcing an assumption and strengthening the propositional content of the root. Identifying denials are used to revise the interlocutor's default assumption of a state of affairs through stereotypically specifying the root and offers a contextual characterization of a state of affairs in the rectification. Positioning denials involve shifting perspectives represented in the root and the rectification, with an aim to manipulate one's physical or psychological positions. Finally, formal denials create an "eliminating" effect by correcting phonological, grammatical, or stylistic mistakes in the root. Each of the four types of denials can be further divided into several subspecies. We have presented a detailed description and illustration of these denials in Chapter 5.

10.1.3 Cognitive Processes Underlying the Derivation of Various Types of MN

Based on the cognitive-linguistic model which brings together useful points in Langacker's model of construal and Verhagen's model of intersubjectivity in a single formulation, this study has presented a cognitively plausible account of cognitive processes underlying the derivation of MN. Based on a distinction between intrasubjective construal adjustment and intersubjective construal adjustment, MN is characterized as involving adjustment of alternate construals between two conceptualizers. Then, we have proposed a new cognitive model of MN termed as the "intersubjective construal adjustment model" of MN. The central assumption of this model is that MN is a linguistic manifestation of the intersubjective coordination activity concerning alternate construals of the same situation. Specifically, the speaker invites the addressee to consider and abandon a particular construal and accept an alternative one.

In Chapter 6, we have analyzed the cognitive activities underlying the meaning construction of five categories of strengthening denials, namely scalar strengthening denials, granular strengthening denials, partonomic strengthening denials, epistemic strengthening denials, and directional strengthening denials. It is found that strengthening denials are conceptually motivated by intersubjective adjustment of alternate construals with varying semantic or informational strength. The five categories of strengthening denials involve intersubjective coordination processes based on a number of parameters of construal, including scale, scope/ attention, level of specificity, epistemic ground of modality, and asymmetrical/ reciprocal action chain. We have argued that, the point of a strengthening denial is that the speaker invites the addressee to consider and abandon a semantic or informational weak construal in some specific manner, and to update the common ground by suggesting another stronger construal of the same situation.

In Chapter 7, we have investigated the cognitive activities underlying the five identifying denials, namely categorical identifying denials, facet identifying denials, relational identifying denials, identity identifying denials, and sequential identifying denials. It is found that identifying denials are also generated through the intersubjective adjustment of alternate construals of the same situation. They share the same cognitive processes in which the speaker invites the addressee to consider and abandon a default construal that gives rise to a more specific proposition, and to update the common ground by suggesting his/her own construal. The intersubjective adjustment processes are based on a number of parameters of construal such as prototypicality of categorization, domain profiling, "trajector/landmark" alignment, epistemic ground of identity, and mental scanning.

In Chapter 8, we have discussed the meaning construction of positioning denials, that is, relativistic positioning denials, causative positioning denials, deictic positioning denials, structural positioning denials, and evaluative positioning denials. It is found that the above five categories of strengthening denials are derived from the cognitive coordination of different perspectives between subjects of conceptualization. However, they share the processes in which the speaker invites the addressee to consider and abandon a particular perspective and to adopt another one. Their meaning construction processes involve parameters of construal such as viewing arrangement, action chain profiles, deixis, individuation, and relationality, as well as frame.

And in Chapter 9, we have characterized formal denials as being motivated by an inappropriate formal realization, which is a special case of categorization. These denials are related to the cognitive principle of "schematicity" and sanctioning relations between the sanctioning structures and the target structures. The speaker and the addressee are engaged in the intersubjective coordination activities of different sanctioning relations between a conventional unit and its target structure.

10.2 Implications

The most important implication is the theoretical one. This study suggests that different cognitive linguistic models can be fruitfully combined for the analysis of pragmatic meaning. The cognitive linguistic approach arises from dissatisfaction with the traditional truth-semantics. As a new theoretical approach, cognitive linguistics can provide novel solutions to many standard pragmatic issues that have been considered mainly as topics of pragmatists (Fauconnier, 2006). However, as Geeraerts (1988) points out, cognitive linguistics is not "one clearly delimited large territory, but rather a conglomerate of more or less extensive, more or less active centers of linguistic research that are closely knit together by a shared perspective". Different theoretical approaches may provide closely related but complementary perspectives on different "cognitive" aspects of the same phenomenon. Considering the complexity and flexibility of linguistic communication and the multifacets of cognition, a single theory that focuses solely on a certain aspect of cognition, or a restricted number of cognitive operations, might fall short of providing an adequate explanation. On many occasions, researchers have to evaluate the explanatory values of different models, explore their potential synergies, and integrate them into a coherent framework.

This study also sheds insights on the further complementarity between the two theoretical models: Langacker's model of construal and Verhagen's model of intersubjectivity. As discussed in Chapter 3, the two models are intimately related because the former serves as an important theoretical basis for the latter. However, there are still other complementary points between the two. On the one hand, broadly speaking, the two models focus on different aspects of human cognition: the former focuses on the "intrasubjective" aspect of cognition, whereas the latter focuses on the "intersubjective" aspect of cognition. Thus, they jointly contribute to our understanding of pragmatic meanings. Therefore, an adequate account of pragmatic phenomena may have to take into consideration both the "intersubjective" and "intrasubjective" aspect of cognition. On the other hand, while the former focuses on the non-constructional representations, i. e. alternate construals of the same situation, the latter focuses on the constructional representations, i. e. grammatical constructions conventionally used for cognitive coordination. Obviously, meaning representations often result from the fusion of constructional and non-constructional representations. For this reason, further dialogues between researchers within the two frameworks will be welcomed.

The methodology adopted in this study also has strengths and implications for future studies of MN. Adopting the usage-based approach, it has presented a variety of interesting data and revealed the diversity of semantic patterns of MN in modern Chinese, providing further proof for the cross-linguistic value of the approach.

Practically, this study offers a promising basis for the instruction of MN. No matter what method of language teaching one employs, the teacher is best served by a clear, accurate understanding of language (Tyler, 2008). Cognitive linguistics offers an account of language structure which is arguably more comprehensive, revealing, and descriptively adequate from the linguistic standpoint (Langacker, 2008). This study advances a conceptually grounded account of the phenomenon, rendering the complex mechanisms of MN in a fairly comprehensible and intuitive way. Teachers and those responsible for developing teaching materials will hopefully benefit from the insights gained in this study in teaching students or developing sensible materials. In this sense, the present study offers support for the effectiveness of teaching MN in an instructed L1 or L2 classroom situation.

10.3 Limitations and Suggestions for Further Studies

Despite its insightful contributions to both descriptive and explanatory studies of MN in modern Chinese, this study presents several limitations that prompt further scholarly inquiry. A primary limitation is the study's narrow focus on the negation marker *bu*, despite acknowledging the existence of other significant markers like *meiyou, nali, hai, and shenme*. These markers are integral to a comprehensive understanding of negation in modern Chinese, as discussed in Chapter 3. The extent to which our theoretical model can be generalized to encompass these varied forms of MN remains uncertain, highlighting a crucial area for future research. Expanding the scope of investigation to include these markers will not only validate the model's applicability but potentially enhance its theoretical robustness.

Additionally, the reliance on existing datasets from modern Chinese poses a challenge to the universality of our findings. It is essential to recognize that models developed within the confines of a single language may not necessarily capture the universal aspects of human language. Future studies should aim to apply and test our model across different linguistic contexts to assess its broader applicability and to refine its theoretical propositions.

Another significant limitation stems from the inherent challenges within cognitive linguistics, the framework underpinning this study. Cognitive linguistics advocates for a linguistic analysis rooted in the understanding of cognitive processes involved in language perception and production. However, the cognitive adequacy of this approach remains heavily debated within the academic community. Critics like Peeters (2001), Dabrowska (2009, 2016), and Niu (2018) question the empirical basis of cognitive linguistic theories, particularly the operationalization and empirical testing of key concepts such as construal operations. Dabrowska (2009) underscores the lack of psychological evidence supporting how speakers perform construal operations, a critique that resonates with the skepticism towards Verhagen's intersubjective perspective on linguistic negation discussed by Hinzen and Lambalgen (2008).

In accordance with Dabrowska's (2009) emphasis on a genuine "cognitive commitment", it is imperative that future research endeavors not only theorize but also empirically substantiate the foundational concepts of cognitive linguistics. The operationalization efforts by researchers like Bergen et al. (2007), Matlock (2004), and Tomlin and Myachykov (2015) exemplify how theoretical constructs can be empirically tested. Future research should continue to derive testable hypotheses from our theoretical frameworks, facilitating rigorous empirical evaluations. This methodological rigor will not only solidify the cognitive linguistic framework but also enhance its practical applicability and relevance across diverse linguistic phenomena.

By addressing these limitations and expanding the empirical base of cognitive linguistics, future research can more effectively bridge the gap between theoretical constructs and their real-world linguistic applications. This will foster a deeper, more nuanced understanding of language as both a cognitive mechanism and a tool for social interaction, thereby enriching the field of pragmatics and its intersection with cognitive studies.

References

AIJMER K, 2013. Understanding pragmatic markers: a variational pragmatic approach[M]. Edinburgh: Edinburgh University Press.

AIJMER K, RÜHLEMANN C, 2015. Corpus pragmatics: a handbook[M]. Cambridge: Cambridge University Press.

ATLAS J D, 1977. Negation, ambiguity, and presupposition[J]. Linguistics and philosophy, 1: 321-336.

ATLAS J D, 1979. How linguistics matters to philosophy: presupposition, truth, and meaning[M]//OH C, DINNEEN D. Syntax and semantics (vol. 2): Presupposition. New York: Academic Press.

ATLAS J D, 1989. Philosophy without ambiguity[M]. Oxford: Oxford University Press.

ATLAS J D, 2004. Presupposition[M]//HORN L, WARD G. The handbook of pragmatics. Oxford: Blackwell.

ATLAS J D, 2005. Logic, meaning, and conversation: semantical underdeterminacy, implicature, and their interface[M]. Oxford: Oxford University Press.

ATLAS J D, 2012. Negation[M]//ALLAN K, JASZCZOLT K. The Cambridge handbook of pragmatics. Cambridge: Cambridge University Press.

BARLOW M, KEMMER S, 2000. Usage-based models of language[M]. Stanford: CSLI Publications.

BERGEN B K, LINDSAY S, MATLOCK T, et al., 2007. Spatial and linguistic aspects of visual imagery in sentence comprehension[J]. Cognitive science, 31

(5): 733-764.

BERGH G, ZANCHETTA E, 2008. Web linguistics[M]//LÜDELING A, KYTÖ M. Corpus linguistics: an international handbook. Berlin: Mouton de Gruyter.

BIBER D, SUSAN C, RANDI R, 1998. Corpus linguistics: investigating language structure and use[M]. Cambridge: Cambridge University Press.

BIQ Y-O, 1989. Metalinguistic negation in Mandarin[J]. Journal of Chinese linguistics, 17(1): 75-95.

BLAKEMORE D, 1992. Understanding utterances: an introduction to pragmatics [M]. Oxford: Blackwell.

BURTON-ROBERTS N, 1989a. The limits to debate: a revised theory of semantic presupposition[M]. Cambridge: Cambridge University Press.

BURTON-ROBERTS N, 1989b. On Horn's dilemma: presupposition and negation [J]. Journal of linguistics, 25: 95-125.

BURTON-ROBERTS N, 1990. Trivalence, gapped bivalence, and ambiguity of negation: a reply to Seuren [J]. Journal of linguistics, 26: 455-470.

BURTON-ROBERTS N, 1999. Presupposition cancellation and metalinguistic negation: a reply to Carston[J]. Journal of linguistics, 35: 347-364.

BYBEE J, 2006. From usage to grammar: the mind's response to repetition[J]. Language, 82 (4): 711-733.

BYBEE J, 2010. Language, usage and cognition[M]. Cambridge: Cambridge University Press.

BYBEE J, 2013. Usage-based theory and exemplar representations of constructions [M]//HOFFMANN T, TROUSDALE G. The Oxford handbook of construction grammar. Oxford: Oxford University Press.

CARSTON R, 1988. Implicature, explicature, and truth-theoretic semantics[M]// KEMPSON R. Mental representations: the interface between language and reality. Cambridge: Cambridge University Press.

CARSTON R, 1996. Metalinguistic negation and echoic use[J]. Journal of pragmatics, 25: 309-330.

CARSTON R, 1998. Negation, "presupposition", and the semantics/pragmatics distinction[J]. Journal of linguistics, 34: 309-350.

CARSTON R, 1999. Negation, "presupposition" and metarepresentation: a response to Noël Burton-Roberts[J]. Journal of linguistics, 35: 365-389.

CARSTON R, 2002. Thought and utterances[M]. Oxford: Blackwell.

CARSTON R, NOH E J, 1996. A truth-functional account of metalinguistic negation, with evidence from Korean[J]. Language science, 18: 485-504.

CHAFE W, 1994. Discourse, consciousness, and time: the flow and displacement of conscious experience in speaking and writing[M]. Chicago: University of Chicago Press.

CHOMSKY N, 1975. Reflections on language[M]. New York: Pantheon Books.

CLARK H H, 1996. Using language[M]. Cambridge: Cambridge University Press

COUPLAND N, 1995. Accommodation theory [M]//VERSCHUEREN J, ÖSTMAN J, BLOMMAERT J, et al. Handbook of pragmatics. Amsterdam: John Benjamins.

CROFT W, 2007. Construction grammar[M]//GEERAERTS D, CUYCKENS H. Handbook of cognitive linguistics. Oxford: Oxford University Press.

CROFT W, CRUSE D A, 2004. Cognitive linguistics[M]. Cambridge: Cambridge University Press.

DABROWSKA E, 2009. Review of the Oxford handbook of cognitive linguistics [J]. Language, 85: 721-724.

DABROWSKA E, 2016. Cognitive linguistics' seven deadly sins[J]. Cognitive linguistics, 27 (4): 479-491.

DAVIS W A, 2010. Irregular negations: implicature and idiom theories[M]// PETRUS K. Meaning and analysis. Basingstoke: Palgrave Macmillan.

DAVIS W A, 2011. "Metalinguistic" negation, denials, and idioms[J]. Journal of pragmatics, 43: 2548-2577.

DAVIS W A, 2013. Irregular negations: pragmatic explicature theories[M]// CAPONE A, LOPIPARO F, CARAPEZA M. Perspectives on pragmatics and philosophy (vol. 1): Philosophy and psychology. Cham: Springer.

DAVIS W A, 2016. Irregular negatives, implicatures and idioms[M]. Cham: Springer.

DEIGNAN A, LITTLEMORE J, SEMINO E, 2013. Figurative language, genre and register[M]. Cambridge: Cambridge University Press.

DUCROT O, 1972. Dire et ne pas dire[M]. Paris: Hermann.

DUCROT O, 1973. La Preuve et le dire[M]. Paris: Maison Mame.

DUIJN M V, VERHAGEN A, 2018. Beyond triadic communication: a three-dimensional conceptual space for modelling intersubjectivity[J]. Pragmatics & cognition, 25 (2): 384-416.

EVANS V, GREEN M, 2006. Cognitive linguistics: an introduction[M]. Edinburgh: Edinburgh University Press.

FAUCONNIER G, 1985. Mental spaces: aspects of the meaning construction in natural language[M]. Cambridge, MA: MIT Press.

FAUCONNIER G, 1997. Mappings in thought and language[M]. Cambridge: Cambridge University Press.

FAUCONNIER G, 2006. Pragmatics and cognitive cinguistics[M]//HORN L, WARD G. The handbook of pragmatics. Oxford: Blackwell.

FAUCONNIER G, TURNER M, 2002. The way we think: conceptual blending and the mind's hidden complexities[M]. New York: Basic Books.

FILLMORE C J, 1977. Scenes-and-frames semantics[M]//ZAMPOLLI A. Linguistic structure processing. Amsterdam: North Holland.

FILLMORE C J, 1982. Frame semantics[M]//Linguistic Society of Korea. Linguistics in the morning calm. Seoul: Hanshin.

FILLMORE C J, 1985. Frames and the semantics of understanding[J]. Quaderni di semántica, 6: 222-253.

FLETCHER W H, 2007. Concordancing the web: promise and problems, tools and techniques[M]//HUNDT M, NESSELHAUF N, BIEWER C. Corpus linguistics and the web. Amsterdam: Rodopi.

FODOR J A, 1983. The modularity of mind[M]. Cambridge, MA: MIT Press.

FODOR J A, 2001. The mind doesn't work that way[M]. Cambridge, MA: MIT Press

FOOLEN A, 1991. Metalinguistic negation and pragmatic ambiguity: some comments on a proposal by Laurence Horn[J]. Pragmatics, 1: 217-237.

FOWLER R, 1985. Power[M]//DIJK T A. Handbook of discourse analysis (vol. 4).

London: Academic Press.

FRIED M, 2010. Construction grammar[M]//ALEXIADOU A, KISS T. Handbook of syntax. 2nd ed. Berlin: Walter de Gruyter.

GAO H, 2003. A cognitive-pragmatic analysis of metalinguistic negation[J]. Journal of Sichuan international studies university (2): 98-102.

GAZDAR G, 1979a. Pragmatics: implicature, presupposition, and logical form [M]. New York: Academic Press.

GAZDAR G, 1979b. A solution to the projection problem[M]//OH C, DINNEEN D. Syntax and semantics (vol. 2): Presupposition. New York: Academic Press.

GEERAERTS D, 1988. Prototypicality as a prototypical notion[J]. Communication and cognition, 21: 343-355.

GEURTS B, 1998. The mechanisms of denial[M]. Language, 74: 274-307.

GIBBS R W, 1994. The poetics of mind[M]. Cambridge: Cambridge University Press.

GILES H, POWESLAND P, 1997. Accommodation theory[M]//COUPLAND N, JAWORSKI A. Sociolinguistics: a reader and coursebook. London: Macmillan.

GOLDBERG A E, 1995. Constructions: a construction grammar approach to argument structure[M]. Chicago: University of Chicago Press.

GOLDBERG A E, 2006. Constructions at work: the nature of generalization in language[M]. Oxford: Oxford University Press.

GRICE H P, 1967. Logic and conversation[J]. Studies in syntax & semantics speech acts, 38(1): 101-136.

HART C, 2013. Constructing contexts through grammar: cognitive models and conceptualisation in British newspaper reports of political protests[M]// FLOWERDEW J. Discourse in context. London: Continuum.

HART C, 2014. Construal operations in online press reports of political protests [M]//HART C, CAP P. Contemporary critical discourse studies. London: Bloomsbury.

HART C, 2015. Discourse[M]//DABROWSKA E, DIVJAK D. Handbook of cognitive linguistics. Berlin: Mouton de Gruyter.

HE Z R, 1991. Pragmatic transference in verbal communication[J]. Foreign language teaching and research (4): 11-15.

HINZEN W, LAMBALGEN M, 2008. Explaining intersubjectivity. A comment on Arie Verhagen, constructions of intersubjectivity[J]. Cognitive linguistics, 19 (1): 107-123.

HIRSCHBERG J, 1991. A theory of scalar implicature[M]. New York: Garland.

HORN L R, 1984. Toward a new taxonomy for pragmatic inference: Q- and R-based implicature[M]//SCHIFFRIN D. Meaning, form, and use in context. Washington: Georgetown University Press.

HORN L R, 1985. Metalinguistic negation and pragmatic ambiguity[J]. Language, 61: 121-174.

HORN L R, 1989. A nature history of negation[M]. Chicago: University of Chicago Press.

HORN L R, 1990. Showdown at truth-value gap: Burton-Roberts on presupposition [J]. Journal of linguistics, 26: 483-503.

HORN L R, 2009. WJ-40: implicature, truth, and meaning[J]. International review of pragmatics, 1: 3-34.

HORN L R, WARD G, 2004. Implicature[M]//HORN L, WARD G. The handbook of pragmatics. Oxford: Blackwell.

HUANG Y, 2014. Pragmatics[M]. Oxford: Oxford University Press.

HUANG Y, 2020. Non-canonical scalar implicatures, face/politeness considerations, and neo-Gricean pragmatics[J]. Foreign language teaching and research (1): 25-39.

JIANG X H, 2011. A cognitive pragmatic study of metonymic expressions: an integrated model of relevance theory and cognitive linguistics[J]. Modern foreign languages (1): 34-41.

JOHNSON M, 1987. The body in the mind: the bodily basis of meaning, imagination, and reason[M]. Chicago: University of Chicago Press.

KARTTUNEN L, PETERS S, 1979. Conventional implicature[M]//OH C, DINNEEN D. Syntax and semantics (vol. 2): Presupposition. New York: Academic Press.

KAY P, 2004. Pragmatic aspects of grammatical constructions[M]//HORN L R,

WARD G. The handbook of pragmatics. Oxford: Blackwell.

KEMPSON R, 1975. Presupposition and the delimitation of semantics[M]. Cambridge: Cambridge University Press.

KILGARRIFF A, GREFENSTETTE G, 2003. Introduction to the special issue on the web as corpus[J]. Computational linguistics, 29 (3): 333-347.

KLEINKE S, 2010. Speaker activity and Grice's maxims of conversation at the interface of pragmatics and cognitive linguistics[J]. Journal of pragmatics, 42 (12): 3345-3366.

KOFFKA K, 1935. Principles of gestalt psychology[M]. New York: Harcourt, Brace & World.

KONG Q C, 1998. The pragmatic mechanism of negation rhetoric[J]. Applied linguistics (1): 59-65.

KÖVECSES Z, RADDEN G, 1998. Metonymy: developing a cognitive linguistic view[J]. Cognitive linguistics, 9 (1): 37-77.

KUNO S, 1987. Functional syntax: anaphora, discourse and empathy[M]. Chicago: University of Chicago Press.

KUNO S, 2004. Empathy and direct discourse perspectives[M]//HORN L, WARD G. The handbook of pragmatics. Oxford: Blackwell.

KUNO S, KABURAKI E, 1977. Empathy and syntax[J]. Linguistic inquiry, 8: 627-672.

LADD D, 1980. The structure of intonational meaning[M]. Bloomington: Indiana University Press.

LAKOFF G, 1987. Women, fire, and dangerous things: what categories reveal about the mind[M]. Chicago: University of Chicago Press.

LAKOFF G, 1993. The contemporary theory of metaphor[M]//ORTONY A. Metaphor and thought. 2nd ed. Cambridge: Cambridge University Press.

LAKOFF G, JOHNSON M, 1980. Metaphors we live by[M]. Chicago: University of Chicago Press.

LAKOFF G, TURNER M, 1989. More than cool reason: a field guide to poetic metaphor[M]. Chicago: University of Chicago Press.

LANGACKER R W, 1987. Foundations of cognitive grammar (vol. 1): theoretical prerequisites[M]. Stanford: Stanford University Press.

LANGACKER R W, 1990. Concept, image, and symbol: the cognitive basis of grammar[M]//Cognitive linguistics research 1. Berlin: Mouton de Gruyter.

LANGACKER R W, 1991. Foundations of cognitive grammar (vol.2): descriptive application[M]. Stanford: Stanford University Press.

LANGACKER R W, 1999. Grammar and conceptualization[M]//Cognitive linguistics research 14. Berlin: Mouton de Gruyter.

LANGACKER R W, 2000. A dynamic usage-based model[M]//BARLOW M, KEMMER S. Usage-based models of language. Stanford: CSLI Publications.

LANGACKER R W, 2008. Cognitive grammar: a basic introduction[M]. New York: Oxford University Press.

LANGACKER R W, 2013. Essentials of cognitive grammar[M]. New York: Oxford University Press.

LANGACKER R W, 2015. Construal[M]//DABROWSKA E, DIVJAK D. Handbook of cognitive linguistics. Berlin: De Gruyter Mouton.

LEE C, 2016. Metalinguistically negated versus descriptively negated adverbials: ERP and other evidence[M]//LARRIVÉE P, LEE C. Negation and polarity: experimental perspective. Berlin: Springer.

LEE H K, 2005. Presupposition and implicature under negation[J]. Journal of pragmatics, 37 (5): 595-609.

LEVINSON S C, 2000. Presumptive meanings: the theory of generalized conversational implicature[M]. Cambridge, MA: MIT Press.

LI F Y, 2008. An introduction to cognitive linguistics[M]. Beijing: Peking University Press.

LITTLEMORE J, 2015. Metonymy: hidden shortcuts in language, thought and communication[M]. Cambridge: Cambridge University Press.

LIU L G, CUI M, 2006. A multi-perspective account of metalingistic negation[J]. Journal of northeast normal university (philosophy and social sciences) (3): 100-104.

LONG L, LU W Z, 2019. A study of scalar implicature denial based on the lexical constructional model[J]. Modern foreign languages (2): 170-181.

LYONS J, 1977. Semantics[M]. Cambridge: Cambridge University Press.

MARMARIDOU S A, 2000. Pragmatic meaning and cognition[M]. Amsterdam: John Benjamins.

MATLOCK T, 2004. Fictive motion as cognitive simulation[J]. Memory and cognition, 32 (8): 1389-1400.

MENDOZA R D, VELASCO D, 2002. Patterns of conceptual interaction[M]// DIRVEN R. PORINGS R. Metaphor and metonymy in comparison and contrast. Berlin: De Gruyter Mouton.

MENDOZA R D, GALERA A, 2014. Cognitive modeling: a linguistic perspective [M]. Amsterdam: John Benjamins.

MENDOZA R D, CAMPO O, 2002. Metonymy, grammar and communication[M]. Granada: Comares.

MEYER C, 2002. English corpus linguistics: an introduction[M]. Cambridge: Cambridge University Press.

MICHAELIS L, 2003. Word meaning, sentence meaning, and syntactic meaning [M]//CUYCKENS H, DIRVEN R, TAYLOR J. Cognitive approaches to lexical semantics. Berlin: Mouton de Gruyter.

MILLER G R, STEINBERG M, 1975. Between people: a new analysis of interpersonal communication[M]. Palo Alto: Science Research Associates.

MOESCHLER J, 2019. Representation and metarepresentation in negation[M]// SCOTT K, CLARK B, CARSTON R. Relevance, pragmatics and interpretation. Cambridge: Cambridge University Press.

NEWMAN J, 2010. Balancing acts: empirical pursuits in cognitive linguistics[M]// GLYNN D, FISCHER K. Quantitative methods in cognitive semantics: corpus-driven approaches. Berlin: De Gruyter Mouton.

NI X H, 1982. The figurative use of negation[J]. Contemporary rhetoric (4): 51-52.

NIU B Y, 2018. New developments in cognitive linguistic research[J]. Modern foreign languages (6): 852-863.

NOH E, 2000. Metarepresentation: a relevance-theory approach[M]. Amsterdam: John Benjamins.

NOH E, HYEREE C, SUNGRYONG K, 2013. Processing metalinguistic negation: evidence from eye-tracking experiments[J]. Journal of pragmatics, 57: 1-18.

NUYTS J, 2001. Epistemic modality, language, and conceptualization: a cognitive-pragmatic perspective[M]. Amsterdam: John Benjamins.

PANTHER K-U, RADDEN G, 1999. Metonymy in language and thought[M]. Amsterdam: John Benjamins.

PANTHER K-U, THORNBURG L, 2003. Metonymy and pragmatic inferencing [M]. Amsterdam: John Benjamins.

PANTHER K-U, THORNBURG L, 2007. Metonymy[M]//GEERAERTS D, CUYCKENS H. The Oxford handbook of cognitive linguistics. Oxford: Oxford University Press.

PEETERS B, 2001. Does cognitive linguistics live up to its name? [M]//DIRVEN R. Language and ideology (vol. 1): cognitive theoretical approaches. Amsterdam: John Benjamins.

PEÑA S, MENDOZA R D, 2017. Construing and constructing hyperbole[M]// ATHANASIADOU A. Studies in figurative thought and language. Amsterdam: John Benjamins.

PITTS A, 2005. Exploring a "pragmatic ambiguity" of negation[J]. Language, 87: 346-368.

RADDEN G, KÖVECSES Z, 1999. Towards a theory of metonymy[M]//PANTHER K-U, RADDEN G. Metonymy in language and thought. Amsterdam: John Benjamins.

RAN Y P, 2007. The pragmatic stance of person deixis, its empathic and de-empathic functions in interpersonal discourse[J]. Foreign language teaching and research (5): 331-337.

RAN Y P, 2013. The metapragmatic negation as a rapport-oriented mitigating device[J]. Journal of pragmatics, 48 (1): 98-111.

RENOUF A, 2003. WebCorp: providing a renewable data source for corpus linguists[M]//GRANGER S, PETCH-TYSON S. Extending the scope of corpus-based research: new applications, new challenges. Amsterdam: Rodopi.

ROMERO-TRILLO J, 2008. Pragmatics and corpus linguistics: a mutualistic entente[M]. Berlin: De Gruyter Mouton.

ROMERO-TRILLO J, 2014. Yearbook of corpus linguistics and pragmatics: new empirical and theoretical paradigms[M]. Berlin: Springer.

ROMERO-TRILLO J, 2015. Yearbook of corpus linguistics and pragmatics: current approaches to discourse and translation studies[M]. Berlin: Springer.

ROMERO-TRILLO J, 2016. Yearbook of corpus linguistics and pragmatics: global implications for society and education in the networked age[M]. Berlin: Springer.

ROMERO-TRILLO J, 2019. Corpus linguistics for pragmatics: a guide for research[M]. London: Routledge.

ROSCH E, 1975. Cognitive representations of semantic categories[J]. Journal of experimental psychology (general), 104: 192-233.

ROSCH E, 1978. Principles of categorization[M]//LLOYD B, ROSCH E. Cognition and categorization. Hillsdale, NJ: Erlbaum.

ROSCH E, MERVIS C, 1975. Family resemblances: studies in the internal structure of categories[J]. Cognitive psychology, 7: 573-605.

RUSSEL B, 1905. On denoting[J]. Mind, 14, 479-493.

SANDT R A, 1991. Denial[J]. Papers from the chicago linguistics society: the parasession on negation, 27 (2): 331-344.

SANDT R A, 2003. Denial and presupposition[M]//KÜHNLEIN P, RIESER H, ZEEVAT H. Perspectives on dialogue in the new millennium. Amsterdam: John Benjamins.

SANDERS T, SPOOREN W, 2007. Discourse and text structure[M]//GEERAERTS D, CUYKENS H. Oxford handbook of cognitive linguistics. Oxford: Oxford University Press.

SCHMID H-J, 2007. Entrenchment, salience and basic levels[M]//GEERAERTS D, CUYCKENS H. Handbook of cognitive linguistics. Oxford: Oxford University Press.

SHEN J X, 1993. An examination of "pragmatic negation" [J]. Studies of the Chinese language (5): 321-331.

SINHA C, 1999. Situated selves[M]//BLISS J, SÄLJÖ R, LIGHT P. Learning sites: social and technological resources for learning. Oxford: Pergamon.

SINHA C, 2005. Blending out of the background: play, props and staging in the material world[J]. Journal of pragmatics, 37 (10): 1537-1554.

SPERBER D, 1994. The modularity of thought and the epidemiology of representations[M]//HIRSCHFIELD L, GELMAN S. Mapping the mind: domain specificity in cognition and culture. New York: Cambridge University Press.

SPERBER D, 2001. In defense of massive modularity[M]//DUPOUX E. Language, brain and cognitive development: essays in honor of Jacques Mehler. Cambridge, MA: MIT Press.

SPERBER D, 2005. Modularity and relevance: How can a massively modular mind be flexible and context-sensitive? [M]//CARRUTHERS P, LAURENCE S, STICH S P. The innate mind: structure and contents (vol. 1). Oxford: Oxford University Press.

SPERBER D, WILSON D, 1981. Irony and the use-mention distinction[M]// COLE P. Radical pragmatics. New York: Academic Press.

SPERBER D, WILSON D, 1986. Relevance: communication and cognition[M]. Oxford: Blackwell.

SPERBER D, WILSON D, 2002. Pragmatics, modularity and mind-reading[J]. Mind & language, 17 (1&2): 3-23.

SPERBER D, CARA F, GIROTTO V, 1995. Relevance theory explains the selection task[J]. Cognition, 57: 31-95.

STEEN G, 2011. The contemporary theory of metaphor: now new and improved! [J]. Review of cognitive linguistics, 9: 26-64.

STEEN G, 2013. Deliberate metaphor affords conscious metaphorical cognition[J]. Journal of cognitive semiotics, 5: 179-197.

STEEN G, 2015. Developing, testing and interpreting deliberate metaphor theory [J]. Journal of pragmatics, 90: 67-72.

STEFANOWITSCH A, 2011. Cognitive linguistics meets the corpus[M]//BRDAR M, GRIES S T, ZICFUCHS M. Cognitive linguistics: convergence and expansion. Amsterdam: John Benjamins.

STEFANOWITSCH A, GRIES S T, 2007. Corpora in cognitive linguistics: the syntax-lexis interface[M]. Berlin: De Gruyter Mouton.

SWEETSER E, 1990. From etymology to pragmatics: metaphorical and cultural aspects of semantic structure[M]. Cambridge: Cambridge University Press.

TALMY L, 1988. The relation of grammar to cognition[M]//RUDZKA-OSTYN B. Topics in cognitive linguistics. Amsterdam: John Benjamins.

TALMY L, 1996. The windowing of attention in language[M]//SHIBATANI M, THOMPSON S. Grammatical constructions: their form and meaning. Oxford: Oxford University Press.

TALMY L, 2000. Toward a cognitive semantics (vol. 1): concept structuring systems[M]. Cambridge: MIT Press.

TAN F F, 2016. A multidimensional comparative study of the structure "不是 a 而是 b" and "not a but b" [J]. Foreign language education (1): 43-48.

TAYLOR J R, 2004. Linguistic categorization: prototypes in linguistic theory[M]. 3rd ed. Oxford: Oxford University Press.

TENDAHL M, 2009. A hybrid theory of metaphor: relevance theory and cognitive linguistics[M]. Basingstoke: Palgrave Macmillan.

TENDAHL M, GIBBS R W, 2008. Complementary perspectives on metaphor: cognitive linguistics and relevance theory[J]. Journal of pragmatics, 40 (11): 1823-1864.

TOMASELLO M, 2003. Constructing a language. A usage-based theory of language acquisition[M]. Cambridge, MA: Harvard University Press.

TOMLIN S, MYACHYKOV A, 2015. Attention and salience[M]//DABROWSKA E, DIVJAK D. Handbook of cognitive linguistics. Berlin: De Gruyter Mouton.

TRAUGOTT E, 1989. On the rise of epistemic meanings in English: an example of subjectification in semantic change[J]. Language, 65 (1): 31-55.

TYLER A, 2008. Cognitive linguistics and second language instruction[M]// ROBINSON P, ELLIS N C. Handbook of cognitive linguistics and second language acquisition. London: Routledge.

UNGERER F, SCHMID H, 1996. An introduction to cognitive linguistics[M]. London: Longman.

UNGERER F, SCHMID H, 2006. An introduction to cognitive linguistics[M]. London: Longman.

VERHAGEN A, 2005. Constructions of intersubjectivity[M]. Oxford: Oxford University Press.

VERHAGEN A, 2007. Construal and perspectivization[M]//GEERAERTS D, CUYCKENS H. The Oxford handbook of cognitive linguistics. Oxford: Oxford University Press.

VERHAGEN A, 2015. Grammar and cooperative communication[M]// DABROWSKA E, DIVJAK D. Handbook of cognitive linguistics. Berlin: De Gruyter Mouton.

VERHAGEN A, WEIJER J, 2003. Usage-based approaches to Dutch[M]. Utrecht, Netherlands: LOT.

VERSCHUEREN J, 1999. Understanding pragmatics[M]. London: Edward Arnold.

WANG Z Y, 2011. A review of studies on metalinguistic negation[J]. Foreign language research (6): 90-93.

WEI Z J, 2019. Pragmatic empathy motivation on metonymic negation construction [J]. Modern foreign languages (1): 13-24.

WEN S L, SHEN Y L, 2012. Construction and function of metonymy negation[J]. Language teaching and linguistic studies (4): 105-112.

WIBLE D, CHEN E, 2000. Linguistic limits on metalinguistic negation: evidence from Mandarin and English[J]. Language and linguistics, 1 (2): 233-255.

WILCE J M, 2009. Language and emotion[M]. Cambridge: Cambridge University Press.

WILSON D, 1975. Presupposition and non-truth-conditional semantics[M]. New York: Academic Press.

WILSON D, 2000. Metarepresentation in linguistic communication[M]//SPERBER D. Metarepresentations: an interdisciplinary perspective. Oxford: Oxford University Press.

WILSON D, 2005. New directions for research on pragmatics and modularity[J]. Lingua, 115: 1129-1146.

WILSON D, SPERBER D, 1988. Representation and relevance[M]//KEMPSON

R. Mental representations: the interface between language and reality. Cambridge: Cambridge University Press.

WILSON D, SPERBER D, 1992. On verbal irony[J]. Lingua, 87: 53-76.

WILSON D, SPERBER D, 2002. Truthfulness and relevance[J]. Mind, 111: 583-632.

WILSON D, SPERBER D, 2004. Relevance theory[M]//HORN L, WARD G. The handbook of pragmatics. Oxford: Blackwell.

WU T G, 1985. A certain form and pattern formed solely by "不"[J]. Linguistic research (1): 57-60.

WU T G, 1986. On the feigned negation[J]. Journal of Zhejiang normal university (social sciences) (4): 142-146.

XU S H, 1994. New Grice's theory of conversational implicature and implicature negation[J]. Foreign language teaching and research (4): 30-35.

XUN E D, RAO G Q, XIAO X Y, et al., 2016. The construction of the BCC corpus in the age of big data[J]. Corpus linguistics (1): 93-109.

YEH L-H, 1995. Focus, metalinguistic negation and contrastive negation [J]. Journal of Chinese linguistics, 23 (2): 42-75.

YOSHIMURA A, 2013. Descriptive/metalinguistic dichotomy?: toward a new taxonomy of negation[J]. Journal of pragmatics, 57: 39-56.

ZENG Z, 2010. The expansion of "枚"[J]. Language planning (10): 43.

ZHANG D Y, 2017. On the quantifier "枚" from "帅哥一枚"[J]. modern Chinese (2): 126-127.

ZHANG H, CAI H, 2005. On the complementarities of cognitive linguistics and relevance theory[J]. Journal of foreign languages (3): 14-21.

ZHANG K D, 1999. The constraints of pragmatic negation in Chinese[J]. Journal of Henan university (philosophy and social science) (1): 66-68.

ZHANG S, ZHANG Y, 2015. Scalar implicature: a Saussurean system-based approach[J]. Language sciences, 51: 43-53.

ZHAO M Y, 2011. The truth-functional nature of metalinguistic negation: a cross-linguistic study[J]. Journal of foreign languages (2): 32-38.